BEGINNER'S GUIDE TO AMAZON KDP SELF-PUBLISHING: 2025 EDITION

By Ann Eckhart

TABLE OF CONTENTS

Beginner's Guide To Amazon KDP Self-Publishing: 2025 Edition By Ann Eckhart

INTRODUCTION

CHAPTER ONE: THE POWER OF SELF-PUBLISHING

CHAPTER TWO: WHY SELF-PUBLISH YOUR BOOK ON AMAZON

CHAPTER THREE: THE ESSENTIAL TOOLS TO SELF-PUBLISH

CHAPTER FOUR: MASTERING AMAZON BOOK CATEGORIES

CHAPTER FIVE: THE FREEDOM OF PEN NAMES

CHAPTER SIX: KINDLE, PAPERBACK, HARDCOVER…OR ALL THREE

CHAPTER SEVEN: THE JOURNEY OF WRITING A BOOK

CHAPTER EIGHT: EDITING YOUR BOOK

CHAPTER NINE: FORMATTING YOUR BOOK FILES

CHAPTER TEN: OPENING AN AMAZON KDP ACCOUNT

CHAPTER ELEVEN: ALL ABOUT ROYALTIES

CHAPTER TWELVE: UPLOADING YOUR BOOK FILES TO AMAZON

CHAPTER THIRTEEN: CREATING BEST-SELLING BOOK COVERS

CHAPTER FOURTEEN: PRICING YOUR BOOKS

CHAPTER FIFTEEN: HOW TO MARKET YOUR BOOKS FOR FREE

CHAPTER SIXTEEN: GETTING BOOK REVIEWS

CHAPTER SEVENTEEN: FACEBOOK ADS FOR AUTHORS

CHAPTER EIGHTEEN: AMAZON ADS FOR AUTHORS

CHAPTER NINETEEN: USING A+ CONTENT TO SELL MORE BOOKS

CHAPTER TWENTY: PUBLISHING ON PLATFORMS OTHER THAN AMAZON

CHAPTER TWENTY-ONE: MAKING MONEY WITH NO-AND-LOW CONTENT BOOKS

CHAPTER TWENTY-TWO: THE EMERGENCE OF AI

CONCLUSION

ABOUT THE AUTHOR

COPYRIGHT 2024 Ann Eckhart

INTRODUCTION

Have you always dreamed of becoming a published author? Whether your stories fill notebooks or simply fill your imagination, you've probably wondered how to turn them into a published book. You may think the process requires an agent and a formal contract. But how do you even begin searching for an agent? What steps are needed to get your book in stores? Will there be costs involved?

Where do you even begin?

Maybe you've seen TV commercials claiming they can help you get your book into print, or you've come across websites offering to publish your work. These companies promise to publish your book for a hefty fee. Maybe you've even bought a guide filled with literary agents' contact information and have researched how to send in proposal letters and a manuscript in the hopes that someone will view your work as valuable enough to publish.

Publishing can seem overwhelming, confusing, and expensive.

But what if I told you there's a much easier, FREE way to publish your book? A way where you keep complete control of your work and the profits?

It might sound too good to be true, but I'm here to tell you that you can self-publish your book for FREE, make it available to hundreds of millions of readers, and keep up to 70% of the profits!

How is that possible?

Through **Amazon's** Kindle Direct Publishing **(KDP) platform**! With KDP, you provide the book files, and Amazon manages the printing, shipping, and distribution. There's no need for an agent or a contract. You are your own agent in control of your own author business.

Now, there is some work beyond just writing your book to publish it. You need to prepare the files – both the interior and cover – but that process is much easier than you may assume. And that is where this book comes in. I will walk you through the entire self-publishing process from start to finish. From writing a book to formatting the file to creating a cover and listing the book for sale on Amazon, this book covers it all in an easy-to-understand format that almost anyone can follow.

Once your book is for sale on Amazon, I'll show you both free and low-cost methods for promoting it to reach more readers and earn more money. I'll also teach you how to publish your book on other platforms, get it into independent bookstores and libraries, and get it onto other eBook platforms.

But why should you listen to me when it comes to self-publishing? Well, since 2013, I've been publishing books on Amazon, and the income I earn from monthly royalties has allowed me to build a full-time author business. These royalties, often referred to as "passive income," are deposited into my bank account every month with minimal ongoing effort on my part. While I do some marketing work to keep sales flowing, Amazon manages the bulk of the operations by printing and shipping books and dealing with customer service issues.

Self-publishing has allowed me to essentially be retired in my 40s!

But let me take you back to where my story began.

As a child, teachers recognized that I was a strong writer as far back in school as I can remember. I excelled in English classes and assumed I would be a writer when I grew up.

I wanted to be a writer.

However, once I got to college, I realized that there were two career paths for writers: journalism or teaching.

While I was on my high school's newspaper, once I was in college, I realized that the hours and low pay of being a journalist weren't for me. I considered magazine writing, but living in Iowa made that difficult since most publications are based in New York, and I wanted to stay in my home state. Fiction writing didn't seem like an option either, as I believed I was more suited for writing nonfiction. Teaching English seemed like the last remaining career option, but I had no desire to do that.

Eventually, I convinced myself that writing couldn't be a "real" job and put my dreams of being a writer behind me. I pursued a "real" job and ended up in the office of a local non-profit, where I stayed for seven years. But the longer I worked there, the more I realized I wasn't cut out to work for someone else. That's when I decided to take the plunge into self-employment.

My first venture was a home-based gift basket business, which eventually led me to sell products online. I began by selling new gift items on both Amazon and eBay, which I sourced from wholesale suppliers. I later transitioned into selling secondhand items such as clothing and vintage collectibles, selling primarily on eBay but also sometimes on Etsy, Poshmark, and WhatNot. I spent weekends at estate sales loading up on antiques and waited for Goodwill sale days to go through their racks of clothes.

Reselling was fine. It paid the bills. And I even started "teaching" reselling to others on my YouTube channel.

However, after nine years of reselling online, I was burned out. The constant cycle of sourcing items, taking and editing photos, writing listings, answering customer questions, and processing orders wore me down. Even though my reselling YouTube videos about reselling brought in an income, I was drained, exhausted, and, frankly, bored. And the fluctuating income was adding to my stress and anxiety.

While holiday sales were great, the summer months were slow. Families were on vacation, kids were out of school, and sales dwindled. There were so many sourcing opportunities at area garage sales. But I had to make sales in order to have the extra money needed to buy more inventory. I felt trapped in a cycle of sourcing, listing, and shipping, all while anxiously waiting for the holiday season when I hoped sales would pick up, making me enough money to carry me through the rest of the year.

Though eBay and YouTube were covering my bills, I knew I needed to find another source of income, not only for the extra cash to put away for retirement but also to give me a creative outlet. Caring for my elderly father required me to work from home, so I had to find yet another home-based business that would make me money and make me happy.

As reselling began to wear me down, I stumbled upon the world of indie authors. To be honest, I can't recall precisely when I realized you could make money by self-publishing Kindle eBooks on Amazon. I might have seen an ad while buying Kindle books for myself, as I was an avid reader, but I can't remember for sure. Regardless of how I discovered it, once I learned that self-publishing was an option, I dove headfirst into learning everything I could about it.

The more I researched Kindle Direct Publishing, the more I wondered: Could I write a book and make money, too? I remember thinking that if I could just earn an extra $50 a month, I'd consider it a success. That would cover my car insurance at the time, which seemed like a reasonable goal.

As I continued exploring the Kindle eBooks available on Amazon, I was surprised to find that many were self-published by the authors themselves rather than by traditional publishers. Tens of thousands of people were making money this way—some as a side income and others full-time—publishing everything from cookbooks to romance novels. If they could do it, surely I could, right?

But then the bigger question hit me: How?

The "how" of self-publishing held me back for quite a while. I had no idea how to format or upload a Kindle book. Would I need specialized word processing software? Would I have to hire someone to format it for me? And what about the cover—how would I design that?

It's important to remember that, at the time, Amazon only offered Kindle eBooks—paperback and hardcover options didn't come until years later. Still, the uncertainty around where to begin with a first book left me stalled. It seemed like everyone else was self-publishing books effortlessly, but I was stuck, not knowing how even to start. That fear of the unknown stopped me from even starting to write a book for months.

Eventually, despite my nervousness and feeling overwhelmed, I forced myself to sit down at my computer and begin researching how to self-publish a Kindle eBook. While there were other platforms available, Amazon KDP naturally appealed to me because I was already familiar with the site as both a shopper and seller, and I read Kindle eBooks myself. I devoured blogs, skimmed discussion forums, and watched countless YouTube videos, overloading myself with so much information that my head felt like it might explode.

At one point, it felt like too much to manage, and I almost gave up before I had even written a single word. But I took a deep breath, figured out how to simplify the process, and soon realized that KDP was actually quite easy. A lot of forums and videos made it seem ridiculously complicated, many because they were also selling expensive courses. However, once I cut through the noise, I realized I could easily self-publish a Kindle eBook on Amazon on my own.

In fact, I figured out how to self-publish my book before I even wrote my first book! Once I had the publishing process down, I finally sat down to write. Since my strength was in nonfiction and I had years of experience selling on eBay, I decided to write my first book on that topic. The content was already in my head; I just needed to put it into words. Or, in this case, type it up in Microsoft Word.

Once I wrote and published my first Kindle eBook, 101 ITEMS TO SELL ON EBAY, the next challenge was promoting it. Initially, I felt overwhelmed by the idea of marketing my book on my own. Big-name authors have agents and publishers to oversee this part of the process, but as an indie author, the responsibility fell entirely on me.

However, it didn't take long before I discovered how to drive sales effectively—quickly, easily, and for the most part, for free—using social media. I already had a modest following on YouTube, and it was my subscribers who were the first to purchase my book. In just one month, I earned $200 from that eBook, far more than the $50 I had hoped for. In my second month, that book earned me $400. The next month, $600. And it just went up from there! I was hooked on Amazon KDP from that point forward.

I continued writing and publishing more books, and soon enough, I wasn't just building a library of titles but also a personal brand. My sales continued to grow. My early books were short, as that was the trend at the time. Today, most of my books are at least 60,000 words, but the first ones were more like booklets, often around 10,000 words.

The first books I published were nonfiction, focused on teaching people how to make money through eBay and YouTube. I also wrote short guides on making money online from other platforms and saving money while shopping. At one point, I even published three travel guides for Walt Disney World. For several years, my books remained in the nonfiction genre, relatively short, and available only as Kindle eBooks.

However, as the Kindle eBook market became increasingly competitive, I noticed my sales beginning to decline. What had started as a full-time income began slipping toward a part-time level, forcing me to rely on eBay again. When I first began self-publishing, the idea of making money from eBooks was still somewhat of a hidden gem. However, as word spread, Amazon became flooded with Kindle books of all kinds, making the marketplace increasingly crowded, and many authors saw their sales dip.

Determined to revive my publishing business, I knew I needed to adapt. That's when I decided to expand into paperback publishing, which Amazon had recently introduced as an option. Much like my initial hesitation with publishing eBooks, I hesitated publishing paperbacks. The formatting process was different—not just the interiors but also the covers. Even though paperbacks had been available for a couple of years, I delayed releasing my own, which ultimately cost me tens of thousands in potential revenue.

But just as I had figured out how to self-publish Kindle eBooks, I soon discovered that publishing paperback books through Amazon was just as straightforward. And once again, I kicked myself for not doing it sooner. The month I launched my first paperback, my royalties quadrupled. And the following year, they doubled when I released updated editions of my books.

Once I had the process down, formatting and uploading additional paperbacks became second nature. I also improved the content, expanding my books to offer more value to readers, which allowed me to increase prices. While I initially priced my Kindle eBooks at $3.99 each, by lengthening them and enhancing their content, I was able to raise the price to $9.99 for eBooks and as much as $18.99 for paperback versions.

As soon as the paperback versions were available, I found that most customers who read nonfiction preferred paperbacks over eBooks. My sales skyrocketed, and today, my paperback sales outpace my Kindle sales by a ten-to-one ratio, providing me with a full-time income. I no longer rely on eBay to pay my bills. However, I still dabble in reselling for extra money and to stay up-to-date on eBay so that I can release a new version of my best-selling book BEGINNER'S GUIDE TO SELLING ON EBAY every year.

At the beginning of my author journey, I was satisfied with my nonfiction books. They sold consistently well, and I released new editions each year. Even older versions continued to sell. However, I began to feel like I had reached a ceiling in writing about home-based e-commerce businesses.

Then, I discovered two other exciting possibilities in the world of publishing: low-content books and fiction books.

My introduction to low-content books came in 2019 when a successful author friend offered an online course. She primarily wrote fiction but had also been creating notebooks, journals, and planners, which she sold on Amazon. These no- and low-content books (so-called because they contain little to no written content) have become quite popular and represent another way for people to make money through KDP.

Note: Although Amazon now publishes paperback and hardcover books, its self-publishing program is still called Kindle Direct Publishing.

Intrigued with the idea of creating low-content books, I took her course and launched a second pen name to publish novelty notebooks, guided journals, and planners featuring fun cover designs. Over time, I expanded this collection to include adult coloring books.

Low-content books have consistently added an extra $1,000 per month to my income. During the holiday season, that number jumps significantly as these books are often bought as gifts. While they don't generate the same sales or profits as my nonfiction books, they provide a steady income for others who focus solely on this type of publishing. Plus, creating these products is both fun and easy, giving me a break from the more labor-intensive and research-heavy nonfiction books, such as the one you are reading now.

After mastering low-content books, I decided to challenge myself further by trying my hand at writing fiction. The same friend who had guided me through low-content publishing also offered a course on writing fiction. Her success was remarkable—she was earning six figures a month from her self-published fiction books—so I knew her advice was legitimate.

Though I had long considered myself only a nonfiction writer, with fiction seeming out of my realm of expertise, I started to reconsider. I had never really entertained the idea of writing fiction beyond a creative writing course in high school. But seeing how much more money fiction authors were making compared to their nonfiction counterparts piqued my interest.

In the summer of 2020, I took the plunge into fiction writing. Through my friend's course, I learned not only how to write fiction but also how to market it. I scoured Facebook author groups, devoured YouTube videos, and soaked up all the information I could. Then, I started writing. By July, I had released my first fiction book, and by the end of the year, I had published three more.

Today, I have nonfiction books under my name, low-content books under one pen name, and fiction books under another pen name. That's right—I have three pen names! I update my two best-selling nonfiction books yearly, but once a fiction book is completed, I never look at it again. All of my books continuously generate passive income, and I regularly add new titles to Amazon, expanding my library. This is work I can do from home on my schedule without the constant need to buy and sell inventory like I need to do for eBay.

Self-publishing truly is one of the best ways to generate passive income! All you need is a computer, basic word-processing software, and an internet connection to get started. While financial success might take time to happen, if you keep publishing new books, your royalties will begin to accumulate.

In this book, I will guide you step-by-step through the entire Amazon KDP process. From understanding the differences between nonfiction, fiction, and low-content books to writing, editing, cover design, formatting, uploading, and marketing both Kindle, paperback, and hardcover editions, this book covers everything, all from someone (ME!) who is doing the work and making a living from it.

The information I share in this book falls into two categories:

- Self-publishing nonfiction and/or fiction Kindle eBooks, paperback books, and hardcover books on Amazon and a few other platforms
- Self-publishing no- and low-content journals, planners, notebooks, and activity books in paperback and hardcover on Amazon

As a bonus, this year, I'm including information about artificial intelligence (AI) and how you can utilize it in your author business.

Everything I share in this book is based on my own experiences and the work I've done to make Amazon KDP my full-time job. While I can't promise overnight success, if you follow the techniques outlined here, you, too, can start making money through self-publishing.

Whether you want to focus on nonfiction books, fiction books, low-content books, or a combination of all three (as I do), this book will guide you through the entire self-publishing process. From writing and editing to formatting and uploading, I will walk you through every step.

In addition, I'll show you how to market and advertise your books, including how to, if you choose to, effectively run Facebook and Amazon Ads. I've created three distinct brands for each of my pen names, and I'll teach you how to do the same.

The best part about self-publishing is the freedom it offers. You have the autonomy to write what you want, when you want, and how you want—and you get to keep up to 70% of the royalties, which are automatically deposited into your bank account every month. You can publish from your couch or on a beach halfway around the world.

Creative freedom and financial security are what I love about Amazon KDP self-publishing!

So, if you're ready to dive into the world of self-publishing, let's get started!

CHAPTER ONE: THE POWER OF SELF-PUBLISHING

The terms **self-publishing** and **indie author** might be new to you. Even for those who are familiar with them, these terms often carry a negative connotation. Some people assume that self-published books aren't "real" books and that writers who independently publish aren't "real" authors.

Many people still believe there's only one legitimate path to becoming a published author: traditional publishing. In this model, you send your manuscript to literary agents and publishing houses, hoping to secure a contract. Random House and Simon & Schuster are two of the largest publishing houses in the United States, and many authors dream of having their books published by either. These publishers, IF they accept a manuscript, which is very rare, take an author's book, edit it, publish it, and then take the lion's share of the profits.

With self-publishing, however, authors retain all control. We can write what we want, when we want, design our own covers, and handle our own marketing. And we keep the majority of profits. However, there are still those who look down on self-published books and indie authors. I've had people I know tell me that self-published books like mine aren't "real books," and I'll be honest—it used to hurt my feelings.

But here's the truth: Tens of thousands of people have read my books. They're sold on Amazon and other major websites. I have stacks of my own paperbacks and hardcovers sitting on my bookshelf. They certainly look and feel like real books to me! And the money that I earn every month is very real, too!

Fortunately, the narrative around self-publishing is shifting, even among traditionally published authors who see their indie author friends earning far more than they do. Let's be honest: writing is an art, but we all need to pay the bills.

However, it is true that self-publishing once had a legitimately poor reputation. Much of that came from shady "vanity presses" that charged authors fees to print their books, leaving them responsible for selling their own inventory. While those options still exist (you may have seen commercials for them), modern self-publishing is different—and, in many cases, far better.

Self-publishing today allows writers to bypass the traditional route of getting their books into the hands of readers. Instead of sending manuscripts to agents and publishers hoping for a book deal, you can upload your work directly to a book distribution platform. There are no rejection letters, no bossy editors, and no rigid expectations. You write your book, upload it to the desired platform, and the platform prints and ships it, depositing the profits into your bank account every month.

And once a book is on a platform, it can sell forever, meaning there is no limit to the money you can earn. Profits from books are called "royalties," and royalties are a form of passive income. Every day, I sell books that I wrote years ago. I don't advertise these books or even think about them. Still, somehow, Amazon customers find them and buy them, providing me with monthly income.

Fortunately, the stigma surrounding self-publishing is fading. However, I still get the occasional comment from people who say they want to write a "real book" that's mass-produced by a publishing house. When they hear about the earnings of self-published authors compared to those who sign away their rights to publishers, their perspective tends to shift.

For example, on Amazon, you can earn up to 70% of the sale price for a Kindle eBook and 60% for a paperback or hardcover. In contrast, traditionally published authors might earn only 10%. While traditional authors may receive a small advance, their royalties only continue as long as the publisher keeps printing the book. Very few books get a second printing, which means most traditionally published authors only make money in the early stages of their book's release. And when an author signs away their rights to a book, it's gone forever. They can't try to self-publish the book themselves.

On the other hand, self-published authors like me continue to make money as long as their books are listed on Amazon and other platforms. I still earn royalties from books I published back in 2013!

Becoming a wealthy author through traditional publishing is a one-in-a-million chance. However, self-publishing offers you a way to cut through the bureaucracy of publishing houses and take control of your work. I know authors who earn six figures per month from their self-published books—that's over a million dollars a year! The vast majority of traditionally published authors barely make minimum wage after everything is said and done. They may get a book or two onto the shelves at Barnes & Noble, but they are essentially working for the publishing house.

But it's not just the money that self-publishing offers; it also gives you the creative freedom to write whatever you want. You can publish short stories or epic novels. You can experiment with genres like romance, thrillers, mysteries, children's literature, young adult fiction, or any niche in non-fiction. If you're passionate about graphic design, creating no-and-low content books like journals, planners, notebooks, or activity books might be the perfect creative outlet for you.

When you self-publish, you're free from publisher deadlines, and you don't have an editor giving you endless corrections you don't want to make. Most importantly, your royalties aren't eaten up by others. You're in control, and the bulk of the money stays with you. My expenses are minimal—some graphic design software and advertising costs. After taxes, the rest of the profits are mine!

That's not to say the responsibility of doing everything yourself isn't overwhelming at times. In addition to writing, you'll need to edit your own work, design your covers, format and upload files, and, of course, advertise your books.

Self-published authors wear many hats: writer, editor, cover designer, and marketer. While you can outsource some of these tasks (which we'll discuss later in this book), the ultimate responsibility falls on you. But even if you choose to hire help, freelancers are much more affordable than the hefty cuts taken by traditional publishing houses.

At first, taking on all of these tasks yourself can feel overwhelming. But I'm here to tell you it's also incredibly empowering and liberating. You get to write what you want, how you want, without anyone dictating the process. You essentially become your own one-person publishing house, and the majority of the income stays in your pocket.

So why self-publish specifically on Amazon? After all, there are other self-publishing platforms out there, which I'll touch on later in this book. The simple answer is that Amazon dominates the book market. They control nearly 50% of the print book market and 75% of the eBook market. The remaining portion is split between traditional publishers and platforms like Apple Books, Barnes & Noble, Kobo, and Google. Since Amazon began as an online bookstore, it has remained the leader in this category and allowing writers to self-publish on its site has only increased its dominance.

Publishing your book on Amazon means having access to the vast majority of readers worldwide. I sell books to customers in the United States, Canada, the U.K., Australia, Japan, Germany, and Italy—all through Amazon's American platform, Amazon.com. Amazon takes care of getting my books in front of international buyers, as well as managing the printing, shipping, and customer service. My only job is to upload my work and if I choose market it via social media or Amazon's advertising platform.

If my books were traditionally published, I would first need to hire an agent to get them in front of publishers. I'd also need a lawyer who understands the publishing world. Even then, my books would probably only be available in the U.S., meaning I'd miss out on the hundreds of dollars I make each month from international sales. If my books became extremely popular, a publishing house might consider expanding sales internationally, but that's never guaranteed.

On top of that, if a book underperforms by a publisher's standards, they'll stop printing and promoting it, and I could be dropped as a client. Or worse, I'd remain under contract and unable to self-publish other books until the contract ended. I've met too many authors who sold the rights to their books to a publisher only to see their books dropped because they needed to meet a certain sales threshold. And as I mentioned earlier, because they signed away their rights to that book, it's gone forever.

When you self-publish, your book stays on Amazon and other platforms as long as you want it to, unless you choose to unpublish it. You can continue promoting it indefinitely and even build on your first book by creating a series. The possibilities are limitless.

One of the best aspects of self-publishing through Amazon KDP is that I don't have to deal with customer service issues. In fact, I have no direct contact with customers. I don't know who buys my books; the only data I receive is the country where the sale was made. I never have to manage customer questions or handle issues like returns. If a customer experiences a problem, such as a delayed shipment or a lost package, Amazon takes care of it. I never even heard about it! This is a huge advantage compared to my other business selling on eBay, where I manage customer service issues daily.

Amazon also offers a great opportunity for authors to earn money from their Kindle eBooks, particularly fiction, through the Kindle Unlimited program. This program allows authors to earn money whenever someone borrows one of their eBooks. This means you can make money both from the sale of your books and from borrowers. Fiction is, unsurprisingly, the largest and most popular category of books. Fiction readers are voracious—once they find a genre they enjoy, they read book after book, often on Kindle. With Kindle Unlimited, readers pay one low monthly fee to access hundreds of thousands of titles, and authors enrolled in the program make money for every page that is read.

We'll dive deeper into the Kindle Unlimited program later in the book.

When you sign up for a KDP account, you cannot only upload your book for sale on Amazon but also upload a new version at any time. Your writing isn't set in stone—if you find mistakes or want to add new information, you simply upload an updated version, which replaces the old one. In contrast, once your book is traditionally published, that's it—you've signed away the rights and have no say in making updates or corrections.

You can also adjust your book's price at any time on Amazon and other platforms. For example, you might start with a Kindle eBook priced at $5.99, but if sales are slow, you can lower the price. As you've likely seen, Kindle eBook prices range from

99 cents to double digits. Your royalty percentage will vary depending on the price you set. You can adjust prices based on market demand, raising them during peak sales periods and lowering them during slower times. And if you choose to be exclusive to Amazon and enroll your book in Kindle Unlimited, you can run free promotions and discounts to attract more readers.

Self-publishing puts you in the driver's seat, and Amazon, in particular, provides you with millions of potential customers and an incredibly user-friendly platform with numerous tools to promote your work.

So the question isn't why would you self-publish, specifically on Amazon, but rather, why wouldn't you?

CHAPTER TWO: WHY SELF-PUBLISH YOUR BOOK ON AMAZON

When it comes to self-publishing, there are numerous platforms available, but the undisputed leader is Amazon, specifically through its Kindle Direct Publishing (KDP) program. KDP has revolutionized the publishing world by giving authors the power to reach readers across the globe without the gatekeeping of traditional publishers.

The vast majority of indie authors not only publish their books on Amazon but also earn the bulk of their income from this platform. But what makes Amazon the best place to self-publish your book? Let's break down the key reasons why Amazon KDP stands above the rest:

Amazon's Global Customer Base: Amazon offers unparalleled reach with millions of customers worldwide. It's not just an online store—it's a global marketplace accessible in many countries. As an indie author, this means your book isn't limited to just your local market; it can be purchased by readers across the globe in the U.S., U.K., Canada, Australia, Germany, Japan, and more.

When you publish your book on Amazon, you're instantly tapping into a massive audience of readers who regularly shop for books. Amazon's algorithms also help your book become more discoverable, showing it to potential readers based on their browsing and buying habits. This kind of exposure is hard to replicate on other platforms.

Amazon Is A Trusted Name in Books: Amazon started as an online bookstore, so it's no surprise they remain the dominant force in the book market today. Readers trust Amazon as a reliable place to discover and purchase books, both in physical and digital formats. Publishing your book on Amazon lends it credibility, as many readers are more likely to take a chance on a self-published book if they find it through a trusted platform.

By being associated with Amazon, you gain access to a marketplace that millions of people already trust for their book purchases, making it easier to build your own reputation as an author.

Free to Publish: One of the most significant advantages of self-publishing on Amazon is the cost—there isn't one! It's completely free to upload and publish your book on KDP. Amazon doesn't charge you upfront fees for distribution or hosting your book on their site. Instead, they take a percentage of your sales, which means you only pay Amazon when you make money.

This low barrier to entry allows you to get started without any financial risk. You can publish your book without worrying about upfront costs, making it one of the most affordable ways to break into the publishing world. Many other self-publishing platforms, which we will discuss later in this book, charge you to upload to their sites. But Amazon allows you to begin your self-publishing journey for free.

A Simple, User-Friendly Platform: Self-publishing on Amazon is incredibly easy, even for beginners. The KDP platform is designed with authors in mind, making it simple to upload your manuscript, format it, and publish it with just a few clicks.

You don't need any technical expertise—Amazon guides you through the entire process, from uploading your book to setting the price.

Even if you're new to self-publishing, Amazon KDP offers detailed instructions and resources to help you navigate the process. Whether it's your first book or your fiftieth, Amazon's platform makes it easy to get your book in front of readers.

Multiple Publishing Formats: Amazon KDP offers flexibility when it comes to the types of books you can publish. Whether you're writing fiction or non-fiction, Amazon allows you to publish in three formats: Kindle eBooks, paperback, and hardcover. This gives you the freedom to cater to different reader preferences, whether they prefer reading on their Kindle or holding a physical book.

Amazon also supports the publication of low-and-no content books, such as journals, notebooks, planners, and activity books. These can be published in both paperback and hardcover formats, making Amazon an excellent platform for a wide range of publishing projects. Whether you're writing novels or designing creative journals, Amazon has you covered.

Kindle Unlimited: For new authors, Amazon's Kindle Unlimited (KU) program can help get books into the hands of readers without the power of a major publishing house behind them. KU is a subscription service where readers pay a monthly fee to access an extensive library of books, and authors get paid based on the number of pages readers consume. The program literally tracks each page that is turned on the reader's device.

Enrolling your book in Kindle Unlimited can help you build an audience while still earning money. You have the flexibility to choose which books to enroll, and the commitment to the program only lasts for 90 days at a time. During that time, you can run free or discount promotions to attract readers. If the strategy works, you can continue in the program or opt-out and "go wide" by publishing your eBook on other platforms.

Amazon Ads: Amazon Ads are a powerful tool to help boost your book sales. You can set up ad campaigns that target specific categories or keywords. Or you can let Amazon automatically show your book to relevant customers. With Amazon Ads, you control how much you want to spend by setting a per-click cost, and you can pause or cancel the ad at any time.

This advertising platform can be especially beneficial for new authors who are trying to get their books noticed. By setting up targeted ads, you increase your book's visibility and attract potential readers who are already interested in similar genres or topics.

Amazon Is Simply The Best: Amazon KDP offers an unmatched combination of global reach, ease of use, and affordability, making it the best platform for indie authors to self-publish their books. Whether you're writing fiction, non-fiction, or creating low-content books, Amazon gives you the tools to get your book in front of millions of readers worldwide. Add to that the flexibility to manage your book's price, edit your content, and use Amazon Ads to grow your audience, and it's clear why Amazon is simply the best choice when it comes to self-publishing!

CHAPTER THREE: THE ESSENTIAL TOOLS TO SELF-PUBLISH

So, you have a book in mind that you want to write, and you plan to publish it through Amazon KDP. If you're like I was, you might worry that you'll need expensive equipment or complicated software to get started. While there are some costly programs out there, you really only need some basic equipment to begin self-publishing:

Computer: A computer with word processing capabilities is the most essential for self-publishing. You can't upload your book to Amazon from a paper notebook or typewriter, and using a smartphone or tablet won't work for the publishing process. You'll need a reliable computer—either a Mac or a PC will do. Personally, I prefer PCs and have written all my books on Dell or HP laptops. Still, many authors work exclusively on Apple computers. The best part is that you can use whatever you already have!

When choosing or upgrading your computer for writing and publishing, here are some key factors to consider:

Screen Size: If you're going to spend long hours writing and editing, a screen that's comfortable for your eyes is crucial. A 13-inch laptop screen might be portable, but it can feel cramped for extended writing sessions. Consider at least a 15-inch screen for a laptop or, if you're using a desktop, a monitor that's 21 inches or larger. If you plan to do graphic design for low-content books or illustrations for children's books, the bigger the screen you can afford, the better.

Processing Power: For basic writing and internet use, almost any modern computer with an Intel i3 or AMD Ryzen 3 processor will suffice. However, if you plan to run graphic design software, such as Canva or Adobe Photoshop, or if you multitask with several applications open, aim for a faster processor like an Intel i5/i7 or AMD Ryzen 5/7. A more powerful processor not only speeds up your current work but also ensures that your computer can handle future software updates and more demanding tasks, such as advanced formatting or video editing for book trailers. I purchase computers with the fastest processing I can afford.

RAM (Memory): For most writing and formatting tasks, 8 GB of RAM is sufficient. However, if you use graphic design or video editing software, 16 GB or more will provide a smoother experience, reducing lag and improving multitasking capabilities. My rule of thumb is to choose a system with as much RAM as you can afford.

Storage: Word processing files are typically on the smaller side. Still, if you're working with high-resolution images for low-content books or children's books, you'll need more storage. A solid-state drive (SSD) is preferable for faster performance and quick file access. A 256 GB SSD is usually enough for writing and basic tasks but consider 512 GB or more if you plan to store large files. Use cloud storage solutions like Google Drive, Dropbox, or OneDrive to back up your work. This not only protects your files in case of a hardware failure but also allows you to access your work from any device.

Portability: If you like to write on the go, a laptop is obviously the best choice. Consider a lightweight model with good battery life if you'll be working in different locations. If you prefer a stationary setup, a desktop computer with a larger monitor might be more comfortable for long writing sessions. These days, laptops come in large sizes with lots of features, meaning you may still choose a laptop even if you have a stationery writing setup. If you are only writing and not using graphic design programs, you can get away with a smaller laptop.

Ergonomics: Whether you use a laptop or desktop, an external keyboard and mouse can improve comfort and reduce strain during extended writing sessions. Look for ergonomic designs that support your hands and wrists. Ensure your screen is at eye level, and your chair provides good back support to maintain a comfortable and healthy writing posture.

No matter what type of computer you have, the key is to make sure it meets your needs and allows you to focus on writing and publishing without technical disruptions. Use what you already have, and only upgrade if your current setup feels limiting. Remember, it's not about having the most advanced technology but rather having tools that support your creative process!

PRO TIP: Even the best computer will only work well if you have a comfortable chair and a solid writing desk. An ergonomic setup will help you write faster and without body pain. I've developed sore wrists and shoulder pain from typing in a chair that is too low. Office supply stores such as Office Max and Staples often have a clearance section of quality office chairs already assembled. You can also find secondhand chairs and desks on the Facebook marketplace, at garage sales, and at thrift stores.

Internet: You'll need internet access to upload your book to Amazon. The faster the connection, the better, but most basic internet services can easily manage file uploads. Since you'll be spending a lot of time on Amazon's KDP site, a stable and reliable internet connection is important. I have high-speed internet through my city's cable provider, but I can also access the internet through the hotspot on my iPhone, which comes in handy when the internet is down due to weather or work in the area.

Microsoft Word: Amazon makes it simple to write and upload books using Microsoft Word. You don't need any fancy writing programs—just standard Microsoft Word, which comes with most computer systems. If Word isn't pre-installed, you can purchase a copy online at Microsoft.com or at any office supply store.

That said, other programs can also be used successfully. Many authors prefer one or more of the following:

Evernote: While not a traditional word processor, Evernote is a powerful note-taking app that's great for planning and outlining your book. You can organize your notes, create outlines, and even write portions of your manuscript on the go. It syncs across devices, making it easy to capture ideas wherever you are. They offer a basic free subscription; if you need more space, you can upgrade to one of several plans.

Google Docs: If you don't have Microsoft Word, Google Docs is a free alternative to obtain word-processing software. While it doesn't offer all of Word's advanced formatting options, it's perfectly fine for writing your manuscript. You can then use a separate formatting program to fine-tune it before uploading. You simply need a Google account to access the program; if you don't have a Google account, they are free and will also give you a free email address ending in gmail.com. As you begin your author journey, you'll want to have a dedicated email address or addresses for your pen names, and signing up for these through Google is free and easy.

Hemingway Editor: Hemingway Editor is a simple, distraction-free writing tool that also acts as an editor. Hemingway highlights complex sentences, passive voice, and other common issues, helping you write clear and concise prose. It's great for self-editing and improving readability. Its website is extremely basic, but it is free to use. However, if you want more features, you can upgrade to a paid plan.

LibreOffice Writer: A free, open-source alternative to Microsoft Word, LibreOffice Writer offers many similar features, including advanced formatting options. It's compatible with multiple file formats, including .doc and .docx. Since it is completely free to use, it's a great option for those who don't have Microsoft Word installed on their computers.

Notion: Notion is a flexible, all-in-one workspace that combines note-taking, task management, and collaboration. Notion is great for organizing research, plotting your book, and drafting content. You can create databases, link documents, and keep all your book-related materials in one place. Notion is free to download.

Pages: Pages is Apple's native word processing software for Mac users. While less feature-rich than Word, it offers a clean and intuitive interface for writing and basic formatting. It can export files in various formats, including PDF and Word. And if you have a Mac, it may already be installed on your system.

Reedsy Studio: Reedsy.com is a platform designed to help authors and publishers navigate the world of self-publishing by connecting writers with professional services such as editors, designers, marketers, and ghostwriters. Their Reedsy Studio is a free online tool specifically designed for authors. Reedsy allows you to write, format, and export your manuscript as an ePub or PDF file. It's user-friendly and provides features for collaboration and editing. It also links to Google, so if you have a .gmail account, it's easy to get started.

Scrivener: Scrivener is a popular word-processing tool designed specifically for authors. It offers features for organization, goal setting, statistics, and custom formatting. Scrivener is available for both Mac and PC and costs less than $50. Scrivener is probably the most popular program for full-time indie fiction authors.

Ulysses: Ulysses is a minimalist writing program for Mac and iOS devices that easily exports files for uploading to Amazon KDP. It costs $5.99 a month.

yWriter: A free writing tool designed by an author for authors, yWriter breaks your novel into scenes and chapters, making it easy to manage large projects. It includes features like word count tracking, scene summaries, and character development tools. yWriter is free to download.

Formatting: You can upload a Microsoft document directly to Amazon KDP. However, most authors prefer to format their books in a separate software program. For years, I uploaded to KDP straight from Word, but in recent years, I have used Kindle Create, as it gives me the right files not just for Amazon but also for other websites I publish to.

Kindle Create: Kindle Create is Amazon's free software for formatting KDP books. It's available for PC and Mac and simplifies the formatting process. We'll cover Kindle Create in detail later in this book, but for now, know that it's an easy, no-cost way to format your book for Amazon.

Paid Formatting Options: While Kindle Create is free, other paid formatting programs offer more features, including:

Adobe InDesign: Adobe InDesign is professional desktop publishing software used for creating complex book layouts. It offers advanced design and formatting tools, making it a great choice for authors with experience in graphic design or those looking to create highly customized layouts. While it's more complex and has a steep learning curve, it provides unmatched control over your book's formatting. It is compatible with Mac and PC and is available as a subscription for $20.99 per month.

Atticus: Atticus is an all-in-one writing and formatting software designed specifically for authors. It allows you to write, format, and export your book in various formats, including Kindle eBooks and print-ready PDFs. Atticus offers a range of formatting options similar to Vellum but is available for both Mac and PC. There is a one-time purchase fee of $147.

Canva Pro: While the free Kindle Create software is great for 6x9-inch fiction and nonfiction books, Canva is a free program that allows you to create books of different sizes or with a lot of graphics, such as children's books. It allows you to create books and save them as PDF files to be uploaded to Amazon. However, if you want to use any of the elements, fonts, colors, or images in Canva, you'll want to upgrade to a monthly Canva Pro subscription.

Jutoh: Jutoh is a versatile eBook creation tool that allows you to import and format your manuscript. It offers a range of templates and styles to create eBooks in various formats, including Kindle, ePub, and others. Jutoh is particularly good for authors looking to create complex eBooks with images and interactive content. Jutoh works on both Mac and PC and has a one-time fee of $49.

Pressbooks: Pressbooks is an online book production tool that offers a variety of templates and customization options for creating eBooks and print books. It's built on the WordPress platform, making it easy to use for those familiar with WordPress. You can export your book in multiple formats, including PDF, ePub, and Mobi. Subscriptions start at $19.99 per month.

Scrivener: Scrivener offers a "Compile" feature that allows you to format and export your manuscript into various eBook and print-ready formats. While less sophisticated than dedicated formatting tools like Vellum, it's a good option for authors already using Scrivener to write their books. It works with both Mac and PC and costs $49 to purchase it outright.

Vellum: Vellum is highly regarded for formatting eBooks and print books, offering beautiful templates and a user-friendly interface. It is only available for Mac users. With Vellum, you can create professional-looking Kindle eBooks and print-ready PDFs for paperback and hardcover books. It supports Kindle, Apple Books, and other eBook formats. Vellum Ebooks, which allows you to create unlimited eBooks, costs $199.99; Vellum Press, which allows you to create unlimited eBooks and paperback books, costs $249.99.

Graphic Design Software: If you plan to design your own book covers, having the right graphic design software is essential. A professional-looking cover is crucial for attracting readers and making your book stand out. I personally use Canva Pro for my cover designs, as it provides a user-friendly interface with all the tools you need to create high-quality book covers.

Canva Pro: Canva is the easiest graphic design software option available. It is a program that most children's book authors use, as well as those who create low-content books such as journals, planners, and coloring books.

Canva is known for its intuitive drag-and-drop interface, making it accessible even for beginners with no graphic design experience. You can easily create stunning book covers without needing to learn complicated design software. There is a free version, but if you plan to use any design elements within the Canva platform, you need to upgrade to a monthly Canva Pro subscription. You can play around with the free version before deciding to pay for the Pro option.

Canva offers pre-sized templates specifically for eBooks, paperbacks, and hardcovers, which are essential for ensuring your cover meets the exact dimensions required by Amazon KDP. You can also create custom-sized templates for other print-on-demand (POD) platforms. With Canva Pro, you gain access to a vast library of high-quality stock photos, illustrations, fonts, and design elements. This allows you to create unique, eye-catching covers without needing to purchase additional graphics or hire a designer.

Canva's powerful editing tools let you customize every aspect of your cover, from fonts and colors to images and layouts. You can also upload your own images and fonts, giving you complete creative control. Canva Pro's Brand Kit feature allows you to save your brand colors, fonts, and logos. This is especially useful if you are creating a series of books and want to maintain a consistent look across all your covers.

Once your cover design is complete, you can download it in high-resolution formats like PNG, JPG, or PDF, ready for upload to Amazon KDP or any other platform.

Adobe Photoshop and Illustrator: These are industry-standard graphic design tools offering advanced features for creating detailed and custom cover designs. Photoshop is great for editing photos and creating intricate designs, while Illustrator is perfect for vector graphics and typography. However, both programs come with a steep learning curve and are subscription-based, which can be costly for new authors.

GIMP: A free, open-source alternative to Photoshop, GIMP offers many of the same features, including photo manipulation, layering, and design tools. It's a good option for authors on a budget who want more control over their cover designs without the cost of Adobe products.

Affinity Designer and Affinity Photo are more affordable alternatives to Adobe products. They offer robust design and photo-editing capabilities without the subscription model. They are one-time purchases and work well for both Mac and PC users.

Hiring a Designer: While creating your own cover can be rewarding, it's not for everyone. Many authors prefer to hire professional cover designers through platforms like Fiverr and UpWork. This option is handy if you want a polished, genre-specific cover that aligns with current market trends.

Hiring a designer can range from $50 to several hundred dollars, depending on the complexity of the design and the designer's experience. It's a worthwhile investment, especially for genres with high cover design standards, like romance or thriller. Look for designers who specialize in your genre and have a portfolio of previous work. Many designers offer pre-made covers, which can be a more affordable option if you're on a tight budget.

Amazon KDP Built-In Cover Designer: Amazon KDP offers a built-in cover designer for authors who want a straightforward solution. While it is a basic program, it's a quick and easy way to create a basic cover that meets Amazon's requirements and can work for nonfiction books and planners with basic covers. You can choose from a variety of templates, fonts, and colors, and it automatically adjusts your cover size based on your book's trim size and page count. While it's free to use and integrated directly into the KDP platform, the customization options are limited, and the covers may look generic compared to those created with more advanced design tools.

And That's It!

Now, I know what you're thinking: *That's it?* Just a computer, internet, word processing software, and cover design tools—either DIY or through a designer—and you're ready to publish?

But yes, it really is that simple! I, too, let the fear of needing complicated software stop me from self-publishing for months. You don't need to make the same mistake. If you have a book to write, open up whatever word-processing software you have and start typing.

MY TOOLS: So, what do I, a full-time indie author, use to write, edit, and format my books? Currently, I use an HP laptop (I've also used Dell in the past) with a fast processor and plenty of storage. I need the extra storage not only for my book files but also for the graphics and illustrations I use in my children's books.

For writing, I use Microsoft Word for my nonfiction books, and I pay for a Grammarly Pro subscription to help with editing. I format my books for Kindle and paperback using Amazon's free Kindle Create program. For designing my book covers, I use Canva Pro, which I also use to lay out my children's books and incorporate elements into the illustrations. Additionally, I use Tangent Templates (which I'll cover later in this book) to design low-content planners.

The tools I use are not only user-friendly but also affordable—and, in some cases, free. Could I upgrade to more advanced software and hire professional designers? Absolutely. But I love managing every step of the publishing process myself. It gives me complete creative control and helps me keep costs down!

CHAPTER FOUR: MASTERING AMAZON BOOK CATEGORIES

As I mentioned in the Introduction, this book covers three main types of books: fiction, nonfiction, and low-content (such as journals, planners, notebooks, and activity books). While some information in this guide applies only to specific types of books, many chapters include elements relevant to all three. This chapter is one of those, as the categories you choose for your books can significantly impact their visibility and discoverability on Amazon.

IMPORTANT UPDATE: In late 2023, Amazon updated their system to allow authors to choose three categories for each format of their books. Previously, authors could select two categories per format during the upload process and then contact Amazon to request inclusion in up to eight additional categories. Now, you're limited to three categories per format. The good news is that the category selection in the listing form now matches the categories on Amazon's website exactly. This means you can choose three categories for the Kindle version of your book and another three for the paperback version—a significant change that I'll discuss in detail throughout this book.

For both fiction and nonfiction books, Kindle, paperback, and hardcover editions often go hand in hand. Most books are first uploaded as Kindle files, and then a paperback version is added to the same listing. Some authors will then add a hardcover version, still within the same listing. If you've browsed books on Amazon, you've probably noticed that many titles are available in multiple formats, such as Kindle, paperback, and even hardcover. The process for uploading paperback and hardcover versions is similar and straightforward.

It's important to note that low-and-no content books are only available in paperback and, if they are long enough, hardcover form. Because these books are meant to be written in, offering an eBook version wouldn't make sense. However, category selection is just as crucial for journals, planners, notebooks, and activity books as it is for fiction and nonfiction books. Choosing the right categories ensures that your book appears in relevant search results, making it easier for customers to find and purchase your work.

Before you can upload a book to Amazon, you must first create it—whether that means writing a fiction or nonfiction manuscript or designing a low-content book. But before you even start this process, you need to decide what type of book you're going to create and the category in which it will be sold. That's why I'm covering this topic before diving into how to format and upload a book. You can't self-publish on Amazon without a complete, so we need to address this foundational step first.

When it comes to authoring books—sometimes referred to as "high content books"—there are two main categories: fiction and nonfiction. Some authors, like me, publish in both categories, while others prefer to focus on just one. There is no right or wrong choice; you should start with whatever works best for you. Remember, when you self-publish, you have the freedom to write in any category as your journey evolves.

Fiction: You're likely familiar with fiction, which the dictionary defines as "literature in the form of prose, especially short stories and novels, which describes imaginary events and people." From classic authors like William Shakespeare and Agatha Christie to modern bestsellers like Danielle Steel and J.K. Rowling, fiction encompasses a broad range of styles and genres.

While you may know the big names in fiction, there are hundreds of thousands of indie authors who self-publish their novels and stories—most of them on Amazon. One of the main reasons authors choose to self-publish is the financial incentive. Amazon typically pays authors nearly three times more than traditional publishers. For those who haven't secured a traditional book deal, self-publishing on Amazon offers an accessible and lucrative alternative. Why spend time sending out countless proposals and dealing with rejection when you can publish your book yourself and start earning royalties right away?

Amazon dedicates an entire section to *Fiction & Literature* books, all of which can be published as both Kindle eBooks and paperbacks. While some authors choose to publish in both formats, many start with just Kindle eBooks. The main categories of Kindle eBook fiction on Amazon include:

- **Absurdist**: Fiction that explores surreal, illogical, or nonsensical themes.
- **Action & Adventure**: Stories packed with excitement, danger, and daring exploits.
- **Adaptations & Pastiche**: Works inspired by or imitating established literature, often in a new context or style.
- **Animals**: Books featuring animal characters or focusing on relationships between humans and animals.
- **Anthologies & Literature Collections**: Collections of short stories, essays, or poetry from various authors or genres.

- **Black & African American**: Literature exploring the experiences and cultures of Black and African American communities.
- **British**: Fiction set in or influenced by British culture, often reflecting the country's history, society, and traditions.
- **Classics**: Timeless works of literature recognized for their enduring cultural or literary significance.
- **Contemporary Fiction**: Modern stories reflecting current life and society, often focused on personal and social issues.
- **Drama & Plays**: Written works intended for theatrical performance, emphasizing dialogue and conflict.
- **Erotica** : Literature focusing on themes of sensuality and intimate relationships, often explicit in nature.
- **Essays & Correspondence**: Nonfiction works featuring essays, letters, and personal reflections.
- **Foreign Language Fiction**: Fiction written in languages other than English, often translated.
- **Genre Fiction**: Books categorized by specific genres such as Romance, mystery, science fiction, and fantasy.
- **Historical Fiction**: Stories set in the past, often integrating real historical events or figures with fictional narratives.
- **Horror**: Fiction designed to evoke fear, suspense, and the supernatural.
- **Humor & Satire**: Books that use humor, irony, or satire to entertain or critique society and human behavior.
- **Literary Fiction**: Character-driven stories that focus on style, themes, and deeper philosophical or social issues.
- **Mythology & Folk Tales**: Stories based on traditional myths, legends, and folklore from various cultures.
- **People with Disabilities**: Books featuring characters with disabilities, exploring their experiences and perspectives.

- **Poetry**: Verses and prose expressing ideas, emotions, and stories through structured or free-form language.
- **Religious & Inspirational Fiction**: Stories that explore faith, spirituality, and moral lessons within religious or inspirational contexts.
- **Short Stories**: Collections of brief, self-contained narratives focusing on a specific theme or character.
- **Small Town & Rural**: Fiction set in small communities, exploring local life, culture, and relationships.
- **United States**: Literature reflecting American culture, history, and society.
- **Women's Fiction**: Stories centered around women's lives, relationships, and personal growth.
- **World Literature**: Fiction from around the globe, showcasing diverse cultures, experiences, and perspectives.

You probably scanned that list and quickly identified the genres that align with your reading preferences. You might also have spotted the category you'd like to write in. Or perhaps you didn't see your favorite genre listed.

Take another look: Did you notice that Romance is missing? Romance is the largest category of fiction books, yet Amazon does not list it under the main Fiction & Literature categories. How can that be? Is this a mistake? What's going on?

There are two possible explanations for this. First, certain genres, like Romance, have their own dedicated sections under the Kindle eBooks tab, separate from the main Fiction & Literature category. So, if you go back and click on the Kindle eBooks tab, you'll find Romance listed there.

The second reason is that some genres are categorized under specific subcategories within more prominent categories. For example, Romance might be found under subcategories like Women's Fiction or Contemporary Fiction. Understanding Amazon's category system is crucial for ensuring your book is listed correctly and reaches its target audience.

Let's take a step back and look at the main Kindle eBook categories on Amazon. It's much easier to explore these categories on a desktop computer rather than a mobile device. To access the categories, follow these steps:

Go to the Amazon homepage. Click on the **ALL** tag on the left-hand side of the page to open a drop-down menu with all of Amazon's categories.

Select Kindle E-readers & Books. Under the **Kindle Store** section, click on **Kindle eBooks**.

Navigate to the main Kindle Books page. At the top of this page, you'll find a tab labeled **Categories**. Click on this tab to see a complete list of all Kindle categories, which include:

- **Arts & Photography**: Books on visual arts, photography, and creative expression.
- **Biographies & Memoirs**: Life stories and personal experiences of notable individuals.
- **Business & Money**: Guides and insights on finance, management, and entrepreneurship.
- **Children's eBooks**: Stories and educational content for young readers.
- **Comics, Manga & Graphic Novels**: Illustrated stories and narratives in various genres and styles.
- **Computers & Technology**: Books on software, hardware, and the latest tech trends.
- **Cookbooks, Food & Wine**: Recipes, culinary techniques, and food and drink culture.
- **Crafts, Hobbies & Home**: Guides on DIY projects, home improvement, and hobbies.
- **Education & Teaching**: Resources for educators, students, and lifelong learners.
- **Engineering & Transportation**: Books on engineering principles, transportation, and related fields.

- **Foreign Languages**: Resources for learning and mastering different languages.
- **Health, Fitness & Dieting**: Guides to physical health, nutrition, and wellness.
- **History**: Books exploring historical events, figures, and eras.
- **Humor & Entertainment**: Books for light reading, humor, and entertainment.
- **LGBTQ+ eBooks**: Literature focusing on LGBTQ+ experiences, themes, and culture.
- **Law**: Books on legal studies, case law, and the justice system.
- **Literature & Fiction**: Novels, short stories, and literary works across genres.
- **Medical eBooks**: Books on medicine, healthcare, and related fields.
- **Mystery, Thriller & Suspense**: Stories filled with intrigue, suspense, and thrilling twists.
- **Nonfiction**: Factual books across various subjects, offering knowledge and insights.
- **Parenting & Relationships**: Guides on raising children and nurturing healthy relationships.
- **Politics & Social Sciences**: Books on political theory, social issues, and cultural studies.
- **Reference**: Comprehensive guides and resources for research and information.
- **Religion & Spirituality**: Books on faith, belief systems, and spiritual growth.
- **Romance**: Love stories and romantic narratives across various subgenres.
- **Science & Math**: Books exploring scientific principles, discoveries, and mathematical concepts.
- **Science Fiction & Fantasy**: Stories set in futuristic, fantastical, or imaginative worlds.
- **Self-Help**: Guides to personal growth, mental health, and achieving life goals.

- **Sports & Outdoors**: Books on sports, outdoor activities, and adventure.
- **Teen & Young Adult**: Literature for teens and young adults, covering diverse genres.
- **Travel**: Books on destinations, travel tips, and cultural exploration.

As you can see, Romance isn't the only genre listed separately from the main Fiction & Literature category. In fact, many genres that one would typically classify as fiction have their own dedicated sections. While Romance may not appear directly under the main Fiction & Literature category, it is a major category in its own right, with nearly 80 subcategories under Kindle eBooks alone.

This setup can be confusing, especially for new authors trying to determine where their book fits best. It's crucial to explore the full range of categories and subcategories available, as choosing the right ones can significantly impact your book's visibility and discoverability on Amazon.

Like any good fiction story, there's a plot twist when it comes to Amazon's book categories. Understanding this twist is vital for finding the best fit for your books. Remember: selecting the correct categories is essential for helping potential readers find your work.

The categories listed earlier are just the main categories for Kindle eBooks. Each main category has numerous subcategories, and your book's genre may fall under several of them.

Take the best-selling novel *The Perfect Couple* by Erin Hilderbrand, which was adapted into a Netflix series. For the Kindle eBook version, Amazon lists it in the following categories:

- **Kindle eBooks:** Literature & Fiction, Women's Fiction, Contemporary
- **Books:** Literature & Fiction, Women's Fiction,

Contemporary
- **Kindle eBooks:** Literature & Fiction, Women's Fiction, Romance

Wait a minute—why is the second category for the Kindle eBook listed under the paperback books category? This is likely an error by the publisher, who may have only selected two Kindle eBook categories. As a result, Amazon possibly placed the Kindle version into the paperback category as a default.

Why does this happen? Well, that's part of the mystery of Amazon's book categories! If you don't select your categories carefully, Amazon will choose them for you. For this book, the publisher should have selected a third Kindle eBook category to avoid this mix-up.

While this isn't an issue for a best-selling book, self-published authors must select three appropriate categories for each format of their book. Doing so increases their visibility and helps them reach more potential readers.

Let's look at the paperback categories for *The Perfect Couple*. To access paperback categories, click on the **Books** tab at the top of any Amazon page. This will take you to the Books at Amazon page. On the left-hand side, you'll see several sections, including **Format**. Under Format, click on **Paperback** to view categories specific to paperbacks. You can also see the categories on a book's listing page, located in the left-hand column about halfway down.

For *The Perfect Couple*, the paperback version is listed in the following categories:

- **Books:** Mystery, Thriller & Suspense; Mystery; Women Sleuths
- **Books:** Literature & Fiction; Genre Fiction; Family Life
- **Books:** Literature & Fiction; Women's Fiction; Domestic Life

These categories are entirely different from those of the Kindle version, which means more customers will see the book as they browse various sections on Amazon. And you may notice that they are categories that many people have even heard of. This is where the power of selecting the proper subcategories comes in, as you can target a specific genre and find readers who are loyal to that troupe.

By carefully selecting the right categories for each format of your book, you can significantly expand your reach and ensure that a wider audience sees your book. This is especially important for self-published authors who rely on visibility to attract new readers. Suppose you only select the main categories for your book. In that case, it will get buried under all of the traditionally published titles. But if you niche down your selections, you can uncover untapped niches that with readers desperate for more books.

Just as we did for Kindle books, let's take a closer look at the paperback categories (note these are also the same categories for hardcover books), specifically those under **Literature & Fiction**. The subcategories include:

- **Action & Adventure Fiction**: Stories filled with excitement, daring exploits, and adventure.
- **Ancient & Medieval Literature**: Literature from ancient and medieval times, reflecting historical themes and cultures.
- **Black & African American Literature**: Fiction exploring the experiences and cultures of Black and African American communities.
- **British & Irish Literature & Fiction**: Stories reflecting British and Irish culture, history, and literary traditions.
- **Classic Literature & Fiction**: Timeless works recognized for their cultural and literary significance.
- **Contemporary Literature & Fiction**: Modern stories

that reflect current life, social issues, and personal experiences.
- **Disability Fiction**: Books featuring characters with disabilities, highlighting their experiences and perspectives.
- **Drama & Plays**: Works written for theatrical performance, focusing on dialogue and conflict.
- **Erotic Literature & Fiction**: Stories focusing on themes of sensuality and intimate relationships.
- **Essays & Correspondence**: Collections of essays, letters, and personal reflections on various topics.
- **Genre Literature & Fiction**: Fiction categorized by specific genres like romance, mystery, and science fiction.
- **Historical Fiction**: Stories set in the past, often incorporating real historical events or figures.
- **Literary Criticism**: Analysis and interpretation of literary works and their themes, styles, and contexts.
- **Humor & Satire Fiction**: Books using humor, irony, or satire to entertain or critique society.
- **Literary Fiction**: Character-driven stories that emphasize style, themes, and deeper meanings.
- **Mythology & Folk Tales:** Stories based on traditional myths, legends, and folklore from various cultures.
- **Poetry**: Verse and prose exploring ideas, emotions, and stories through structured or free-form language.
- **Short Stories & Anthologies**: Collections of brief, self-contained narratives focusing on various themes or characters.
- **American Literature**: Literature reflecting American culture, history, and society.
- **Women's Literature & Fiction**: Stories centered around women's lives, relationships, and experiences.
- **World Literature**: Fiction from diverse cultures, showcasing global perspectives and narratives.

Look closely at this list. Are there any major fiction categories missing? For example, where is Romance? Just as Romance isn't listed under Literature & Fiction for Kindle eBooks, it's also absent from the paperback subcategories.

Why is this the case? Similar to Kindle categories, the paperback categories are structured differently. Not all genres are included under Literature & Fiction. Instead, you may need to explore the broader main categories to find your specific genre.

For instance, because Romance is the most popular type of book, it often has its own main category, separate from Literature & Fiction. This organization of categories can be confusing, especially for new authors. Still, it's essential to navigate it effectively to ensure your book appears in the right sections where readers are looking.

If you go back to the main Books categories, you'll notice that Romance is listed as a main category, just as it is under Kindle eBooks. This is because Romance is such a popular genre that it warrants its own primary category. However, **Romance also appears as a subcategory within other main categories**, including:

- **Christian Books & Bibles**: Love stories that focus on faith-based relationships and Christian values, often highlighting spiritual growth alongside romantic development.
- **Comics & Graphic Novels**: Illustrated narratives that explore romantic themes and relationships, often blending visual storytelling with emotional and dramatic elements.
- **Religion & Spirituality**: Stories that combine Romance with themes of faith, spirituality, and personal beliefs, reflecting how love and religion intersect in characters' lives.
- **Self-Help**: Books that provide advice and guidance

on building and maintaining healthy romantic relationships, focusing on self-improvement and emotional well-being.
- **Teen & Young Adult**: Romantic stories targeted at teens and young adults, often exploring first loves, relationships, and personal growth during adolescence.

Are you feeling confused? Stick with me—I promise I'll help you make sense of it all! But hold on because we're about to take a bit of a journey first.

When you upload a Kindle eBook to Amazon, you'll need to select three categories for it to be listed under. Then, when you upload the paperback and hardcover versions of that Kindle eBook, you'll need to choose three categories for each of those two formats as well. Sometimes, the same categories and subcategories are available for both formats. Still, as we discussed earlier, they can sometimes differ.

Oh, and those subcategories? Here's another plot twist: Many subcategories have additional subcategories, and some of those even have more subcategories under them. We're talking sub-sub-sub-categories in some cases!

So, how do you find the best fit for your book among thousands of potential categories? And why does it even matter? Why not just pick the three most relevant categories and move on? If you're writing purely for fun and don't care about selling many books, then, sure, pick whatever categories you want. But suppose you're serious about making money through self-publishing. In that case, it's crucial to understand your book's primary categories and how to position it within Amazon's complex category system.

Correctly categorizing your book increases its chances of being discovered by the right readers, which can lead to more sales and, ultimately, more income. The fiction book market on

Amazon is enormous, so readers tend to search for specific sub-genres, often called "tropes," that match the types of stories they enjoy. This is where self-published authors can gain an advantage—by **writing to market.**

Writing to market means that authors deliberately choose specific tropes to target a dedicated audience for their books. By focusing on these unique sub-genres, they often find a more loyal readership and make more money than they would by writing in a more general category.

Take the *Romance* genre, which we've established as the largest book category both on and off Amazon. Romance can be found under numerous main Kindle and paperback categories and subcategories. To illustrate this, I'll show you how to navigate these subcategories.

Start by clicking on **Books** at the top of the Amazon homepage. On the left side of the page, under the **Department** section, you'll see the main book genres, which I listed earlier. I'll click on **Romance.** Amazon will take me to a new page with several sub-genres to choose from:

- **Action & Adventure**: Love stories filled with excitement, danger, and daring exploits, where Romance unfolds amidst high-stakes action and thrilling adventures.
- **Amish**: Romantic tales set within Amish communities, focusing on love, faith, and traditional values while exploring the unique challenges of this lifestyle.
- **Billionaires:** Stories centered around wealthy protagonists, often featuring themes of luxury, power dynamics, and finding true love beyond riches.
- **Black & African American**: Romantic narratives that explore the love lives, experiences, and cultures of Black and African American characters.
- **Clean & Wholesome**: Love stories that avoid explicit content, focusing on emotional connection and

meaningful relationships without steamy scenes.
- **Collections & Anthologies**: Curated collections of short romantic stories or novellas, often featuring multiple authors or varied themes within the romance genre.
- **Contemporary**: Modern love stories set in the present day, exploring current relationship dynamics, societal issues, and personal growth.
- **Erotica**: Romantic tales with explicit sensual content, focusing on physical intimacy and passion between characters.
- **Fantasy**: Romantic stories set in fantastical worlds with magical elements, mythical creatures, and epic adventures alongside love and passion.
- **Gothic**: Dark and mysterious love stories set in eerie, atmospheric settings, often featuring elements of suspense, the supernatural, or brooding characters.
- **Historical**: Romantic tales set in various historical periods, blending love with the cultural, social, and political contexts of the time.
- **Holidays**: Romantic stories centered around holidays, such as Christmas or Valentine's Day, often highlighting themes of love, family, and celebration.
- **Inspirational**: Faith-based love stories that focus on spiritual growth and personal faith, often incorporating themes of redemption, forgiveness, and divine love.
- **Later in Life**: Romantic narratives featuring older protagonists, exploring love, companionship, and new beginnings in later stages of life.
- **LGBTQ+**: Love stories featuring LGBTQ+ characters, focusing on their relationships, experiences, and the unique challenges they may face.
- **Medical**: Love stories set in medical settings, such as hospitals or clinics, often featuring doctors, nurses, and healthcare workers finding love amidst their

demanding careers.
- **Military**: Romantic tales involving soldiers, veterans, or military settings, highlighting love, duty, and sacrifice.
- **Multicultural & Interracial**: Stories celebrating love across different cultures, ethnicities, and backgrounds, exploring the challenges and beauty of diverse relationships.
- **New Adult & College**: Romantic stories focused on young adults navigating love, life, and relationships during their college years and early adulthood.
- **Paranormal**: Love stories featuring supernatural elements, such as ghosts, witches, or otherworldly beings, where Romance intertwines with the mysterious and unknown.
- **Rockstar Romance:** Romantic tales featuring musicians or celebrities exploring the highs and lows of love in the limelight.
- **Romance in Uniform**: Love stories featuring characters in uniform, such as police officers, firefighters, or military personnel, highlighting duty, honor, and passion.
- **Romantic Comedy**: Lighthearted, humorous love stories that mix Romance with comedy, often featuring witty dialogue and amusing situations.
- **Romantic Suspense**: Love stories laced with tension and danger, where Romance develops alongside thrilling mysteries or suspenseful plots.
- **Science Fiction**: Romantic narratives set in futuristic or technologically advanced worlds, blending love with science fiction elements.
- **Sports**: Love stories set in the world of sports, featuring athletes, coaches, or enthusiasts, where romance blossoms amidst competition and teamwork.
- **Time Travel**: Romantic tales involving time travel, where characters find love across different time

periods or eras.
- **Vampires**: Love stories featuring vampire characters, exploring themes of immortality, forbidden love, and the supernatural.
- **Werewolves & Shifters**: Romantic tales featuring werewolves or shape-shifting characters, blending love with the allure and danger of the supernatural.
- **Western & Frontier**: Love stories set in the American West or frontier settings, often featuring cowboys, ranchers, and pioneer life.
- **Writing**: Stories that revolve around writers, authors, or the literary world, exploring love, creativity, and the challenges of storytelling.

Let's take **Historical Romance** as an example. *Outlander* and *Bridgerton* have made this a popular sub-genre, but it doesn't stop there. Within Historical Romance, there are even more subcategories:

- **20th Century**: Love stories set in the 1900s, exploring Romance against the backdrop of significant events like World Wars, the Roaring Twenties, and the mid-century social changes.
- **American**: Romantic tales set in various periods of American history, from colonial times to the Civil War and beyond, highlighting the unique cultural and social landscapes of the U.S.
- **Ancient World**: Romance set in ancient civilizations, such as Egypt, Greece, or Rome, blending historical intrigue with passionate love stories.
- **Gilded Age**: Love stories set during the late 19th century, focusing on themes of wealth, society, and the changing American landscape.
- **Medieval**: Romantic tales set in the Middle Ages, featuring knights, castles, and chivalrous love amidst the backdrop of feudal society.

- **Regency**: Love stories set during the early 19th century in England, often involving aristocracy, social conventions, and the elegance of the Regency period.
- **Renaissance**: Romantic narratives set during the Renaissance, highlighting art, culture, and the rebirth of intellectual and creative pursuits.
- **Scottish**: Stories of love set in the Scottish Highlands or historical Scotland, often featuring clan rivalries, rugged landscapes, and passionate characters.
- **Tudor**: Romance set during the Tudor dynasty in England, featuring courtly intrigue, royal romances, and the turbulent politics of the era.
- **Victorian**: Love stories set during the 19th-century Victorian era, exploring themes of societal expectations, industrial change, and romantic ideals.
- **Viking**: Romantic tales set in the Viking Age, featuring adventurous Norsemen and fierce heroines, often blending conquest and passion.

Further down the page, readers can narrow their search by selecting specific types of **Romantic Heroes**, such as:

- **Alpha Males**: Dominant and assertive heroes who exude confidence and strength in their romantic pursuits.
- **BBW (Big Beautiful Women)**: Love stories featuring plus-size heroines celebrated for their beauty and confidence.
- **Bikers**: Romantic tales featuring rebellious biker heroes, often set in the world of motorcycle clubs and outlaw culture.
- **Cowboys**: Stories of rugged, hardworking cowboys who embody the spirit of the American West and win hearts with their loyalty and charm.
- **Criminals & Outlaws**: Romance with heroes who live on the edge of the law, adding danger and intrigue to

their love stories.
- **Doctors**: Love stories featuring dedicated medical professionals who balance the demands of their careers with their romantic lives.
- **Firefighters**: Heroes who risk their lives to protect others, bringing bravery and passion to their romantic relationships.
- **Highlanders**: Stories of fierce and honorable Scottish warriors known for their loyalty, strength, and passionate love.
- **Pirates**: Romantic adventures featuring daring and roguish pirate heroes who live by their own rules.
- **Royalty & Aristocrats**: Love stories involving kings, queens, princes, and nobles, often filled with intrigue, duty, and forbidden romance.
- **Spies**: Heroes with a taste for danger, navigating intrigue and secrecy as they fall in love while on a mission.
- **Vikings**: Romantic tales featuring bold and fearless Norse warriors, blending adventure and passion in their quests for love.
- **Wealthy**: Romance with affluent heroes who navigate love, power, and privilege in high-society settings.
- And then there are various **Romantic Themes**, including:
- **Amnesia**: Romantic stories where one or both characters lose their memory, creating unique challenges and emotional rediscovery in their love story.
- **Beaches**: Love stories set on or around beach locations, often highlighting sun-soaked Romance, relaxation, and scenic backdrops.
- **International**: Romance that spans across different countries or cultures, exploring love amidst travel, language barriers, and cultural differences.
- **Love Triangle**: Stories involving three characters

caught in a complex romantic entanglement, leading to tension, conflict, and difficult choices.
- **Medical**: Romantic tales set in healthcare environments, featuring doctors, nurses, and medical professionals balancing love and their demanding careers.
- **Second Chances**: Stories about rekindling love, where characters reunite and rediscover each other, often overcoming past misunderstandings or heartbreak.
- **Secret Baby**: Romance with a hidden child, where one character discovers they have a child they didn't know about, adding emotional depth and unexpected twists.
- **Vacation**: Love stories that blossom during travel or holidays, where characters experience Romance in new and exciting locations.
- **Wedding**: Romantic tales centered around weddings, including planning, ceremonies, and the emotional journey leading up to the big day.
- **Workplace**: Stories of love and relationships developing in professional settings, navigating the complexities of Romance and career ambitions.

Is your mind a bit blown by all of these subcategories? Mine sure was the first time I began learning about them! But there's more research to do to help you narrow down exactly the type of book you should write that will sell.

For example, if you search for Secret Baby under Romance, you'll find over 50,000 results. But if you narrow it down further by choosing Highlanders, the number of books drops to under 400. So, suppose you've been dreaming of writing a juicy secret baby Highlander romance. In that case, you'll only be competing with a few hundred books, not tens of thousands.

Narrowing down these tropes is how you help readers find you —not by burying your book under one broad genre or sub-genre, but by choosing the most niche category possible. And nothing is more niche than a historical romance featuring a Highlander and a secret baby!

By now, I'm sure your head is spinning. Categories, genres, tropes... and all with multiple layers of subcategories. Plus, the choices vary between Kindle and paperback/hardcover lists. But consider all this data a gift, as it can help you focus on your book's theme before you even start writing!

Instead of sitting down and writing a generic romance novel that might get lost among thousands of others, you now have a roadmap to success. By targeting a specific niche, you'll be able to attract customers more effectively and increase the likelihood of them purchasing your book.

The same strategy applies if you create low-and-no content books such as journals, planners, notebooks, and activity books. Let's say you want to publish a cat-themed adult coloring book. The most logical category for this type of low-content book would be Coloring Books for Grown-Ups: Animals, a category that currently has over 70,000 results. But since you can choose two additional categories, you have the opportunity to reach even more buyers, especially if you select categories that aren't as crowded. In fact, it's better to select three subcategories than give one of those precious slots to a main category where your book will be buried under those that are traditionally published.

But how do you find those less crowded categories? The first step is to look at the bestsellers in the category of book you plan to publish. For example, let's use Harry Potter as a case study. Suppose you type Harry Potter into the Amazon search bar. In that case, it will bring up everything related to Harry Potter—not just the books, but also movies and merchandise. To narrow down your search, click on Books under the Department section on the left-hand side of the page.

For this example, let's look at *Harry Potter: The Complete Collection*. Clicking on the title takes you to the book's information page. Typically, the Kindle version is highlighted by default, as it was for me during my research.

Scrolling down the product page, you'll find a section titled **Product details**. This section includes all the technical aspects of the book, from the ASIN and publication date to the language and print length.

At the end of this block of information, you'll find the **Best Sellers Rank**, which shows the three categories in which the book is listed. For the Kindle version of this Harry Potter book, the categories are:

- **Fantasy Anthologies**
- **Teen & Young Adult Wizards & Witches Fantasy eBooks**
- **Children's Fantasy & Magic Adventure**

Those last two categories are quite specific, aren't they? Did you even know such categories existed? It's because they are subcategories, not main categories. Clicking on the **Teen & Young Adult Wizards & Witches Fantasy eBooks link** will open a new page, showing you how this subcategory breaks down from the main category of **Teen & Young Adult**.

Here's how the category sequence works:

Kindle eBooks > Teen & Young Adult > Science Fiction & Fantasy > Fantasy > Wizards & Witches

Understanding this breakdown is essential. For authors, this sequence shows how deeply a book can be categorized within Amazon's structure. By navigating these layers, you can pinpoint the most precise category for your book, improving its chances of being found by the right readers.

Choosing specific subcategories is a powerful strategy that can help your book stand out in a crowded market. It's not just about being listed in broad categories; it's about finding your unique niche and positioning your book where your ideal readers are looking.

Every category and subcategory on Amazon has its own bestsellers list. While it's great to see your book ranked high in a category that perfectly matches its theme, you can also leverage smaller niche categories—even those that aren't an exact match—to increase your chances of making it onto a bestseller list.

But beware: the days of manipulating the system to achieve a number-one rank by placing your book in completely irrelevant categories are over. Amazon now closely monitors book categories to prevent authors from gaming the system. It used to be that authors could request Amazon to place their books into obscure subcategories with little competition just to earn a bestseller badge. However, with the new rule requiring authors to select only three categories during the upload process, this loophole has been closed.

The strategy now is to find categories that are relevant yet not as obvious. Let's go back to the example of the cat-themed adult coloring book. You could list it in three coloring book categories, all of which are extremely competitive. But you could also place it in one of the cat reference categories, which are less crowded and might offer a better chance of ranking higher.

PRO TIP: When I'm uploading a new book, I choose the most obvious categories for my first two selections. For the third category, I look for a relevant but less crowded option. I examine the best-selling books that are similar to mine and check which categories they are listed in. Then, I assess the competition in those categories. If a category appears too crowded, I keep looking until I find one where my book has a better chance of ranking higher. Even if I can't reach the number-one spot, having my book in the top ten means it will be prominently displayed at the top of the page when someone is browsing that category.

Nonfiction: The dictionary defines "nonfiction" as "prose writing that is based on facts, real events, and real people, such as biography or history." Similar to fiction, nonfiction Amazon books have a variety of categories and subcategories for both Kindle eBooks and paperback Amazon.

Just as I did for fiction books, let's explore the nonfiction categories for both Kindle and paperback/hardcover. The key difference is that Amazon offers Nonfiction as a primary category for both formats. However, many other main categories also cover nonfiction topics. Selecting the primary Nonfiction category will reveal numerous subcategories. For this example, we'll focus on those subcategories, but keep in mind that for my nonfiction books, I often choose from both main categories and their respective subcategories.

Here are the Nonfiction subcategories for Kindle eBooks:

- **Arts & Photography**: Books covering visual arts, photography techniques, and creative expression in various artistic disciplines.
- **Biographies & Memoirs**: Personal accounts of individuals' lives, offering insights into their experiences, achievements, and challenges.
- **Business & Money**: Guides and advice on finance, entrepreneurship, leadership, and management strategies for business success.
- **Children's eBooks**: Educational and entertaining eBooks designed for young readers, covering various topics and interests.
- **Comics, Manga & Graphic Novels**: Illustrated nonfiction works exploring real-world topics, memoirs, and educational content through graphic storytelling.
- **Computers & Technology**: Books on programming, software, hardware, and the latest developments in the tech industry.

- **Cookbooks, Food & Wine**: Guides on cooking techniques, recipes, food culture, and wine pairings for culinary enthusiasts.
- **Crafts, Hobbies & Home**: DIY guides, home improvement projects, and hobbyist books for creative and practical pursuits.
- **Education & Teaching**: Resources for educators, students, and lifelong learners covering teaching strategies, learning theories, and academic skills.
- **Engineering & Transportation**: Books on engineering principles, technology, and transportation systems, including automotive and aerospace topics.
- **Foreign Languages**: Books and guides for learning and mastering different languages, including grammar, vocabulary, and conversation skills.
- **Health, Fitness & Dieting**: Guides on physical health, exercise, nutrition, and wellness strategies for a healthy lifestyle.
- **History**: Books exploring historical events, people, and periods, providing insights into the past and its impact on the present.
- **Humor & Entertainment**: Nonfiction works that entertain, amuse, or explore the world of entertainment and popular culture.
- **LGBTQ+ eBooks**: Nonfiction books covering LGBTQ+ history, culture, personal experiences, and issues relevant to the community.
- **Law**: Books on legal principles, case law, and the justice system aimed at legal professionals and general readers interested in the law.
- **Literature & Fiction**: Nonfiction works exploring literary analysis, criticism, and studies of classic and contemporary fiction.
- **Medical eBooks**: Resources on medical topics, healthcare practices, and patient care, written for both professionals and general readers.

- **Mystery, Thriller & Suspense**: Nonfiction books examining the genres, authors, and history of mystery, thriller, and suspense literature.
- **Nonfiction**: A broad category encompassing a wide range of factual books on various topics, from history and science to personal development and more.
- **Parenting & Relationships**: Guides on child-rearing, family dynamics, and building strong, healthy relationships.
- **Politics & Social Sciences**: Books exploring political theory, social issues, cultural studies, and current affairs.
- **Reference**: Comprehensive guides, encyclopedias, and resources for research and information across various subjects.
- **Religion & Spirituality**: Books on faith, belief systems, and spiritual growth, covering diverse religious traditions and practices.
- **Romance**: Nonfiction books exploring the genre, its history, themes, and the craft of writing Romance.
- **Science & Math**: Books explaining scientific concepts, discoveries, and mathematical principles for a general or academic audience.
- **Science Fiction & Fantasy**: Nonfiction works examining the genres, authors, and impact of science fiction and fantasy literature.
- **Self-Help**: Guides offering advice and strategies for personal growth, mental health, and achieving life goals.
- **Sports & Outdoors**: Books on sports techniques, athletic training, and outdoor activities, including adventure and exploration.
- **Teen & Young Adult:** Nonfiction books aimed at teens and young adults, covering topics like self-discovery, academic skills, and social issues.
- **Travel**: Books on travel destinations, tips, cultural

insights, and experiences from around the world.

Just like with fiction, each main category has numerous subcategories. For example, most of my nonfiction books fall under the Nonfiction category, then the Business & Money subcategory. Within Business & Money alone, there are over twenty subcategories. I typically publish under Business Development & Entrepreneurship. Still, even within that subcategory, there are additional layers of subcategories to choose from.

When I upload a nonfiction book to Amazon, I select three categories for the Kindle version, three for the paperback version, and three for the hardcover version. I always research the competition to determine which categories are the best fit for my books and which have the most potential for higher rankings.

All this talk of categories may sound overwhelming, but trust me, it will make more sense once you're choosing categories for your own books. It all comes together when you have a finished book ready to publish. As you publish more and more books, you'll see firsthand how the categories you choose influence your book's visibility and rankings.

Why am I even talking about these categories if they will only matter once you are ready to upload? Well, I want to give you an idea about all the different types of books you can self-publish. From Romance and horror to cookbooks and self-help, in order to self-publish, you just need to find your niche and go from there. You may already have a book in mind, but knowing about categories can help you hone in on a niche trope. Or you may want to make money self-publishing but need to figure out what sells. Understanding Amazon's categories helps in both situations.

If you already have a book idea, knowing about categories can help you refine your concept into a specific niche or trope that will attract readers. On the other hand, if you want to make money through self-publishing but need to figure out what sells, exploring Amazon's categories is an excellent way to discover popular genres and trends.

In both cases, a clear understanding of Amazon's categories will help you craft a book that fits well within the market, increasing your chances of success.

Current Popular Fiction Categories Among Readers: To get you thinking, here are the top troupes for both fiction and nonfiction for the current year that you may want to consider if you want to make money from your books:

<u>Romance</u>

- **Billionaire Romance:** Stories featuring wealthy protagonists who navigate love and power dynamics.
- **Enemies-to-Lovers:** A classic trope where characters start off as adversaries but gradually fall in love.
- **Fake Dating/Marriage:** Characters pretend to be in a relationship for various reasons, only to develop genuine feelings.
- **Second Chance Romance:** Ex-lovers reconnect and rekindle their Romance after being separated by time or circumstances.
- **Small-Town Romance:** Often set in a cozy, close-knit community, focusing on love and relationships in a small town.
- **Romantic Suspense:** Blends romance with elements of mystery or thriller, where love and danger go hand-in-hand.
- **Fantasy Romance:** Incorporates magical or fantastical elements, often set in fictional worlds with unique creatures and abilities.

<u>Mystery, Thriller & Suspense</u>

- **Psychological Thrillers:** Focus on the unstable

emotional and mental states of the characters, often featuring unreliable narrators.
- **Domestic Thrillers:** Set within homes or close relationships involving secrets, betrayal, and suspense.
- **Cozy Mysteries:** Lighthearted mysteries, often featuring amateur sleuths and small-town settings, without graphic violence or adult themes.
- **Police Procedurals:** Stories that follow law enforcement officers solving crimes, with a focus on the investigation process.

Science Fiction & Fantasy

- **Space Opera:** Large-scale adventures set in space, often featuring interstellar battles and political intrigue.
- **Dystopian/Post-Apocalyptic:** Depicts worlds in decline or after catastrophic events, focusing on survival and societal breakdowns.
- **Epic Fantasy is a genre of expansive** narratives set in fictional worlds, often involving quests, complex characters, and magical elements.
- **LitRPG/GameLit:** Combines elements of role-playing games with traditional storytelling, where characters might be aware they're in a game or use game mechanics to solve problems.

Young Adult

- **Coming-of-Age:** Focuses on the personal growth and development of young protagonists as they transition into adulthood.
- **Fantasy/Adventure:** Young characters embark on epic journeys, often in magical worlds, facing challenges that lead to self-discovery.
- **Contemporary YA:** Deals with real-life issues such as identity, relationships, and mental health, set in a modern context.

Current Popular Non-Fiction Categories Among Readers: While most writers write fiction, I am a full-time self-published non-fiction author. There is good money to be make in the non-fiction categories, including:

Self-Help

- **Personal Development:** Books focusing on self-improvement, motivation, and productivity.
- **Mindfulness & Mental Health:** Guides on meditation, mental wellness, and coping strategies for anxiety and depression.
- **Habit Formation:** Strategies for building and maintaining healthy habits, often based on behavioral psychology.

Business & Money

- **Entrepreneurship:** Advice on starting and growing a business, with a focus on innovation and scalability.
- **Personal Finance:** Guides on managing money, investing, and achieving financial independence.
- **Leadership & Management:** Insights on effective leadership, building team culture, and navigating corporate environments.

Health, Fitness & Dieting

- **Plant-Based Diets:** Recipes and guides focusing on vegan and vegetarian lifestyles.
- **Holistic Health:** Books on alternative medicine, integrative health, and natural wellness practices.
- **Fitness & Exercise:** Training programs and exercise routines, often targeting specific demographics like seniors or beginners.

Biographies & Memoirs

- **Celebrity Memoirs:** Personal stories from public

figures, often exploring themes of resilience and personal growth.
- **Inspirational Stories:** Accounts of individuals overcoming adversity, achieving greatness, or making a significant impact.
- **True Crime:** Deep dives into real-life criminal cases, often exploring the psychology of criminals and their impact on victims.

Parenting & Relationships

- **Parenting Techniques:** Guides on effective parenting styles, from attachment parenting to Montessori methods.
- **Marriage & Couples Therapy:** Books focused on building healthy relationships, improving communication, and resolving conflicts.
- **Family Dynamics:** Exploring family roles, sibling relationships, and intergenerational issues.

CHAPTER FIVE: THE FREEDOM OF PEN NAMES

Understanding Amazon categories and sub-categories can help you narrow down a niche. But what's even better than choosing a niche is knowing that you don't have to stick with just one. Many full-time self-published writers explore various genres using different pen names. Yes, Amazon and other self-publishing platforms allow you to publish under any name you choose—whether it's your legal name or a pen name you create.

I currently use three pen names and could add more if I wanted. I write business non-fiction under my name. I have a separate pen name for my print-on-demand books, such as planners, journals, notebooks, and activity books. And I use another pen name for my fiction books.

Why use different pen names for different genres? The answer is simple: branding.

Creating a distinct brand is essential for selling books. It's what keeps readers coming back for your new releases. I've built a brand around my legal name that focuses on teaching people about self-employment and making money online. Adding unrelated books under this name would confuse my readers and dilute my brand.

For instance, the non-fiction books I write under my name are listed under the business categories on Amazon. It wouldn't make sense for me to also publish thriller novels or children's joke books under the same name. Customers would visit my author page and wonder why someone writing about eBay is also writing futuristic murder mysteries. Publishing books in vastly different genres under the same name can erode consumer confidence in your brand overall.

(Note: I don't actually write about futuristic murder mysteries; I'm just using that as an example. But hey, murder mysteries are extremely popular!)

A lot of what happens with books, especially on Amazon, is that customers latch onto an author and will read all their titles. I often hear from readers who have read all my business books because that is the content they are most interested in. They do not follow me for my fiction books; most do not even know I write fiction under a pen name, and I prefer to keep it that way.

On the flip side, my fiction readers follow me for the type of fiction books I write. They do not follow me for e-commerce books, nor do they know that I create journals, planners, and notebooks under a different pen name. To them, I am simply the author of the fiction trope they enjoy reading. My fiction books represent a different brand than my non-fiction books.

Similarly, my planners, journals, notebooks, and activity books are under yet another pen name with its own distinct brand. It's a completely separate business from my non-fiction and fiction author brands. I treat my pen names as though they are independent businesses, even though they are all managed under a single Amazon KDP account.

I should mention that I do promote my low-content books to those who follow me for my non-fiction work. Many of my non-fiction readers have been following my content for years, so

I feel comfortable sharing the other "business" I have created with them. However, I do not promote my fiction books on my non-fiction or low-content platforms. While there is some overlap between non-fiction and low-content books, fiction is an entirely different genre that wouldn't make sense to mix with my other products.

As I mentioned, I could create additional pen names if I decided to write in different fiction genres. I don't want to confuse or alienate potential readers by lumping different genres under one pen name. For instance, consider how well-known James Patterson is for his thrillers. It would be odd if he suddenly started publishing cookbooks or children's picture books under the same name. Many well-known authors use multiple pen names to differentiate between their various genres and brands.

Pen names are quite common in the publishing business for both self-published and traditionally published authors. For example, romance author Nora Roberts writes her romantic suspense series under her name, but she uses the pen name J.D. Robb for her futuristic crime thrillers. This strategy helps her keep her different audiences separate. It allows each pen name to maintain its own unique brand identity.

A tip about pen names: Many authors use variations of their legal names to create their pen names. For example, author Nora Roberts uses her initials and married name to write as J.D. Robb for her futuristic crime novels. George R.R. Martin, best known for *Game of Thrones*, also wrote under the name George Raymond to separate his earlier works. Similarly, author Lemony Snicket, known for *A Series of Unfortunate Events*, is a pen name for Daniel Handler, who uses his real name for his adult fiction books. Other writers might use a nickname for one pen name, their full first name for another, or even their initials for a third. Some choose to blend family names, mix celebrity names, or simply use names that resonate with them.

Can you have too many pen names? You might be wondering if managing multiple pen names would be too difficult. The truth is that most self-publishers use multiple pen names to upload all kinds of books. Amazon and other self-publishing platforms allow multiple pen names under a single account and make it easy to manage them. When you upload a book on Amazon, you simply enter the name you want to use. The only restriction is that you can't use a famous author's name—so you can't upload your books as *Stephen King.*

That said, you don't have to write in multiple genres or use various pen names. It's best to start by focusing on publishing one book—just one! Some authors publish exclusively under one pen name, while others have dozens. Categories and pen names are two elements of self-publishing that you have complete control over.

For example, you might start by writing historical romance novels. After publishing a few books in that genre, you may decide you want to write cookbooks instead. No problem! You can create another pen name and upload your cookbooks under that new identity.

Whether you choose to stick with one pen name or expand to multiple ones, the decision is entirely up to you. There's no right or wrong approach, and you can always change your mind as you go. I never thought I would write fiction or publish print-on-demand products. Still, eventually, I decided to explore those areas. Now, I have three pen names, with more planned for the future. The freedom to publish whatever you want and to create unique identities for each genre is one of the greatest advantages of self-publishing.

Do You Need to Copyright Your Pen Name? A common question many new authors have is whether they need to copyright their pen names. The short answer is no. Once you publish a book, the pen name you use is automatically associated with your work and becomes your identifier.

Copyright law protects the content of your book—your writing —not the name you use. It's important to note that copyrighting a name itself isn't possible; instead, you will need to trademark it if you want exclusive rights to use that name in the context of publishing or other goods and services.

However, it's not always necessary to trademark a pen name, especially if you're just starting out. Many authors use names that are common or similar to others. In fact, it's not unusual for several people to share the same name, and there's no legal issue unless there's a direct intent to mislead or impersonate.

While I personally don't trademark my pen names, I do take other steps to protect my brand. For instance, I purchase the domain names for my pen names, such as AnnEckhart.com. Owning the URL for your name helps ensure that no one else can create a website under your author's name and confuse your readers. It also gives you a professional platform to promote your books and connect with your audience.

Ultimately, whether or not you decide to trademark or copyright anything related to your pen name depends on your goals and comfort level. Suppose you plan to build a significant brand around your pen name or think there's a potential for others to misuse it. In that case, you might consider consulting with a legal professional about trademarking. But for most self-published authors, simply publishing under your chosen pen name and securing related URLs is sufficient protection.

Suppose your books really take off, and you're selling tens of thousands of copies each month. In that case, it's a good idea to consult a lawyer to discuss any steps they may recommend for protecting your work. At that point, it might make sense to consider trademarking your pen name or exploring other legal protections.

In addition, if you're making a significant income, meeting with an accountant and financial advisor is also advisable. They can help you manage your earnings, plan for taxes, and make strategic financial decisions.

What a great problem to have!

CHAPTER SIX: KINDLE, PAPERBACK, HARDCOVER... OR ALL THREE

So, you have a computer with internet access and Microsoft Word (or another word processing software). You've either already come up with an idea for a book or have been inspired by browsing through Amazon's book categories. You understand that you can use multiple pen names to explore different genres. You're almost ready to start writing.

Well, almost!

While it's natural to think ahead to the formatting and uploading process, there's no need to worry about those details until you have an actual book to publish. There are still some important decisions to make before you begin or complete your book.

Because you're self-publishing, you have the freedom to write any type of book you want—whether it's fiction or nonfiction, 24 pages or 2,400 pages. You're your own publisher and editor, so the decisions are entirely yours. Maybe writing novels isn't your thing, and instead, you want to create fun notebooks and planners. That's perfectly fine!

Perhaps you want to write a cookbook filled with family recipes. Go for it! Maybe you have an idea for a historical romance series. Do it! Or perhaps you want to design children's activity books. You can absolutely make it happen! Whatever you're passionate about, you can bring your creative vision to life with Amazon KDP.

But let's not forget the important factor of wanting to make money from your books. At least, I hope you do—because there's definitely money to be made! Writing a book is just one step in the process of earning an income as an indie author.

There are two different schools of thought when it comes to publishing nonfiction and fiction books for profit on Amazon:

Publish Many Short Kindle eBooks: This approach focuses on quantity over length. You publish multiple short eBooks and make most of your money from Kindle Unlimited page reads. These books are often too short to be eligible for paperback or hardcover formats, so the emphasis is on eBooks only.

OR

Publish Fewer, Higher-Quality Books: This strategy involves publishing longer, more polished books that can be offered in Kindle, paperback, and hardcover formats. With longer books available in multiple formats, you can charge higher prices and reach a wider audience.

Both business models can be successful for self-publishing. Some writers choose one approach, while others mix both strategies. For many years, I did a combination of both. I published several short "booklets" on Kindle and longer books available in Kindle, paperback, and eventually hardcover formats. I made money from the shorter books through Kindle Unlimited while generating sales from the books not enrolled in Kindle Select.

Oh, I suppose we need to discuss Kindle Select, don't we? Because that adds an entirely new layer to self-publishing on Amazon. But first, a little backstory.

As I mentioned earlier in this book, when I first started self-publishing on Amazon, Kindle eBooks were the only option available. That's why the program is called Amazon KDP, which stands for Kindle Direct Publishing. Paperback options had yet to be introduced. Back then, most Kindle eBooks were short and inexpensive, typically priced around $2.99. Amazon also allowed Prime members to download one free Kindle eBook per month, and authors were paid the same amount for those free downloads as they were for regular sales.

Initially, I made a lot of money from Prime members choosing my book as their monthly "free" Kindle title. Amazon paid authors like me out of the Prime membership fees, so I didn't lose out on revenue, and plenty of other customers were willing to purchase my books as well.

In my first month of self-publishing on Amazon, I made $200 with just one 10,000-word book. Within four months, I was earning a full-time income from several $2.99 Kindle eBooks. At the time, these short books—or booklets—were the norm. I could easily write a new book every month, and there seemed to be no limit to how high my income could grow as long as I kept consistently publishing short Kindle books.

Then came Kindle Unlimited, which drastically changed Amazon's self-publishing landscape.

Kindle Unlimited Explained: Kindle Direct Publishing (KDP) is the program you use to upload and sell books on Amazon. Even though authors can upload eBooks, paperbacks, and hardcovers, the name remains Kindle Direct Publishing.

KDP Select is an optional program you can opt into when uploading your book. Enrolling in KDP Select means committing that your book's digital (Kindle eBook) format will be available exclusively through Amazon for at least 90 days. This exclusivity allows those with a Kindle Unlimited subscription to download your book at no additional cost.

When you enroll a book in KDP Select, you cannot publish its digital format on any other website for the duration of its enrollment. This is referred to as being "exclusive to Amazon." However, you can still publish the paperback version of the book elsewhere, as KDP Select only applies to the Kindle eBook format. Kindle Unlimited subscribers can "borrow" KDP Select books but must "buy" paperback books.

You have the flexibility to enroll individual books in KDP Select rather than your entire catalog, which means you can decide which titles you want to be part of Kindle Unlimited. Kindle Unlimited subscribers pay $11.99 per month and can borrow up to 20 books at a time. The subscription fees are pooled together, and authors receive a share of the profits based on the number of pages read from their books.

You may be thinking that you don't want anyone to borrow your book; you want them to buy it. However, for new authors, enrolling in KDP Select can help get your books into the hands of more readers. When you enroll your book in KDP Select, Amazon pays you every time someone borrows and reads your book. Each month, Amazon allocates money from the Kindle Unlimited subscription fees into the KDP Select Global Fund, which is then divided among the authors whose books have been borrowed and read.

The key word here is read. Customers must now actually read the book they download, not just borrow it, for the author to be paid. Let me explain:

Before Kindle Unlimited, the average payout to authors was around $2 per book borrowed, regardless of whether the customer actually opened or read the book. Simply downloading the book triggered a payout. For books priced at $2.99, authors earned roughly the same amount whether their book was purchased or borrowed.

However, in 2015, Amazon made significant changes to how authors were compensated for borrowed books, fundamentally altering the profit distribution. Instead of being paid for downloads, authors would now only be paid when readers actually engaged with their books.

Amazon launched Kindle Unlimited in 2015, a subscription service that allowed members to borrow an unlimited number of eligible books for a monthly fee. Most of the books available in Kindle Unlimited come from self-published authors who have opted into KDP Select. Most traditional authors and big-name publishers don't have their books available for borrowing. Hence, the vast majority of Kindle Unlimited offerings are from indie authors.

When I first started self-publishing, I priced my books at $2.99 and earned about $2.07 per sale. I also averaged around $2 for each book borrowed by Amazon Prime members, who could download one free Kindle book per month. At that time, authors were paid whether or not the book was read, making it easy to earn from both sales and borrows.

With the introduction of Kindle Unlimited, readers could now borrow multiple books, and authors were paid only if readers made it through 10% of the book. The payouts came from the Kindle Unlimited subscription fees, which allowed customers to access thousands of books for a flat monthly fee. Self-published authors were still making money on both sales and borrowings of their books, and the setup seemed ideal until the system was exploited.

Kindle Unlimited soon experienced what established authors called the "scam-phlet" craze, short for "scam pamphlets." Internet marketers realized they could make quick money by publishing extremely short books that met the 10% reading threshold with minimal content. Since Kindle Unlimited subscribers could download as many eligible books as they wanted, marketers flooded the market with these short books, knowing they only needed readers to open the file to the cover page to get paid.

An entire small industry of "Kindle Publishers" (who were not actual writers) emerged, exploiting the system by publishing hundreds of short, low-quality books in niche sub-categories. For example, they might produce a short 10-page booklet on a specific cooking technique or ingredient with a catchy title and cover. These marketers were more interested in generating downloads than in providing valuable content.

Kindle Unlimited subscribers felt they were getting "free" books, so they downloaded almost anything that seemed interesting. Marketers capitalized on this by constantly uploading new content, sometimes hundreds of books per month. They used various tactics to boost visibility, such as giving away free copies, paying for reviews, and spamming keywords. A reader only had to "read" 10% of the book, meaning a publisher was paid for a 10-page book just for the reader opening the file.

While some scammers claimed to be making six figures on Kindle, what they didn't reveal was the significant money they spent producing, promoting, and reviewing these books. They then sold courses to teach others how to use the same tactics, resulting in thousands of new "publishers" flooding the Kindle platform.

Soon, the Kindle market was flooded with so much junk that legitimate books were pushed down in the search results. The "scam-phlets," with their spammed keywords and fake reviews, rose to the top of reader lists, resulting in more downloads and pushing genuine authors' books out of visibility. My own sales ranks plummeted.

Once Kindle Unlimited customers started downloading these low-quality books, negative reviews began to pile up. But the scammers kept churning out short new reads, making money just by getting them opened. Since Amazon allows unlimited pen names, they would simply switch to a new niche and pen name to continue gaming the system. It became a never-ending cycle of junk books flooding the market. In just a few months, I went from earning a full-time income to barely making enough to cover my car payment.

Fortunately, it didn't take long for Amazon to catch on to the "scam-phlet" scheme, mainly because Kindle Unlimited customers were not only complaining about the poor quality of books but were also canceling their memberships. Just as Prime memberships are a major revenue source for Amazon, Kindle Unlimited subscriptions have also proved to be a lucrative business. Amazon knew they needed to save the program—and fast.

To retain subscribers, Amazon had to discourage junk books. Most of these short reads were profiting merely because readers were opening them to the cover, meeting the 10% read threshold. To combat this, Amazon drastically changed the payout structure. Instead of paying authors based on a book reaching the 10% mark, they switched to paying based on the number of *pages* read, requiring readers to make it through the entire book.

But, as with any system, scammers found a workaround. They began placing links on the first page of the book, enticing readers to click through to the last page with promises of a secret tip, freebie, or some other incentive. This tricked Amazon's system into marking the book as fully read, triggering the full payout for the borrower. It was another blow to legitimate authors who continued to struggle as their books were buried beneath these deceptive practices.

In response to increasing complaints from both authors and readers, Amazon cracked down on these tactics by targeting another widespread practice: paying for book reviews. Positive reviews are crucial for online sales, and Kindle eBooks are no exception. Many people on sites like Fiverr.com were selling "gigs" to leave positive reviews for as little as $5 each. Amazon responded by filing lawsuits against over a thousand Fiverr sellers for violating the site's terms of service by leaving paid reviews.

These lawsuits were a turning point. While the scammers themselves weren't sued, they realized they could be next. Many of the "Kindle publishers" left the platform, pulling their scamphlets and halting their paid courses on how to "get rich" with Kindle. Although some bad actors persisted, the reputation of self-published authors had already suffered significant damage.

Finally, Amazon revised the Kindle Unlimited program one more time, implementing measures that helped eliminate junk books but also made it more challenging to earn money through KDP Select. Now, authors are paid per page read, and Amazon's software tracks the actual turning of the pages. Skipping straight to the back of the book no longer counts. Only when a customer physically "flips" through the virtual pages does it register as being read.

While this was a welcome development in curbing junk books, the per-page payout remains low. Currently, authors earn around half a cent per page read—that's one penny for every two pages. This is a significant decrease from the over $2 per borrowed book that authors used to make. If someone only skims a handful of pages, authors in KDP Select are lucky to earn just a few cents. And if a customer downloads a book but never reads it (which is common with Kindle Unlimited subscribers), the author earns nothing at all.

However, it's not all doom and gloom when it comes to publishing your book on Kindle and opting into Kindle Select. Despite the drop in author profits, Kindle remains the leading platform for eBook self-publishing. Enrolling in the Kindle Select program means your book's digital format can only be published on Kindle. The good news is that you can decide this on a book-by-book basis rather than for your entire catalog. You might choose to enroll one book in Kindle Select *while* opting out with others, and the commitment period is only 90 days.

And there are still plenty of customers who purchase books outright, even if they have a Kindle Unlimited membership. None of my nonfiction books are currently enrolled in Kindle Select. Between Kindle and paperback sales, I earn a full-time income—much more than when I first started self-publishing. The success you achieve really depends on the categories you're publishing in and whether you've established a strong brand. I began with Kindle Select, but once I built a loyal audience, I was able to opt-out and focus solely on sales. Expanding into paperback formats, however, is what truly boosted my earnings.

While my nonfiction books aren't in Kindle Select, I do enroll my fiction books in the program. Since fiction is a newer venture for me, enrolling in Kindle Select helps get my books into readers' hands. For me, it's more about gaining exposure and building a following than immediate profit. Kindle Select is an excellent way to launch a pen name with the hope that, over time, you'll grow a large enough audience to eventually opt out of the program and rely on sales alone.

Since Amazon still dominates the eBook market, my advice is to enroll your fiction or nonfiction books in Kindle Select for at least the initial 90-day period. Monitor your book's performance; if you're getting a lot of borrows with many pages read, you might find that you earn more from borrows (even at one penny per two pages) than from publishing your book on less popular platforms. See if other authors in your niche enroll their books in Kindle Select. If the vast majority of authors in a category are enrolled in the program, you will likely have to as well in order to compete.

However, if you're not satisfied with the results after the 90-day period, you can always opt out of Kindle Select. You could also then upload your book to other platforms, such as Draft2Digital, as your eBook would no longer be exclusive to Amazon. However, if you want to remain exclusively on Kindle but without the borrowing option, you can simply remove your book from Kindle Select, making it available only for purchase.

As we've discussed, the paperback and hardcover versions of your books are only available for sale, not for borrowing. There's no Kindle Select program for paperbacks or hardcovers. In my experience, nonfiction books sell better in paperback, while fiction readers tend to prefer the Kindle format. Fiction customers are often avid readers who consume book after book, which is great for fiction authors since the demand for their work is consistently high. Regardless, though, since there is no exclusivity for paperback and hardcover books, you can "go wide" with them regardless of the status of your Kindle book. This means that you can have your eBook enrolled in Amazon's Kindle Select, which means it can only be sold on Amazon. Still, you can publish the paperback version to Amazon and any other platforms you choose, as there is no exclusivity for paperback books on Amazon.

I know some authors who remain exclusive to Amazon even though their books aren't enrolled in Kindle Select. For a long time, I did the same. Even after I removed my books from the Kindle Select program, it took me a couple of years to upload them to Draft2Digital for distribution to Apple, Barnes & Noble, and other platforms.

I'll talk more about Draft2Digital and other publishing platforms later in this book.

If you do choose to enroll your books in Kindle Select, two potentially valuable marketing tools are available: **Kindle Countdown Deals** and **Free Book Offers**.

Kindle Countdown Deals allow you to discount your book on a timed "countdown" basis. For example, if your book is normally priced at $6.99, you could offer it for 99 cents on the first day, $1.99 on the second day, $2.99 on the third day, and so on until the promotion ends. *Kindle Countdown Deals* can be run for up to five days within each 90-day enrollment period.

The **Free Book** promotion tool lets you offer your book for free for up to five days within each 90-day period. This promotion isn't limited to Kindle Unlimited subscribers; it's available to anyone browsing Amazon's website. You can choose to offer your book for free for up to five consecutive days, or you can split the promotion into separate days. For example, you could run the promotion for two days now and three days later in the same 90-day cycle. You can also cancel the promotion at any time if you change your mind.

Personally, I find that free book promotions are most effective when offered in two- or three-day blocks, as this gives potential readers time to discover your book but also gives you two different times to run the offer over the 90 days. I often run a two-day free promotion and then a three-day promotion a month or so later. If I decide to keep the book enrolled in Kindle Select, I'll repeat the promotions in the next 90-day cycle. However, if the book is performing well, I might opt out of Kindle Select and make it available for sale only.

Unless you're creating **no-and-low content books** such as journals, planners, notebooks, and activity books, which aren't eligible for Kindle, you'll likely be creating Kindle versions of your books. This means you'll need to format your book file for Amazon. As we discussed earlier, many new authors use Microsoft Word to write their books.

Kindle Book Formatting in Microsoft Word:

1. **Select Text**: Highlight the text you want to format. To apply these settings to the entire document, press **Ctrl + A** to select all the text.
2. **Open the Paragraph Settings**: Go to the **Home** tab on

the ribbon. Click on the small arrow in the bottom-right corner of the **Paragraph group** to open the **Paragraph** dialog box.

3. **Set Indentation**: In the **Paragraph** dialog box, find the **Indentation section**. Set the **Left** and **Right** indent values to 0. For **Special**, choose **First line** from the drop-down menu and set the **By** box to **0.2 inches**. This creates a 0.2-inch first-line indentation for each paragraph.
4. **Set Line Spacing**: In the same **Paragraph** dialog box, find the **Spacing section**. Under **Line spacing**, select **Single**. Ensure the **Before and After** spacing is set to 0 pt to avoid extra space between paragraphs.
5. **Apply Heading Styles to Chapter Titles**: Highlight your chapter title (e.g., **Chapter 1: Introduction**). Go to the **Home** tab on the ribbon and click on **Heading 1** (or **Heading 2**, etc., based on your preference) in the **Styles** group. Repeat for each chapter title.
6. **Create a Table of Contents**: Place your cursor where you want to insert the Table of Contents, usually at the beginning. Go to the **References** tab, click on **Table of Contents**, and choose a style from the drop-down menu.
7. **Create Clickable Links for Chapter Titles**: A Table of Contents created with the built-in feature will automatically generate clickable links. If the links aren't working, highlight the text you want to link (e.g., **Go to Chapter 1**), right-click, and select **Hyperlink**. In the **Insert Hyperlink** dialog box, choose **Place in This Document** on the left, select the chapter heading, and click **OK**.
8. **Save & Export Your eBook**: Save your document as a **.docx** file. While you can upload it directly to Amazon, I recommend using Kindle Create for optimal formatting.
9. **Kindle Create**: Download and open Amazon's free

Kindle Create software. Click on **+ Create New** and then **Choose**. Find the saved **.docx** file on your computer and follow the on-screen steps to upload.

Kindle Create offers various formatting options, such as fonts and layouts. When finished, click **Export** and choose **KPF**. Save this file where you can easily locate it when completing your Amazon listing. If you plan to list your book on other platforms, you can also download an **EPUB** file for sites that require it.

Remember, your files are never permanent; you can always go back to Word, make changes, and start fresh in Kindle Create. Frequent revisions are common, and you can upload updated versions at any time.

Paperback & Hardcover Books: Whether you choose to enroll your eBooks in KDP Select or not, it's typically assumed that most authors will start by publishing their fiction and/or nonfiction books in eBook format. But what about paperback and, more recently, hardcover books?

At the beginning of this chapter, I mentioned that one self-publishing business model is to produce a large number of shorter books and generate income through Kindle Unlimited page reads. While I've cautioned against publishing "scamphlets"—the low-quality, short books favored by scammers—this doesn't mean that shorter, well-written Kindle books can't be a profitable strategy. In fact, many authors successfully use this "quantity of quality books" approach to make a living.

However, producing longer books opens up the opportunity to offer your work in multiple formats, including paperback and hardcover. There are several nonfiction categories where books perform better in these physical formats compared to Kindle alone. Consider books that take longer to read or that people like to make notes in, such as technical manuals, cookbooks, or travel guides.

I also publish guided journals under a pen name in both

paperback and hardcover formats. These low-content books, filled with blank lined pages and question-and-answer prompts for users to write in, don't qualify for Kindle because they have more blank space than written words, and Amazon doesn't allow these to be published as eBooks.

Paperback Book Formatting: While Kindle books are one size and can feature as many or as few pages as you want, the requirements for paperback books are much different. While most authors will use the same formatting options for their paperback books as they did the Kindle versions, no-and-low-content books are typically different sizes. All paperback books must have a minimum page count of 24 pages and cannot exceed 828 pages for most trim sizes.

Paperback Sizes (in inches): The most popular paperback book size is **6 x 9**, which is the standard size that Kindle Create will produce for you. However, other sizes are available, including:

- **5 x 8**: fiction novels, poetry collections, memoirs, novelty coupon books
- **5.06 x 7.81**: pocket-sized fiction, novellas, self-help books, small-format journals, or planners
- **5.25 x 8**: personal development, small-format nonfiction, guided journals, gift books
- **5.5 x 8.5**: young adult novels, trade paperbacks, nonfiction, gratitude journals, habit trackers.
- **6 x 9**: Standard size for most genres, including fiction, nonfiction, memoirs, notebooks, and portable planners.
- **6.14 x 9.21**: academic texts, technical manuals, detailed nonfiction, specialized journals
- **6.69 x 9.61**: detailed nonfiction, biographies, business books, workbooks
- **7 x 10**: workbooks, educational texts, activity books, guided journals
- **7.44 x 9.69**: larger-format novels, academic books, art

- collections, children's activity books
- **7.5 x 9.25**: children's books, instructional guides, journals, interactive notebooks
- **8 x 10**: cookbooks, photography books, children's educational books, coloring books, activity books
- **8.25 x 6**: landscape-oriented books like art collections, photo books, themed notebooks
- **8.25 x 8.25**: children's picture books, photo books, gift books, interactive journals
- **8.5 x 8.5**: children's books, art books, scrapbooks, keepsake journals.
- **8.5 x 11**: This is a standard letter size, perfect for textbooks, workbooks, reference books, coloring books, and planners.
- **8.27 x 11.69**: academic papers, research, technical manuals, educational workbooks

Hardcover Book Formatting: While you can usually use the same file as your paperback book to create a hardcover edition, there are two things to keep in mind. First, hardcover books must have a minimum page count of 55 pages and cannot exceed 550 pages. Second, hardcover trim sizes are limited to the following:

Hardcover Sizes (in inches)

- 5 x 8
- 5.5 x 8.5
- 6 x 9
- 6.14 x 9.21
- 7 x 10
- 8.5x11

While there are numerous book size options, the majority of fiction and nonfiction books are formatted at 6 x 9. This size is the default for most self-published titles on Amazon. If you use Amazon's free *Kindle Create software*, it will automatically format your paperback and hardcover books to this standard 6 x

9 size.

The other sizes listed are more suitable for different no-and-low-content books. For example, composition notebooks are commonly 7" by 10", while coloring books are usually 8.5" by 11". Smaller formats, such as 5" by 8", are often used for novelty coupon books or purse-sized planners.

If you plan to publish a fiction or nonfiction book using *Kindle Create,* it will default to the 6" by 9" format. However, if you want to use a different size, you'll need to create and format your manuscript in another program, which we'll cover later in this book.

When I was publishing solely on Kindle, my average word count was around 15,000 words. Today, my nonfiction books average 60,000 words, which works well for both Kindle and paperback formats. A typical paperback length is about 225 pages. Keep in mind that page counts for Kindle books vary, as readers can adjust the font size, which changes the total number of pages displayed.

My books are primarily nonfiction. Readers expect different minimum page counts for different genres, such as:

Fiction Page Counts

- Flash Fiction: 100 to 1,500 words
- Short Story: 1,500 to 7,500 words (up to 30,000 words for longer short stories)
- Novella: 30,000 to 50,000 words
- Novel: 50,000 to 100,000 words (Generally, 80,000 to 100,000 words is preferred for most adult genres)
- Children's Chapter Books: 4,000 to 10,000 words
- Children's Picture Books: 300 to 800 words (some may go up to 1,000 words)
- Children's Early Readers: 200 to 3,500 words
- Middle Grade (Children's Books): 20,000 to 55,000 words

Nonfiction Page Counts

- Memoirs: 60,000 to 80,000 words
- Self-Help: 30,000 to 70,000 words (usually around 40,000 to 50,000 words)
- General Nonfiction: 70,000 to 100,000 words

Fiction Genres with Specific Word Count Expectations

- Mainstream Romance: 70,000 to 100,000 words
- Romance Subgenres (e.g., Contemporary, Historical, etc.): 50,000 to 90,000 words
- Science Fiction/Fantasy: 90,000 to 120,000 words (Epic Fantasy can exceed 150,000 words)
- Historical Fiction: 80,000 to 100,000 words (can be longer for complex narratives)
- Thrillers/Horror/Mysteries/Crime: 70,000 to 90,000 words
- Young Adult: 50,000 to 80,000 words

No-and-Low Content Boks

- Journals: 100 to 200 pages, depending on design and purpose.
- Planners: Typically 120 to 200 pages
- Notebooks: 100 to 150 pages
- Adult Coloring Books: 50 to 120 pages
- Children's Coloring Books: 30 to 80 pages
- Activity Books for Adults: 80 to 150 pages
- Activity Books for Children: 30 to 100 pages
- Logbooks: 100 to 200

Size To Market: Do you see the genre you would like to write in listed above? If you do and feel overwhelmed by the expected word counts, remember that these are guidelines and averages. I have nonfiction books that fall short of the 40,000-word mark and fiction books that fall somewhere between novellas and full-length novels. The key is to have an understanding of what readers in your chosen genre expect. After all, they are the ones you hope will purchase your book. For instance, historical fiction tends to be quite long, so a book that is only 20,000 words might not meet reader expectations in that category.

The length of your book directly influences how much you can charge for it. It's difficult to sell a book for $10 that is only a few thousand words unless it falls into the no-or-low content category, such as a complex planner or coloring book.

Having your books available in paperback and hardcover also opens the door to wider distribution opportunities. As mentioned earlier, if your Kindle eBooks are enrolled in Kindle Select for Kindle Unlimited subscribers to borrow, the eBook version must remain exclusive to Amazon. However, this restriction does not apply to the paperback or hardcover versions. You can "go wide" with your print books, making them available through Apple, Barnes & Noble, and even libraries through sites such as Draft2Digital, IngramSpark, or Lulu.

So, should you publish in Kindle, paperback, hardcover, or all three formats? Each has its own dedicated reader base, and each format can be a profitable avenue. Personally, I prefer the "quality over quantity" method for self-publishing. I may not have hundreds of nonfiction and fiction books. Still, the ones I do publish are high-quality enough to be available in multiple formats, including eBook, paperback, and hardcover.

For my children's books, I stick to Kindle and paperback formats because they don't meet the page length requirements for hardcover. Most of my no-and-low-content books are available only in paperback. However, I've begun offering some of my best-sellers in hardcover as well.

If you plan to write fiction or nonfiction, it can be tempting to focus solely on Kindle versions and bypass the work of formatting physical books and creating additional covers. However, by doing so, you may be missing out on significant revenue opportunities. Offering your books in paperback and hardcover can broaden your reach and increase your earnings. Later in this book, I'll walk you through the step-by-step process of uploading your book in all three formats. I promise—it's easier than you might think!

When Amazon first introduced the paperback option, I hesitated for nearly two years before deciding to publish in that format. That hesitation cost me tens of thousands of dollars in lost royalties. Don't make the same mistake! Providing multiple format options can significantly increase the likelihood of your book reaching more readers, and the more books you sell, the more money you will make!

eBooks vs. Printed Books: eBooks are still extremely popular, but paperback and hardcover books also have an audience. eBooks continue to attract readers due to their convenience and portability. Features like adjustable fonts and integrated dictionaries make them accessible to a wide audience. The ability to store thousands of titles on a single device is a significant advantage for avid readers.

As of 2024, 42% of Amazon eBook sales were self-published titles. The KDP Select *Global Fund*, which pays authors for Kindle Unlimited borrows, reached $56.1 million in June 2024.

Despite the rise of eBooks, printed books maintain a strong presence. In the U.S., hardcover and paperback sales still dominate the market, with annual sales of approximately $3 billion and $2.5 billion, respectively.

Readers still value the tactile experience of holding a book and turning its pages, especially in genres such as children's books, cookbooks, and art books, where the visual and physical aspects are crucial. Plus, physical books make for popular gifts.

Younger readers, particularly Millennials, are engaging more with a mix of eBooks, audiobooks, and print books compared to older generations. In terms of genre popularity, fiction genres like mystery, thriller, and classics dominate eBook sales. At the same time, nonfiction topics such as biographies, history, and self-help are popular in both eBook and print formats.

The great thing about Amazon KDP is that they offer formats that work for whatever type of book you want to publish!

PRO TIP: Many people think you need an Amazon Kindle device to read Kindle books, but that's not the case! Kindle books can be read on any device using Amazon's free Kindle app. I have a Kindle device, but I also use the Kindle app on my laptop and phone so that I can read anywhere. When promoting a Kindle book, I often say, "No Kindle? No problem! Simply download Amazon's FREE Kindle reading app to your computer, smartphone, or tablet!" Then, I provide a direct link to the app, which is available for Apple, Android, PC, and Mac.

CHAPTER SEVEN: THE JOURNEY OF WRITING A BOOK

So, you've got the essentials—computer, internet access, word processing software, and you're ready to design your own book covers or hire someone to do it. You've explored the book categories and found ones you're excited to write in. You understand pen names and the differences between Kindle, paperback, and hardcover formats, as well as the pros and cons of Kindle Select.

You're familiar with the basics of self-publishing, but now comes the challenging part:

YOU NEED TO WRITE A BOOK!

(Or create a no- or low-content book like a journal, planner, notebook, or activity book. I'll cover those in a later chapter, but for now, we'll focus on writing fiction and nonfiction books.)

So, how do you go about writing a book? Not just one that you'll enjoy writing, but one that millions of potential readers will want to buy—a book that can actually make you money?

For many, writing a book is the hardest part of the self-publishing journey. It's not about a lack of talent but the fear of failure. I've seen many would-be authors struggle even to begin because they're overwhelmed by fear of the unknown. They have great book ideas but have yet to get them onto paper.

But don't let fear hold you back! Millions of people around the world are successfully self-publishing books and making money from them—including me. There's no reason you can't join us. You just need to start writing. And the key to writing a book is simply to START!

If you're like me, you might already have your first book mapped out in your head long before you start typing. I spent weeks thinking about my first book before finally sitting down to write it. But even if you're still undecided on a topic, you can still come up with an idea that works.

Here's a little secret: my first book was terrible! It was very short, as was typical for Kindle books at the time, but it was subpar compared to my current work. I didn't even have a nice cover—just a basic one from Amazon's Kindle Cover Creator, which only offered solid colors and a standard font. It was as bare-bones as a book could be, and I'm amazed anyone bought it. Thankfully, those readers stuck around and bought my subsequent books, which, in my humble opinion, are a million times better!

One of the perks of being an indie author is that you can revamp any book as many times as you want. Later in my career, I completely overhauled that first book, including redesigning the cover and putting it into paperback and large print. It's still one of my top-selling books, even after all of these years. Since it isn't exclusive to Amazon, I also have it published on Draft2Digital and IngramSpark so that shoppers outside of Amazon can buy it.

Today, when people ask what I write about, I explain that I write books on making money on platforms like eBay, Etsy, YouTube, and Amazon. I always get the sense that they're hoping I'll say I write spicy romance and are disappointed when I say nonfiction!

Nonfiction topics come naturally to me, but fiction has always been a challenge. I've started and stopped numerous fiction books over the years. With nonfiction, I outline everything beforehand, but with fiction, I often start with a basic plot and see where it takes me. Most authors stick to either fiction or nonfiction, but I've tried both to expand my catalog and sharpen my skills.

Adding no-and-low content books to my collection has boosted my income by an average of $1,000 a month on top of what I earn from nonfiction. When it comes to self-publishing, quantity matters. Few authors strike gold with their first book, even with a traditional publisher. I have hundreds of books under my three pen names, but most of my income comes from just 20% of those titles. This is the 80/20 effect: 80% of your books may not sell much, but the successful 20% can provide a steady income.

Here are some tips to get you started writing your first book:

Brainstorm: Remember how teachers encouraged you to brainstorm in school? I still use that technique for my books. If you're new to writing or experiencing writer's block, brainstorming can help.

Start with a topic and write down anything that comes to mind, even if it doesn't make sense. Keep going until you're out of ideas. This list isn't set in stone; you'll refine it as you continue writing.

For example, when writing about reselling on eBay, I'll jot down ideas like "account setup," "sourcing," and "customer service." Some of these will be combined, others removed. It's just a starting point.

Brainstorming often sparks ideas for other books. When I brainstorm fiction, potential plots emerge that I note for future use. This means I always have a list of ideas ready to be developed into new books.

Outline: After I finish brainstorming, I turn that list into an outline. You probably remember creating outlines in school, and

I use a similar format for my books.

I start by dividing my brainstorming list into sections or chapters, placing related topics under each section. I then expand on those topics with more bullet points until most of the information is organized.

For example, let's create an outline for a nonfiction book about gardening:

Chapter 1: Getting Started with Gardening

- Introduction to Gardening: Benefits of gardening, both physical and mental.
- Choosing the Right Location: Sunlight, soil type, and space considerations.
- Basic Tools and Equipment: Essential gardening tools and their uses.

Chapter 2: Understanding Soil and Plant Needs

- Types of Soil: Sandy, clay, loam, and how to improve soil quality.
- Testing Soil pH: Importance of pH and how to test and amend the soil.
- Composting Basics: Creating and using compost for healthy plants.

Chapter 3: Planning Your Garden

- Choosing the Right Plants: Annuals vs. perennials, understanding hardiness zones.
- Companion Planting: Benefits and common pairings.
- Garden Design: Layout ideas for vegetable, herb, and flower gardens.

Chapter 4: Planting and Growing Techniques

- Starting from Seeds vs. Transplants: Pros and cons, and how-to guides for each.

- Watering and Fertilizing: Best practices for plant health and growth.
- Pruning and Maintenance: Techniques to keep plants healthy and productive.

Chapter 5: Managing Pests and Diseases

- Common Garden Pests: Identification and organic control methods.
- Preventing Plant Diseases: Best practices and natural remedies.
- Attracting Beneficial Insects: How to encourage pollinators and predators.

Chapter 6: Seasonal Gardening Tips

- Spring Preparation: Starting seeds, preparing soil, and early planting.
- Summer Care: Watering, mulching, and managing heat stress.
- Fall Harvest and Cleanup: Tips for harvesting and preparing the garden for winter.
- Winter Planning: Indoor gardening and planning for the next season.

Chapter 7: Specialty Gardens

- Container Gardening: Best practices for small spaces and patios.
- Raised Bed Gardening: Building and maintaining raised beds.
- Herb and Kitchen Gardens: Growing herbs and veggies for cooking.

Chapter 8: Troubleshooting Common Issues

- Yellowing Leaves, Wilting, and Poor Growth: Diagnosing and fixing problems.
- Overwatering vs. Underwatering: Signs and solutions.

- Nutrient Deficiencies: Identifying and correcting with fertilizers.

Chapter 9: Harvesting and Using Your Garden's Bounty

- When and How to Harvest: Optimal times for different crops.
- Preserving Your Harvest: Canning, freezing, and drying methods.
- Cooking and Enjoying Fresh Produce: Simple recipes and storage tips.

Chapter 10: Gardening for the Future

- Sustainable Gardening Practices: Water conservation, organic methods, and permaculture basics.
- Expanding Your Garden: Tips for adding new plants and structures.
- Building a Year-Round Garden: Extending the growing season with greenhouses and cold frames.

For fiction, let's create an example of an outline for a cozy mystery novel:

Chapter 1: The Setup

- Introduce the Protagonist: Describe the main character, their background, and their role in the community.
- Establish the Setting: Small town or village, cozy and inviting atmosphere.
- Hint at the Conflict: Introduce tension, such as a rivalry or local issue.

Chapter 2: The Crime

- Introduce the Victim: Someone connected to the protagonist or community.
- Discover the Body: The protagonist or close friend finds the victim.

- Initial Reaction: Shock, confusion, and the protagonist's resolve to get involved.

Chapter 3: The Suspects

- Introduce Suspects: Include at least 3-5 suspects with possible motives.
- Reveal Backstories: Short scenes or dialogues showing why each could be guilty.
- Red Herrings: Misdirect the reader with false leads.

Chapter 4: The Investigation

- Protagonist Begins Sleuthing: Casual conversations, eavesdropping, and light snooping.
- Conflict with Authorities: The protagonist clashes with the official investigator.
- Suspect Interactions: The protagonist interviews the suspect, uncovering clues and motives.

Chapter 5: Uncovering Clues

- Discover Important Clue: An object, overheard conversation, or hidden message that shifts the focus.
- Protagonist Faces Danger: The antagonist becomes aware of the investigation and tries to deter the protagonist.
- Support from Friends: Friends help the protagonist make connections and provide assistance.

Chapter 6: The Twist

- Revelation: A major twist that points the investigation in a new direction.
- Suspect Eliminated: One suspect is cleared, leading to renewed focus on others.
- Doubt: The protagonist questions their judgment and feels pressure to solve the case.

Chapter 7: The Confrontation

- **Build-Up to the Showdown:** The protagonist pieces together the final clues.
- **The Confrontation:** The protagonist confronts the true culprit.
- **Dangerous Situation:** Tension escalates; the protagonist may be put in physical danger.

Chapter 8: The Resolution

- **Culprit Revealed:** Final revelation of the criminal and their motives.
- **Justice Restored:** The culprit is apprehended or escapes with consequences.
- **Community Reaction:** The community heals or reacts to the events.

Chapter 9: The Aftermath

- **Wrap-Up Loose Ends:** Address any unresolved subplots or lingering questions.
- **Personal Growth:** The protagonist reflects on the experience and what they've learned.
- **Tease Future Mystery:** Hint at a possible new mystery or adventure.

Outlines aren't set in stone, but they can provide a structure to guide your writing and can evolve as you progress. My final drafts rarely follow my initial outlines exactly but having them helps me stay organized and focused.

Write: Once my outline is done, I start writing, fleshing out each section of my outline. Most fiction authors will tell you that the best way to write is to just WRITE! Let the words flow, and don't worry about spelling, grammar, or sentence structure, as you can fix all those things later. Stopping to correct every misspelled word will interrupt your flow, and you will lose steam. As long as the words are coming to you, keep on writing!

And remember, you can write any way that works best for you.

You can write on paper, type on your computer, use your phone, or even dictate your book out loud. There is no one "right" way to write—do what works best for you

Of course, you cannot write all day and night; you need to take breaks. If you are on a hot streak, write for as long as you can. However, if you have writer's block, step away from the computer. Clear your head by doing something else, anything else. Go for a walk. Clean the house. Take a nap. Watch a movie. Forget about your book for a while, even for the rest of the day, so that you can return to it refreshed. Even if that means you do not get back to it for a few days or even a week.

That being said, don't take too long of a break. You want to maintain interest in your own story. I periodically feel completely burned out from writing and tell myself I need a few weeks off, only to return to my book the next day after a good night's sleep. If the story is there, the words will eventually come.

However, if the words aren't coming, try changing course with your story. Remember, this is YOUR book. If a character or plot isn't working, you can change either or both. Review your outline, if you made one, to remind yourself where you are going with your book. If you still need to start with an outline, you can still create one after you start writing. It may be easier to develop an outline after you have already written a few pages, as you likely have a better idea of the location, characters, and plot.

Depending on your book, the writing process could take days, weeks, or even years. The longer the book, the longer it will obviously take to write. However, don't mistake quantity for quality. A book with a large word count doesn't mean it's a good book. Focus on QUALITY, no matter how many words you write or pages you end up with. Quality always sells more than quantity in the long term.

Story Structure: When you start writing fiction, you may come across the terms *Pantsers*, *Plotters*, and *Plantsers*. These refer to different approaches to storytelling.

Pantsers "fly by the seat of their pants," meaning they start writing without a clear plan. They let the story and characters evolve naturally. For example, Stephen King often writes without knowing the ending of his books, allowing the narrative to unfold on its own. While this method can lead to unexpected twists, it can also result in hitting a wall or having an inconsistent plot.

Plotters take the opposite approach. They plan out their stories in detail before they begin writing. J.R.R. Tolkien meticulously outlined the entire mythology and events of Middle-earth before penning *The Lord of the Rings*. Plotters often avoid writer's block because they have a clear roadmap. Still, they might feel constrained by their outline if the story naturally veers in a different direction.

Plantsers blend both methods. They may start with a loose outline but are open to letting the story evolve as they write. J.K. Rowling planned the broad arc of the Harry Potter series but allowed individual book plots to develop more organically. Many writers identify with this style because it offers both structure and creative freedom.

I am a Plantser. I start with a rough outline for my books, but I constantly expand on that as I write, adding additional topics within chapters and even adding new chapters.

There's no right or wrong way to approach writing. Your process may evolve over time or change based on the book you're writing. You don't need to label yourself as any one type. Some authors may start as plotters but become more flexible over time, or vice versa. The key is to find a process that helps you get your ideas down and finish your book. Remember, the most important thing is to keep writing, no matter what your method!

The W Plot: An author friend introduced me to the **W Plot** method for crafting fiction. This structure not only simplifies the writing process but also aligns with what readers expect in a story.

The W Plot has three acts:

Act I: Start with a **Trigger Event** to draw the reader in, then establish the protagonist's problem. The plot begins at a high point and descends to the **1st Turning Point**, the story's lowest moment, just like the first downward stroke of a W. For example, Jane is coming home after losing her job only to find her husband in bed with her best friend. He tells her he wants a divorce and kicks her out of the house. That's about as low as a character can go!

Act II: The protagonist recovers from the initial setback. The plot ascends, reaching a peak where the **Second Triggering Event** occurs. This leads to another decline, ending in a deeper problem at the **2nd Turning Point**. Using our example, Jane decides to head back to her small hometown, where she starts a bakery and meets a new man. Life is looking up until she discovers her new boyfriend has a big secret: he was once in jail! Then, her ex-husband showed up, demanding a share of her bakery profits. Jane is now as low as she was at the end of Act I.

Act III: From the **2nd Turning Point**, the story ascends again towards resolution. The final stroke of the W concludes with the problem's resolution, offering either a satisfying ending or a "happily ever after...for now" scenario. For Jane, she learns that her boyfriend was set up for a crime he didn't commit. Even though he was released from jail, people still believe he is guilty. Jane works to help him clear his name, they get married, and her bakery is named the best in the state. Her husband and her best friend split up and are both miserable. The end!

In a "happily ever after...for now" book, you would continue the story as a series by creating new drama for Jane and her new husband in the second book or shifting focus to a new character within the same setting. For example, the second book could feature Mary, an employee at Jane's bakery who has her own story. During the course of the book, readers would get to see where Jane and her husband are now, and Jane would be helping Mary. But the story would be Mary's, and she would get her happy ending. And then book three would follow someone else in Jane and Mary's orbit in the town.

If your book is part of a series, you can also end on a cliffhanger but be cautious. While cliffhangers can drive sales for the next book, they may also frustrate readers if the sequel isn't readily available. My first fiction book ended on a cliffhanger, and I received negative feedback because the second book wasn't immediately available. If you choose a cliffhanger, ensure the next book is published or available for pre-order with a release date within a month.

PRO TIPS: Every writer is different, and I firmly believe there is no right or wrong way to write a book. My writing technique has continued to evolve over the years. Here are some tips and tricks that may (or may not!) work for you:

Set a Writing Schedule: Establish a daily or weekly writing schedule. Consistency is key, even if you only write a few hundred words a day. It adds up! Some authors set a timer, while others set a word count goal. I don't write every day; I need to take breaks, or else I burn out. But some authors can't go a day without writing. Do what works best for you!

Create a Dedicated Writing Space: Find a quiet, comfortable place where you can focus on your writing without distractions. It helps to have a specific area where your brain knows it's time to get creative. However, make sure that you have an ergonomic setup. Writing on your laptop while slouched on the couch may sound relaxing, but your back and shoulders will soon tell you they would rather you sit in a chair and put your laptop on a table that supports your forearms while you type.

Read Your Competition: Read books in your genre to understand what works and what doesn't. It also helps to inspire new ideas and improve your writing style. It may be worth it to subscribe to Kindle Unlimited for a month or two to read what other self-published authors are putting out, especially in subcategories that aren't usually found in traditional bookstores. Self-published books in niche troupes follow a very specific pattern and have similar covers, so you need to know exactly what readers expect from books in those categories.

Join a Writing Group: Engaging with other writers can provide feedback, encouragement, and accountability. You can find online writing communities or local groups. There are even YouTube channels where you can live stream with other writers or watch those streams back while you write.

Read Aloud: Reading your work aloud helps catch awkward phrasing, repeated words, and other issues you might miss when reading silently. While I use Grammarly Pro and Microsoft Editor to check my work, reading my books aloud (even in a whisper) helps me catch those last few errors before I hit publish.

If you don't like reading out loud, you can let your computer read to you. I frequently use the **Read Aloud** feature (located under the **Review** tab) in **Microsoft Word** to help me catch errors.

Take Breaks: Writing burnout is real. Step away from your book from time to time. A fresh perspective often leads to better ideas and clearer writing. Whether this means you take a coffee break on your porch or take a trip overseas, time away from your project can help inspire new ideas and get you excited about writing again.

Keep a Notebook Handy: Ideas can strike at any time. Having a notebook or note app on your phone allows you to jot down thoughts whenever inspiration hits. I often have ideas in bed at night, even in my dreams! I can quickly open up the notes app on my phone and turn on the microphone to record my ideas.

Be wary of others' opinions: Facebook is filled with author groups, and to be honest, many of them are brutal. There are a lot of people who fancy themselves writers even though they've never published anything. Instead, they throw around big words and like to intimidate new authors. I bet you picked up this book because you want to write AND make money. And those two things combined aren't always welcome in the world of writers. But I am proof that you can love what you write and make a living from your work. And if I can, so can you!

CHAPTER EIGHT: EDITING YOUR BOOK

When I first started writing books, I would power through without stopping to correct errors, resulting in a rough first draft of about 30,000 words. I'd then go back and make corrections, usually adding another 20,000 words, making this second draft the longest part of the process. I'd repeat this process with a third or even fourth draft, constantly refining and adding content.

It was an exhaustive process, but I followed the same schedule as many authors who often spend more time editing than writing. For those like me, who tend to get stuck in an endless cycle of edits, it's easy to feel like the work is never truly finished.

One major downside of this approach was burnout. After working through multiple drafts, I often became overwhelmed and frustrated. I found myself nitpicking every sentence, and the process became less about improving the book and more about trying to find something to fix. It felt like I was chasing perfection, which ultimately slowed my progress and drained my creativity.

I realized that this endless cycle of editing was affecting my productivity and motivation. I began to dread the editing phase, and I knew I needed to change my approach. That's when I decided to experiment with writing in a more focused and deliberate manner.

Now, I take a whole new approach to writing and editing. Instead of racing through the first draft, I take my time, perfecting each paragraph before moving on to the next. While it may seem slower, it actually cuts my workload in half and helps me complete books faster without burning out. Before, after the third draft, I could barely see the words on the page. Now, I usually only do two drafts—writing slowly and carefully the first time and then doing a thorough edit afterward. It's been a game changer for me, allowing me to complete books faster and not burn out!

Ultimately, both methods have their pros and cons. Some authors thrive on getting the rough draft out quickly and then refining it later, while others, like me, find it more productive to write carefully from the beginning. The key is to see what works best for you and to remember that self-publishing gives you the flexibility to choose your own path. Whether you prefer to speed through a rough draft or take your time crafting each sentence, the most important thing is to keep writing and improving your craft.

For me, whether I'm speeding through a first draft or writing more slowly, I always dedicate a second draft to editing. I start from the beginning, carefully reading through my work to make corrections and add new content. This phase isn't just about fixing typos; it's about refining the book's overall structure and improving the flow.

Even if I have an outline, I often rearrange sections during editing—sometimes moving entire chapters. Remember, nothing is set in stone. The beauty of self-publishing is that you can always revise and improve your book, even after it's published.

However, even if you are a skilled proofreader, it's hard to edit one's work. Having a second or third set of eyes review your work is always helpful. And there are software editing options you can access to help catch spelling, grammar, and punctuation errors. Here are some options:

Grammarly: Grammarly is the most well-known tool for catching spelling, grammar, and punctuation errors. The free version is helpful for basic corrections, but the Grammarly Pro subscription offers much more. With Grammarly Pro, you can edit for clarity, conciseness, and overall readability. It also provides suggestions for improving sentence structure and word choice, which can significantly enhance your writing.

Grammarly Pro recently added AI features, but I've found these to be error-prone. While they may improve over time, I recommend using these tools cautiously. Another useful feature is the plagiarism checker, which ensures your content is original and helps avoid accidental inclusion of copyrighted material, such as song lyrics. This is particularly helpful for children's books.

You can download Grammarly, which integrates with your word processing software and internet use. I use it when writing emails, creating Facebook ads, and writing anything in Word.

Microsoft Word Proofreading: Microsoft Word is one of the most commonly used tools for editing books, offering features like spell check, grammar check, and readability analysis. The built-in spelling and grammar check helps catch basic errors. At the same time, the Review feature allows you to track changes and add comments as you edit. Word also includes tools like "Read Aloud," which reads the text to you, making it easier to catch mistakes you might miss when reading silently. I use both Word Proofreading and Grammarly Pro as both programs catch different mistakes. For me, using both is like having two additional people reviewing my work.

ProWritingAid: ProWritingAid is a comprehensive writing tool that goes beyond basic grammar and spell-checking. It provides detailed reports on various aspects of your writing, including grammar, style, sentence structure, and readability. The tool offers suggestions for improving sentence variety, word choice, and consistency. It also highlights issues like passive voice, overused words, and complex sentence structures.

ProWritingAid integrates with platforms like Microsoft Word, Google Docs, and Scrivener, making it a good choice for those who use different writing programs. You can test out a free version before deciding whether to pay for the service.

Hemingway Editor: The Hemingway Editor is a user-friendly tool designed to help writers create clear and concise content. It highlights complex sentences, passive voice, adverbs, and difficult-to-read phrases, making it ideal for refining your writing style. The editor uses color-coded highlights to identify problem areas: yellow for hard-to-read sentences, red for very hard-to-read sentences, and blue for adverbs that could be omitted. It also offers readability scores and suggests simpler alternatives to enhance clarity. Hemingway Editor is available as both a web-based tool and a desktop app and offers both a free online version and a paid desktop app.

Ginger: Ginger software is an editing tool designed to enhance your writing by checking grammar, spelling, punctuation, and sentence structure. It offers features such as grammar and spelling checks, sentence rephrasing, translation (great if you are publishing books in multiple languages), and the ability to have your work read aloud to you via their text reader. Ginger has a free version with limited features and a premium version that offers advanced tools and services.

Slick Write: Slick Write is an online writing tool that helps with grammar, spelling, punctuation, and style checks. It is designed to improve the quality of your writing by identifying issues related to sentence structure, word variety, and readability. In addition to grammar and spell check, it also features style analysis to highlight redundant phrases, passive voice, and other stylistic concerns. It can also analyze sentence length and structure for better readability. Slick Write is free to use and accessible online without the need for downloads or installations.

WhiteSmoke: WhiteSmoke is an advanced writing tool designed to enhance grammar, spelling, punctuation, and style. It provides various features that help improve writing quality, including checking grammar, spelling, style, and punctuation. Like Ginger, it also offers translation options. WhiteSmoke is available as a browser extension, desktop application, and mobile app. It requires a subscription for full access to its features.

Hiring Proofreaders & Editors: If you want a live person to review your work, you can hire freelancers from numerous websites, the most popular of which are Fiverr and Upwork.

A **proofreader** and an **editor are** two different people. A proofreader focuses on correcting surface-level errors, such as spelling, grammar, punctuation, and formatting issues. They ensure the final manuscript is free of typos and mistakes before publication. An editor provides more in-depth feedback, addressing content, structure, clarity, and flow.

Here are some tips when looking at hiring proofreaders and editors on Fiverr and Upwork:

Fiverr: Fiverr started as a website that offered freelance work for $5 per "gig." It has evolved, with experienced users charging hundreds, if not thousands, of dollars. However, new users always sign up on the site who sell their services for much less to get their foot in the door.

When searching Fiverr for proofreaders and editors, use specific keywords like "book editor" or "proofreader" and filter by ratings and budget. Look for high ratings, positive reviews, and any samples they've provided. Begin with a small project, like editing one chapter, to test their quality before committing to a full manuscript.

I have found Fiverr excellent for hiring graphic designers to create book covers more so than for proofreaders. If you choose to hire a proofreader on Fiverr, make sure they are native speakers of the language in which your book is written. I wouldn't look for an editor on Fiverr, as the best editors are on Upwork.

Upwork: Upwork, in my opinion, is a more sophisticated platform than Fiverr. You are more likely to find highly qualified proofreaders and editors here than on Fiverr. When searching for freelancers on Upwork, you can review profiles to submit proposals to and post your job for people to apply to.

When posting a job, describe your needs in detail, including genre, word count, and specific requirements (e.g., familiarity with fiction or non-fiction). Look for relevant experience and client feedback. Upwork's profiles often showcase detailed work history and ratings. Ask specific questions about their experience with similar projects and request a short sample edit if possible.

When using Fiverr or Upwork, make sure you specify deadlines, budget, and any unique needs upfront. Get confirmation on whether you can submit additional corrections. For example, many graphic designers on Fiverr specify how many book cover corrections you can request. The more drafts of a cover you want, the more you will pay.

Additional Self-Editing Tips: Even when you use proofreading programs and hire editors, you still want to review your work. Here are some strategies you can use:

Read Your Work Out loud: Reading your book aloud is an effective way to catch mistakes that might slip by during silent reading. Speaking the words helps identify awkward phrasing and errors. I often use Microsoft Word's Read Aloud feature, which reads the text back to me and gives me a fresh perspective on my writing.

Print Out Your Manuscript: Reading from a printed page helps you see the work in a new light and catch errors you may have missed on the screen. Grab a highlighter or red pen to mark the corrections you want to make.

Change Font and Layout: Changing the font or text size can help you spot mistakes more easily. If you typically use Ariel, switch to Times New Roman just for the editing process. You'll be surprised at how many mistakes suddenly pop out at you.

Read Backwards: Reading your manuscript from end to beginning helps you focus on each sentence, making it easier to spot typos and awkward phrasing. This is a tedious task, but it really does work.

Track Repeated Words: Use the **Find** function in your word processor to identify overused words or phrases and replace them with alternatives. I overuse the word "actually;" Grammarly has been helpful in providing me with alternative words.

My Process: After I have completed my book's draft, I run the document through Microsoft Word's spell and grammar checks and Grammarly Pro. Grammarly provides more in-depth suggestions for sentence structure and word choice. While it can be time-consuming, I carefully review each suggestion and decide what to implement based on the context. I will then have a friend or family member read my work to see if they can catch any additional errors.

Editing is a time-consuming and sometimes tedious process. But it is imperative that you check, double-check, and even triple-check your work before hitting publish. Unedited books result in negative reviews, which will tank your overall sales.

CHAPTER NINE: FORMATTING YOUR BOOK FILES

After your book is written and edited, the next step is to format it for upload to Amazon KDP. This was the part of the self-publishing process that scared me the most, but I learned that it is really quite simple. Once you've formatted one book, the ones after that will be so much easier!

Font & Style: Amazon insists that you keep the font and style of your books simple. Not all fonts and styles translate to Kindle, meaning your book will look like a mess once it is uploaded.

I use **Calibri (Body) 12** for my text and simple features such as **Bold** and *Italic*. I then chose **Heading 1** for my chapter headings and **Subtitle** for my author name.

I select **Open** under **Paragraph Spacing** and **12 pt spacing** between each paragraph. When it comes to self-publishing books, white space is commonly thought of as preferred. I have found that it works best for my nonfiction books as it breaks up the content and does not overwhelm the reader. Look at how books in your category are laid out to see what paragraph spacing and indentations look like so you can follow suit.

The only other style feature I use is to **Center** headings; otherwise, my books are **Align Text Left**.

Page Breaks: You want to add Page Breaks between chapters. This feature is found under **Insert** at the top of every Word document.

To insert **Page Breaks**, you simply place your cursor after the last word of the previous page. Click on the **Insert tab** at the top of the page in Microsoft Word and then click the **Page Break** icon. The text following where your cursor is positioned will move down to a separate page. Continue going through your book and adding page breaks where needed.

Note that you can undo page breaks simply by placing your cursor next to the first letter of the text and hitting the **Backspace** key on your computer until the text returns to the page it was originally on.

Page breaks give your Kindle book the look and feel of actual paper pages, breaking up the text so that it all does not run together. To get an idea of where your page breaks should be, look at an actual paper book. Note that the first pages – the title, author, Copyright, and table of contents – are all on their own pages. Sometimes, the chapter titles are on their page, with the actual chapter contents starting on the next page. The formatting will transfer to both Kindle and paperback book files.

For my books, I insert a page break after the **Title** and **Author** page. The next page is Copyright, and I insert another page break after that. I then include my **Table of Contents**, inserting a page break after that. Next comes my **Introduction**, followed by each chapter. Finally, I always have a **Conclusion** and **About the Author** page.

Table of Contents: Every book needs a Table of Contents, and with Kindle eBooks, that table needs to contain active links so that users can click on each chapter and be taken directly to it. While you should be able to create a table using Amazon's free Kindle Create software, I frequently run into issues and must manually create a TOC in my Word documents. Fortunately,

Amazon provides step-by-step instructions for this process:

Instructions for creating a Kindle Interactive TOC in Word:

PC Instructions:

1. **Apply chapter styles:** Highlight your first chapter title. Go to the **Home** tab. In the **Styles** section, click **Heading 1**. Repeat these steps for all chapter titles.

2. **Insert TOC:** Click where you want to insert your table of contents. Go to the **References** tab and click **Table of Contents**. Choose **Automatic Table 1**. Click **Table of Contents** again, but this time, choose **Custom Table of Contents**. In the dialog box that appears, clear the **Show Page Numbers** box. Set **Show levels** to **1** and click **OK**. When asked if you want to replace the table of contents, click **OK**.

3. **Add Bookmark:** Highlight the Table of Contents. Go to the **Insert** tab. In the Links section, click **Bookmark**. In the **Bookmark name** field, enter **toc**, and click **Add**. Insert a page break after your table of contents.

Mac instructions:

1. **Apply chapter styles:** Highlight your first chapter title. Go to the **Home** tab. Under **Styles,** click **Heading 1**. Repeat these steps for all chapter titles.

2. **Insert TOC:** Click where you want to insert your table of contents. Go to the References tab and click **Table of Contents**. Choose **Classic**. Click **Table of Contents** again, but this time, choose **Custom Table of Contents**. In the dialog box that appears, clear the **Show Page Numbers** box. Set **Show levels** to **1** and click **OK**. When asked if you want to replace the table of contents, click **Yes**.

3. **Add Bookmark:** Highlight the table of contents with the title Table of Contents. Go to the **Insert** tab. Click the **Links** section and choose **Bookmark**. In the **Bookmark name** field, enter **toc**, and click **Add**. Insert a page break after your table of contents.

Kindle Create: Amazon offers Kindle Create, a free desktop program that will format your books as eBooks or paperbacks. It can be downloaded on PCs and Macs.

You can use Kindle Create to format your books if you write in Microsoft Word, Google Docs, Apple Pages, or Open Office. You can also import .rtf and .txt files created from applications like WordPad and Notepad or copy and paste your content. I prefer to format my book files in Word and make minimal changes in Kindle Create. Note that you can always start over in Kindle Create if you spot an error. Simply make the changes in your word processing document and start the process over.

Kindle Create is very intuitive. It will walk you through the entire process and show you a preview of your book layout. Amazon frequently updates Kindle Create. Once you download it, the system will automatically alert you when a new version is available.

Kindle Create offers several different themes and features, such as adding chapter titles, drop caps, and image placements. I recommend that you play around with the various layouts and options offered within Kindle Create. Again, you aren't locked into anything; you can redo your choices and simply re-download new versions at any time. Since the formatting options are limited, you also don't have to worry about being overwhelmed with unlimited choices. This is just another reason why it's an excellent option for beginners. And even though I am no longer in the beginning phase of my writing career, I still use Kindle Create because it's so easy!

Format In Vellum: A popular book formatting program in the author community is Vellum, which is available for purchase at Vellum.com. Vellum packages start at $199.99, so it is a hefty investment. However, Vellum offers advanced features that Kindle Create does not, including:

- Custom Drop Caps
- Ornamental Flourishes
- Box Sets
- Advance Copies
- Links for Social Media
- Store Links
- Formatting for Apple, Kobo, etc.

Hiring Someone to Format Your Book: If formatting your Kindle eBooks and paperback books yourself feels too overwhelming, you can hire someone to do the work for you. During my first couple of years as an author, I paid freelancers on **Fiverr** to format my Kindle books for me. For $5, I was able to format my books and have them ready to upload to Amazon. You can also hire people to format books on **UpWork**. While it's easy to format an all-text book yourself, you might find you need help if you have a complex layout, such as books with full-color photos or eBooks with interactive elements.

These days, I format all of my fiction and nonfiction books—Kindle, paperback, and hardcover—myself using Kindle Create. I also use Tangent Templates and Canva Pro to format my low-content books—journals, planners, and coloring books—which we will discuss later in this book.

Doing my own formatting allows me more freedom to make changes to my files. However, suppose you are just starting out self-publishing books and are feeling the pressure of publishing your first book. In that case, there is absolutely nothing wrong with paying someone a few dollars to do it for you.

Converting my Word document into a format I could upload to Amazon was something that held me back from self-publishing. I was convinced that the process was too complex for me. Hopefully, I have shown you that it really is quite simple.

Whether you choose to do it yourself or pay someone to do it for you, formatting your book file is one of the easiest parts of self-publishing and one that I am now a little embarrassed to admit I was ever scared of!

CHAPTER TEN: OPENING AN AMAZON KDP ACCOUNT

Before you can upload your book to Amazon, you must create a **KDP account,** which you will remember stands for **Kindle Direct Publishing**. Whether it is a non-fiction, fiction, or low-content book, or if it is a Kindle eBook or paperback, you can only have one KDP account under which all the books you publish will fall.

Amazon's Terms & Conditions: *No Multiple Accounts. You must ensure that all information you provide in connection with establishing your Program account, such as your name, address, and email, is accurate when you provide it, and you must keep it up to date if you use the Program. You may maintain only one account at a time. If we terminate your account, you will not be able to establish a new account. You will not use false identities, impersonate any other person, or use a username or password you are not authorized to use. You authorize us, directly or through third parties, to make any inquiries we consider appropriate to verify account information you provide. You also consent to us sending you emails relating to the Program and other publishing opportunities from time to time.*

You must agree to these Terms & Conditions when you create

your Amazon KDP account. Understanding that you can only have ONE account is critical to keeping it. Any attempts to create multiple accounts will result in your being permanently suspended from the KDP program.

Note that the account you use to shop on Amazon is different from your KDP account. So don't worry if you already have an account for buying, as that is entirely different than the one you need to self-publish books. However, if you already have an Amazon selling account for the Fulfilled by Amazon (FBA), Merchant Fulfilled, or Merch by Amazon programs, you will log in under that account first. But again, you are about to create a new account just for Kindle publishing.

You will need to create an account in the Kindle Direct Publishing program, which is at **kdp.amazon.com.** Once on the KDP website, you simply click on the yellow **Get Started** button, which will take you to the account setup page.

Also, remember that Amazon calls its self-publishing platform KDP because, in the beginning, Kindle was the only format available. Now, however, paperback and hardcover books are also included. The KDP name has not changed, but the formats available have.

The process of setting up your Kindle Direct Publishing account will likely be the longest part of publishing your first book. There are several screens you will need to go through to fill in all your information, including (if you are an American) your **Social Security number** (after all, if you are going to be making money with Kindle, you will owe taxes on that money) and your **bank account routing numbers** (so you can get your royalty payments directly deposited into your account every month).

If you are located in a country outside of the United States, Amazon will walk you through the process of uploading your identification and banking information.

Once you have completed the sign-up process, you will have

access to your very own personalized Kindle Direct Publishing area. I have this page bookmarked so that I can easily access it throughout the day to monitor sales and pending uploads. There are four tabs at the top of your KDP account page:

- **Bookshelf**
- **Reports**
- **Community**
- **Marketing**

Bookshelf: Your Bookshelf is where all your books are located. You can choose for the system to show you ten books per page, twenty-five books per page, or fifty books per page. I currently have forty-six pages of books with the ten books per page option selected! You have editing features next to each of your books, which we will review in a bit.

Your Bookshelf is also where you upload new books. At the top of the page is a yellow + **Create button.** Clicking on this button will open a new page titled **"What would you like to create?"**

Here, you can choose from the following:

- **Kindle eBook**
- **Paperback**
- **Hardcover**
- **Series page**
- **Kindle Vella**

In this book, we are focusing on the first three options: Kindle eBook, Paperback, and Hardcover. However, I want to note the **Create series** page link. Here, you can link books in a series together, which makes it easy for readers to go from one book to the next. You can also **View existing series** to view all the titles in a series and edit series details.

We have already discussed how most books start with a Kindle version. A paperback version is added within the same listing, and sometimes, a hardcover edition is also added. However, for print-on-demand planners, journals, and notebooks, which we will discuss in the last chapter of this book, publishers would only need to choose paperback or hardcover to get started.

Back on the main page of the Bookshelf is your list of books, where all your titles under all of your pen names are listed.

You can change the default layout under View, Sort by, and Filter by:

View:

- **Your titles:** all active titles that are currently for sale on Amazon. This is the default selection and the one I personally use the most.
- **Series titles:** If you have created any series, only books within a series will be shown here.
- **Archived titles:** I have older books that I have unpublished and archiving them removes them from the list. However, I can select this option to find them.
- **All titles:** All of your books, regardless of status.

Sort by:

- **Last modified:** The most recently added or edited books will show up first. This is the default option, which I personally rarely change.
- **Date submitted:** The most recently published will appear first.
- **Title:** Books will be sorted alphabetically.
- **Contributor:** Books will be sorted alphabetically by pen name.
- **eBook price:** Kindle books will sort with the lowest prices first.
- **Paperback price:** Books will be sorted with the lowest prices first.

- **Hardcover price:** Sorted with the lowest prices on your hardcover books first.

Filter by:

- **All:** All your books under all pen names.
- **Draft:** Unpublished books.
- **In Review:** Books that Amazon is reviewing.
- **Publishing:** Books that have passed Amazon's review process and are in the process of being uploaded to the site for sale.
- **Live:** Books that are live and for sale on Amazon's website.
- **Blocked:** A book you or Amazon has made unavailable to edit or publish.

There is also a **Search** feature on the Bookshelf page where you can quickly locate a book by title or pen name. I often use this feature to narrow down my fiction books from my non-fiction titles by entering one of my pen names.

Reports: I spend a lot of time in the Reports section of my KDP account; after all, that is where I can see how much money I am making! Clicking on Reports will bring up a page with the following options on the left:

Orders: Here, you will find a screenshot of estimated royalties, orders, and KENP read pages today, yesterday, and this month. As you scroll down the page, you will find more data, including a breakdown of orders, book formats sold, top-earning books, and marketplaces where your book has made sales. Amazon.com is Amazon's American marketplace; each country has its own.

KNEP Read: This report shows Kindle Edition Normalized Pages (KENP) read by customers who borrow your book from Kindle Unlimited (KU) and the Kindle Owners' Lending Library(KOLL). You can also see a report showing how many pages were read for each title. If your books aren't enrolled in Kindle Select, you won't have any data here.

Month-to-Date: In this section, you can compare sales data from the past month with the current month.

Promotions: This report shows the results of any Kindle Countdown Deals or Free Book promotions you may have run if your books are in Kindle Select.

Pre-orders: This report shows you information about your book's pre-order history. You can schedule Kindle eBooks to be released on a specific day, allowing customers to play pre-orders. As of this printing, Amazon does not have the pre-order option available for paperback or hardcover books.

Royalties Estimator: This is my favorite section of my KDP account, as I can see my current monthly royalties and look back at past weeks, months, and years. I'm not embarrassed to admit that I check my sales numbers at least twice a day!

Kindle Vella: Kindle Vella is a platform for authors to publish serialized stories in a format designed for mobile reading. It allows writers to release their stories one episode at a time, similar to how TV shows are aired in episodes. Each episode can range from 600 to 5,000 words.

Readers can access the first few episodes for free and then purchase tokens to unlock additional episodes. The platform also includes interactive features like "thumbs up" for episodes and the ability to crown a favorite story each week. Kindle Vella is currently available for U.S. authors and readers only.

Authors on Kindle Vella make money in two ways: by earning tokens that readers purchase, authors receive 50% of the revenue, and by bonuses that Amazon awards based on reader engagement.

Prior Months' Royalties: Download statements from the money you earned from the previous month.

Payments: Download statements of your sales data. You can filter the results based on the marketplace, sales period, and book status.

Community: The next tab at the top of your KDP account page is Community. Here, you can find announcements from Amazon and forums for authors to ask questions for other authors to answer. As with many online communities, the forums can be a bit harsh to newcomers. However, you can learn a lot just by reading the posts.

I feel the Amazon **Help** section, which is linked at the top of all KDP account pages, is more helpful than the forums. Here, you can find in-depth answers to any account questions you may have. This page also has a database of tutorials and user guides available for every section of the KDP site.

Marketing: The fourth and final tab at the top of your KDP account page is Marketing. Here, you can perform several tasks under **Marketing Resources:**

Marketing tips: Amazon will suggest books for you to advertise, even if you are already advertising them. This is a new section of the page, so hopefully, they will improve on it soon.

KDP Select: We discussed the pros and cons of the KDP Select program earlier in this book. You can enroll an eBook into KDP Select within the actual book listing under Bookshelf or here. The nice thing about this section is that Amazon will show you all the books that are not enrolled but are eligible.

Amazon Ads: Once you have set up your account, you can access the Amazon advertising portal here or directly. I will include an entire Amazon Advertising chapter later in this book.

Author Central: You can access Author Central here or directly once you have set up your page. Author Central is a dedicated page where you can view your books, sales rankings, and customer reviews from one single portal. If you have multiple pen names, you can easily toggle back and forth between them. I frequently check my Author Central page to see where my books are currently ranked.

A+ Content: A+ Content allows you to add images, text, and comparison tables to your product detail page to engage readers and give more information as they consider buying your book. This link leads you to an entirely new page with tutorials on creating these features in your product pages. I will discuss this feature further later in this book.

Run a Price Promotion: Here, if your Kindle eBook is enrolled in Kindle Select, you can create **Kindle Countdown Deals** and **Free Book Promotions**. You can also create these offers directly within your book's listing on the Bookshelf page by choosing **Promote and Advertise** under **Kindle eBook Actions**.

Nominate your eBooks: Amazon frequently runs contests for authors, as well as including them in special promotions. You can **Nominate a book for a Kindle Deal,** which is a limited-time discount offered on select eBooks. You can also **Nominate a book for Prime Reading**. Amazon offers a rotating selection of eBooks available to Prime Members to read for free. There is no harm in opting to have your book nominated. If selected, Amazon will email you, and you can decide if you want to opt into the deal they want to offer or not. Note that this program is still in Beta testing and may not be available to all publishers.

More Marketing Resources: Here, you can learn more about Kindle Pre-Order, Gifting for Kindle, and Kindle Instant Book Previews.

Your Account Data Your Way: Just like self-publishing gives you the freedom to write what you want, once you familiarize yourself with your KDP account page, you'll learn what works best for your when accessing your data. Maybe you have books enrolled in Kindle Select and want to monitor page reads and book promotions. Perhaps you want to edit categories after you've published a book.

Or you might be like me and want to look at the Reports section multiple times a day to see how much money you are making!

KDP provides a lot of options and data for authors, However, all of the information can seem overwhelming. Figure out what works best for you and your business and don't worry if you don't access certain features. The most important part of publishing is that you get your work published!

CHAPTER ELEVEN: ALL ABOUT ROYALTIES

In my opinion, getting paid is the best part of self-publishing! There's nothing better than tracking book sales, watching the numbers grow, and seeing your royalties increase. However, understanding how and when you get paid can be a bit confusing when starting with KDP.

You can track your royalties in the Reports section of your KDP account. The reports are estimates and update around three times a day. Thanks to additional sales from international buyers, which tend to lag in the reporting, I typically end up earning more than what the report shows.

The money you earn from your books is called **Royalties**. Amazon offers two royalty rates for Kindle eBooks:

- **70% Royalty Option**: For eBooks priced between $2.99 and $9.99. A file delivery fee, based on the eBook's size, is deducted.
- **35% Royalty Option**: This option applies to eBooks priced below $2.99 or above $9.99 and to books sold in certain countries.

Authors earn 60% of the list price for paperback and hardcover books minus printing costs, which vary based on page count, ink color, and paper type.

We'll discuss pricing strategies in an upcoming chapter. For now, remember that because of printing costs and Amazon's cut, you'll need to price paperback and hardcover books higher than Kindle versions to earn similar royalties.

Payment Schedule: Amazon distributes your royalties two months after they are earned. For example, if you earn royalties in December, you won't receive payment until the end of February. If you start self-publishing in June but only earn $99, you won't get paid in August. Your June earnings will carry over into July, and if you then earn $100, your total earnings of $199 will be paid in September.

While it can be frustrating to wait, once your books are selling consistently, payments will become regular. The more books you publish, the more consistent your monthly payments will be.

Amazon usually deposits royalties at the end of the month. I typically get a notification around the 29th, but payments often arrive earlier. Payments are made separately for each country, so you may receive multiple deposits. They typically arrive within a few days of each other.

Receiving Payments: Amazon issues payments via direct deposit to your bank account, which is why you need to provide your bank routing number when setting up your account. Depending on your country and bank, the transfer can take from one day to a week. Since I'm in the United States using a U.S. bank, my payments usually clear within one day.

Passive Income: You've likely heard the term passive income, and royalties are one of the best ways to continually earn money on something you worked on at one time. Once your book is published on Amazon, it can continue generating income for years without additional work. This is one of the greatest advantages of self-publishing: a book you publish today can keep selling and earning royalties for as long as it remains listed.

While you are earning passive income from your published

books, you will be free to focus on creating new books while your existing ones continue to generate income. Moreover, as your catalog grows, so do your earnings since each new book can lead to more sales of your other titles. This "set it and forget it" model means that your initial investment of time and effort can pay off for years, providing a steady stream of passive income.

Thanks to the passive income from my KDP royalties, I was able to semi-retire in my 40s. While I still engage in side hustles like selling on eBay and making YouTube videos to bring in extra spending money and keep my skills sharp, my goal is for my royalties, combined with Social Security and savings, to support a comfortable retirement. I view my royalties almost like a pension, providing monthly income.

And after I'm gone? I've set up a trust to ensure my family will continue receiving my royalties, offering financial support for several years, even without new books or ads. Royalties are a much better gift to leave your loved ones the dusty old antiques!

CHAPTER TWELVE: UPLOADING YOUR BOOK FILES TO AMAZON

If you're feeling nervous about uploading your book to Amazon, you're not alone—I felt the same way! I was convinced it would be an overwhelming and complicated process, to the point that I almost gave up before even starting.

But here's the good news: I was completely wrong!

Uploading your book to Amazon is actually one of the easiest steps in the self-publishing process. It's quicker and more straightforward than writing, formatting, or promoting your book. Once you've created your KDP account, it only takes a few minutes to get your book live and ready for sale.

To upload your book to Amazon, log in to your KDP account. After signing in, you'll land on your personal KDP page, where you'll find several tabs: **Bookshelf**, **Reports**, **Community**, and **Marketing**. The page defaults to **Bookshelf**, which is where you can upload new books. Look for the **Create** section with the prompt **Create a new title or series**.

In 2022, Amazon revamped this process, making it more streamlined. Now, you can publish in various formats, including eBook, paperback, hardcover, or even Kindle Vella, and create series pages if needed.

Let's begin by uploading a Kindle book. The process is slightly different for Kindle books than for paperback or hardcover books, so I will cover the Kindle version first and note the differences for paperback later.

First, click on the yellow **+ Create** button. A new page titled **"What would you like to create"** will open.

Under the **Kindle eBook** section, click on the yellow **Create eBook** button. This will bring up three pages, starting with the first one titled **Kindle eBook Details**, where you'll need to complete various sections to fill in your book's information.

The first field is **Language**, which defaults to the language of the Amazon site you are registered under (typically English for U.S. users). However, you can also publish books in Afrikaans, Alsatian, Arabic (Kindle only), Basque, Bokmål Norwegian, Breton, Catalan, Chinese (Kindle only), Cornish, Corsican, Danish, Dutch/Flemish, Eastern Frisian, Finnish, French, Frisian, German, Gujarati (Kindle only), Hebrew (paperback only), Hindi (Kindle only), Icelandic, Irish, Italian, Japanese (Kindle only), Latin (paperback only), Luxembourgish, Malayalam (Kindle only), Marathi (Kindle only), Manx, Northern Frisian, Norwegian, Nynorsk Norwegian, Portuguese, Provencal, Romansh, Scots, Scottish Gaelic, Spanish, Swedish, Tamil (Kindle only), Welsh, and Yiddish (paperback only).

As you continue your self-publishing journey, you may consider publishing your books in multiple languages. While English is the primary language in the United States, Spanish is spoken by a significant portion of the population, many of whom shop on Amazon's U.S. site, including for books in Spanish. You can hire translators on platforms like Fiverr.com and UpWork.com to translate your books into various languages. You can also list your books directly on international platforms such as

Amazon's Mexico and Canada sites.

Book Title: In the Book Title field, you will need to input your main title and any subtitle. While Kindle book titles can be edited after publication, paperback titles cannot. It's crucial that your paperback title and subtitle match your cover exactly, or Amazon will not publish it.

However, this isn't a requirement for the Kindle version. Self-published authors often add keywords to their titles, particularly in non-fiction and low-content books like planners or journals, to improve discoverability. Striking a balance between search-friendly and accurate titles is critical to success.

Amazon has specific guidelines for creating book titles. Your title must appear exactly as it does on your book cover, and your Kindle and paperback titles should be the same to ensure they're linked on the identical product page. It's crucial not to use unauthorized references to other books or authors, trademarked terms, or misleading phrases like "bestselling."

Subtitles are optional and should only be used if your book needs additional context beyond the main title. Keep the combined length of your title and subtitle under 200 characters. The subtitle is meant to provide extra information, but it's best to use this field sparingly.

You've likely seen Amazon listings with overly long subtitles stuffed with keywords, which some authors use in an attempt to improve search rankings. However, both Amazon and many potential customers view these as spammy and unprofessional. While adding keywords to your subtitle can be helpful for discoverability, it's essential to balance that with readability and keep the title/subtitle relevant to your book's content. Instead of cramming in keywords, focus on creating a concise, appealing title that still includes essential terms your audience might search for.

Series: Adding a book to a series allows readers to find related titles that you have written on a single page, making it easier for them to navigate and purchase your books. You can either add your new book to an existing series or create a new one, and you can always edit or adjust the series details later. When setting up a series, ensure common elements like characters, plot, or setting link the books. If you have different formats of a title (eBook, paperback, etc.), link them together so readers can easily choose the format they want.

Edition Number: When you upload a new version of an existing book, whether it's to replace a current copy or to offer an updated yearly edition, you can specify the edition number. For example, if your book is being published for the first time, you would mark it as Edition 1. If you later update or revise that book, you can upload the changes and mark it as Edition 2. For books like my yearly editions, each new release gets a fresh listing with an updated edition number, such as Edition 4 for my 2025 guide.

Note that Edition Number is an optional field; you can skip it if you wish.

Author: This field is where you enter the **First Name** and **Last Name** of the primary author or contributor, whether it's your legal name or a pen name. Keep in mind that once your book is published, this field cannot be changed for either Kindle or paperback editions. This name is also used to create your Amazon Author Page, Series Page, and other related features on Amazon's platform.

While the paperback setup page allows for a middle name, prefix, or suffix, the Kindle setup does not. Still, you can contact Amazon to request changes if needed.

Contributors: If others contributed to your book, you could list them in the Contributors section by selecting their roles, such as author, editor, foreword, illustrator, introduction, narrator, photographer, preface, or translator. However, if you are the author, only your name should be entered under the Author section, not repeated here. It's best to avoid adding unnecessary names. There's no need to add the name of a Fiverr designer you hired. You would only add additional contributors if you signed a contract with them stating you would do so. This isn't something most self-published authors have to do.

Description: After your cover and book title, the description—also called a "blurb"—is the most important part of your book's listing. This is where you sell your book to readers and convince them to make a purchase.

Your description needs to be both compelling and informative. Summarize your book in a way that grabs potential readers' attention and motivates them to buy. You can format the text using **bold**, *italic*, underline, and other basic styles to make the description visually appealing. You can also use bullet points and numbered lists.

For fiction books, focus on the book's main plot, themes, or topics while keeping the description brief and engaging. Avoid giving away the entire plot but offer just enough to pique the reader's curiosity. For non-fiction and low-content books, highlight the practical benefits of your book, such as what readers will learn, how the book can solve a problem, or what experience it provides.

Keep your description simple and easy to understand. Use clear sentences that are accessible to a wide range of readers, including those who may not be native English speakers. Avoid using complex words or phrases that could confuse potential customers. The goal is to ensure that anyone browsing your book can quickly grasp the value it offers without struggling to interpret your message. As I learned in journalism class, write as if your audience reads at an 8th-grade level.

To grab readers' attention from the start:

1. Write an engaging opening sentence that immediately

hooks them.

2. For fiction, emphasize the protagonist's dilemma or the story's central conflict in a way that sparks curiosity.

3. For non-fiction, consider starting with a bold statement or question that highlights the book's main benefit.

4. Make the first three lines bold to stand out but avoid bolding the entire description—Amazon may ask for revisions if you do.

PRO TIP: Utilizing an AI program such as ChatGPT has helped improve my book descriptions. I've never been great at sales pitches, but by providing my book information to ChatGPT and asking it to generate a compelling book description that will help me sell more books gives me great options that I can then edit. We'll discuss using AI in your author business in the last chapter of this book.

Keywords play a crucial role in helping customers find your book, so naturally integrate them into your description. Instead of listing them directly, weave them into your sentences. For example, if your book is about eBay selling, instead of simply stating, "eBay, work from home, reselling," you could write, "Learn how to start a successful work-from-home business by reselling on eBay."

The first four lines of your description are the most important, as they are visible immediately to customers. Make these lines count by clearly communicating your book's value and enticing readers to click the "read more" option. This is where you should be strategic and confident in what your book delivers, using strong and actionable language.

To help with this, look at best-selling books in your genre and observe how their descriptions are written. You'll notice a mix of engaging language, well-placed formatting, and effective keyword use.

Finally, avoid prohibited content in your description, such as external URLs, requests for reviews, or promotional material. Keeping your description professional and clean helps ensure that your book is not flagged or removed.

Publishing Rights: In this section, you need to choose one of two options:

I own the copyright, and I hold the necessary publishing rights (select this if you wrote the book yourself or hold exclusive publishing rights).

OR

This is a public domain work (choose this for content that is freely available, like a translation of a public domain book).

If you wrote your book, select the first option. Under U.S. copyright law, your work is protected as soon as it's written. Copyright ensures no one can legally publish or copy your work without permission. Avoid plagiarism at all costs; while no idea is entirely new, it's crucial not to replicate another author's words or content.

Primary Audience: You will need to disclose if your book contains **Sexually Explicit Images or a Title**. If you select Yes, the **Reading age** will automatically lock in at 18. If you select No, you can select the **Reading age**, although it is optional in most categories. Children's books are the one category where selecting an age range is mandatory, as Amazon will place books into age-specific categories.

Primary marketplace: Here, you select the country from which you expect the majority of your book sales to come. The system will default to the country you selected when you set up your account. For U.S. authors, this means the Amazon.com marketplace will be the default option.

Many international authors have changed their locations to the American market, too, as that is where the bulk of sales occur. However, depending on the format of your book, you may also be able to offer it on other Amazon marketplaces. You will see this on the third page of the listing form under **Pricing**.

Categories: Selecting the correct categories for your book is crucial to its discoverability on Amazon. You can choose three categories for each format—Kindle, paperback, and hardcover. While you used to be able to add more categories by contacting Amazon, this is no longer possible. However, you can edit your book categories any time after your book is published if you feel it isn't performing well in those that you selected.

Keywords: Keywords are essential for making your book discoverable on Amazon. You can select up to seven keyword fields, but instead of using single words, it's more effective to fill each field with keyword phrases. For instance, rather than just listing "eBay," "reselling," and "home business," you could combine these into "eBay reselling guidebook home-based business ideas."

Start by brainstorming relevant keywords and testing them on Amazon's search bar to see what comes up. You can also use tools like **Publisher Rocket** or free options like **Kindleranker** to generate more ideas.

Amazon has guidelines for keywords, emphasizing logical word order (e.g., "military science fiction"), avoiding subjective claims, spelling errors, and program names like "Kindle Unlimited." You also can't use other author's names or book titles in your keyword fields.

Use relevant plot themes, character types, or settings in your keywords. For example, "Highlanders" could be an excellent keyword for a historical romance set in Scotland. When filling out the keyword fields, try to include phrases that would work even if rearranged. For instance, the keyword field "KDP

Amazon self-publishing guide book help" could match up with searches like "KDP," "Amazon KDP," "self-publishing books on Amazon," and "guide books on KDP." This makes your book more discoverable on Amazon and other search engine websites.

You can change keywords as often as you like, which gives you the flexibility to update your metadata if you feel your book isn't getting enough attention or if you discover new keywords that may be a better fit.

Pre-order: Pre-orders are essential for fiction authors with a fan base, particularly for books in a series. Pre-orders allow readers to pre-order the next release, helping boost early sales and, hopefully, early reviews. While pre-orders are standard for fiction, I don't always use them for my non-fiction books, especially since Amazon doesn't offer pre-orders for paperback or hardcover. I prefer to release all formats simultaneously, so I often hold off until all versions are ready.

You have two options here: **Release my book now** or **Make my Kindle eBook available for Pre-order.**

WARNING: Missing the pre-order upload deadline results in a year-long loss of pre-order privileges. I made this mistake a couple of years ago when I was positive I had uploaded the file for a book I had on pre-order. I only realized my error when I got a message from Amazon telling me that I couldn't offer pre-orders for an entire year since I hadn't uploaded the file. This would have been devasting had it been a fiction book!

Save and continue: Once you have completed the first page of the listing form, click on the yellow **Save and continue** button. Note that you can still go back and edit these fields before you publish your book. Some fields, such as the keywords and categories sections, can be edited at any time, even after you publish your book. But some, such as your author name, cannot.

Manuscript: On the second page, the first field is for Manuscript. In this section, you will do two things:

Digital Rights Management: This feature restricts unauthorized distribution of your Kindle book. Most self-published authors, including myself, choose **NO** for DRM, as we prefer to encourage purchases rather than borrowing. Once published, you cannot change your DRM selection.

Upload manuscript: This is where you upload your book's file. You may have created your file in Word and saved it as a .DOCX file, used Kindle Create or another formatting program, or had someone else create it for you. Whichever method you use, simply click the yellow button and select the file from your computer.

Remember, you can upload a new version of your book at any time, even after it's published.

If Amazon detects a spelling error in your manuscript file, an alert will appear here. You can click on the possible spelling error to check if it's a legitimate mistake or slang that Amazon doesn't recognize. If it's an error, correct it in your document and upload the updated file. If the word is correct, simply click the **Ignore** button.

Kindle eBook Cover: The following field is for uploading your book's cover. I'll discuss creating covers in an upcoming chapter. Amazon offers two options in this section:

- Use **Cover Creator** to design your cover (you can use Amazon's templates or upload your own image and overlay text). OR
- Upload a cover you already have (JPG/TIFF only).

We'll explore these options further later, but for now, this is where you'll upload your cover file. Note that Kindle covers don't have a spine or back cover, so you'll need different covers for your Kindle and paperback/hardcover versions.

AI-Generated Content: A new field in the listing form addresses **AI-Generated Content**. Amazon is now collecting information about the use of Artificial Intelligence (AI) tools in creating content, which they define as text, images, or translations made by AI-based tools. According to Amazon's KDP Content Guidelines:

AI-generated content refers to text, images, or translations created by an AI tool. Even if substantial edits are made afterward, the content is still considered AI-generated.

AI-assisted content refers to work you've created yourself but improved using AI-based tools for editing, refining, or brainstorming. In this case, you don't need to disclose the use of AI

You are responsible for ensuring that all AI-generated or AI-assisted content complies with copyright and intellectual property rights.

With AI platforms like ChatGPT and MidJourney rising in popularity, their use has opened Pandora's box of issues in the publishing industry. Many people use these tools to create books. While Amazon is currently only collecting information on AI-generated content, how they will handle this in the future remains to be seen.

In late 2023, Amazon responded to the flood of AI-generated books by limiting authors to uploading only three books per day. This rule change aimed to curtail the overwhelming number of low-quality, AI-created books that appeared on the site. For authors like me, this is a welcome change. When Kindle Unlimited was introduced, the platform was swamped with poorly written, junk books. It took a few years to get that situation under control. Now, Amazon is acting more swiftly with AI, but further regulations will likely follow.

Despite the challenges AI presents, there are also helpful AI tools that can assist self-published authors, which we'll explore later in this book.

Preview: After uploading your manuscript and cover, you'll need to launch Amazon's Previewer tool to review your files. Keep in mind that it can take a while for Amazon to process these files. I usually save my draft and come back later to preview the book once everything has been processed.

Kindle eBook ISBN: You don't need an ISBN for a Kindle eBook, but it's something to consider purchasing. According to Amazon, an ISBN (International Standard Book Number) is not required for Kindle eBooks, and if you do enter one, it won't appear on the detail page, as only the ASIN will. Additionally, you can't use the same ISBN from your print edition for your eBook version—it has to be unique. If you want to include one, you can purchase it through services like Bowker.com.

Most self-publishing platforms, including Amazon, will offer you a free ISBN for paperbacks, but there's a trade-off. If you opt for Amazon's free ISBN, you can only use it on KDP, and it limits your ability to publish the book on other platforms. I used Amazon's free ISBNs when I started out, but now I buy my own for my fiction and non-fiction titles, especially since I self-publish on platforms outside of Amazon. I invest in bulk, purchasing 100 ISBNs for $500, but this ensures complete control over my books.

However, if you only plan on publishing short Kindle eBooks, making your money through Kindle Select page reads, or focusing on no-and-low content books like planners or journals, owning your ISBNs isn't as crucial unless you plan to distribute outside of Amazon.

Paperback ISBN: Unlike eBooks, paperback books do require an ISBN. All ISBNs assigned after 2007 are 13 digits long. You can choose between using Amazon's free ISBN (which can only be used for KDP distribution) or buying your own. Owning your own ISBN allows you to publish your book elsewhere without restrictions. But if you're only publishing on KDP, Amazon's free option is perfectly fine.

Publisher: Next, there is an optional field to enter a Publisher. If you purchased your own ISBN, the Publisher name needs to match exactly what you submitted when you bought the ISBN. Many authors run into problems here because if the names don't match, Amazon will push your book back to Draft mode without specifying the issue. Nine times out of ten, it's due to the Publisher name mismatch.

Save and Continue: Once you've approved your book and cover files and completed the fields on the second page, click **Save and continue** to move to the final page. You can still change most of this information later if needed.

KDP Select Enrollment: At the top of the third and final page is KDP Select Enrollment. One of the biggest decisions you'll make when publishing your Kindle books to Amazon is whether to enroll them in Kindle Select, which is Amazon's Kindle Unlimited program.

I've already covered KDP Select earlier in this book, but here's a brief recap:

Amazon customers can pay a monthly subscription fee to join Kindle Unlimited, allowing them to borrow as many eligible Kindle books as they want. The key word here is eligible, as an author must voluntarily enroll their book in the program to make it available for Kindle Unlimited subscribers. It's rare to see traditionally published books in KDP Select; the vast majority are self-published.

Amazon collects the Kindle Unlimited subscription fees and divides the revenue among authors whose books were downloaded. As of now, the payout is around half a cent per page read (or one penny for every two pages read). Amazon counts a page as having been read only when the reader physically turns it, so the days of skipping to the end of the book and being paid for all pages are over.

Books are enrolled in KDP Select for 90 days. You can opt to renew automatically or turn off automatic renewal and re-enroll manually. KDP Select has three distinct benefits:

- The opportunity to make money from page reads, not just sales
- Free Books Promotions (five free days per book per 90-day enrollment period)
- Kindle Countdown Deals (five per book per 90-day enrollment period for books priced between $2.99 and $24.99)

Enrolling in KDP Select can be quite beneficial for new self-publishers. In fiction, especially when it's tough for new authors to gain traction, KDP Select allows readers to try out books without committing to a purchase.

When KDP Select first launched, I enrolled all of my books. However, none of my non-fiction titles are in the program today. I've built my brand as a business author, and customers now buy my books outright.

On the other hand, my fiction books remain in KDP Select. As I'm still new to fiction writing, most of my income from fiction comes from page reads. Over time, as I grow my fiction readership, I may remove my fiction books from KDP Select, but for now, it's a valuable revenue stream.

Remember, if you enroll in KDP Select, your eBook must remain exclusive to Amazon for the 90 days. This means you can't publish the eBook on other sites like Draft2Digital or IngramSpark (more on these later). However, you *can publish* the paperback version elsewhere. Only the eBook is required to stay exclusive to Amazon while in KDP Select.

Territories: Choose **All territories (worldwide rights)** if you own the full rights to your book and want it available globally. This option allows customers worldwide to purchase your title through various Amazon marketplaces, including the U.S., UK, Germany, Japan, Brazil, and more. If you don't hold global rights, select Individual territories and indicate where you have distribution rights. For most authors with original content, selecting worldwide rights is typical.

If you wrote the book yourself, selecting worldwide rights is usually the best option.

Primary Marketplace: Simply choose the website where you expect most of your books to sell. The selection will default to the country where you created your account. If you are in the United States, this will be Amazon.com.

Pricing, royalty, and distribution: Next is the section where you set the price and determine how you'll earn money. I'll cover pricing strategies in depth in another chapter, but here are the basics:

Amazon offers two royalty options for Kindle eBooks:

- **35% Royalty:** This applies to books priced below $2.99 or above $9.99. There's no delivery fee, which makes this option good for very short or large file-sized books.
- **70% Royalty:** This option is available for books priced between $2.99 and $9.99. A delivery fee of 15 cents per megabyte applies. This is the standard range for most Kindle eBooks on Amazon.

Most authors prefer the 70% royalty rate, especially for books in the $2.99 to $9.99 range. Non-fiction books can sometimes command a higher price, but fiction is typically priced lower to attract readers due to competition. However, fiction readers often purchase multiple books by the same author, so you can make up the difference in volume. For example, if you have ten books at $2.99, you could earn $2.10 per sale, making $21 if one customer buys all ten books.

In contrast, non-fiction buyers often only purchase one or two books based on the topic. I price my non-fiction Kindle books higher, around $9.99, and earn about $7 per sale. While you earn less per book with fiction, higher sales volume makes up for it compared to non-fiction.

Amazon automatically adjusts pricing for international distribution. The pricing section allows you to view royalty comparisons based on different territories. Remember, pricing can be updated anytime, just like your book files. I used to price my Kindle books at $3.99 but raised them to $9.99 as my catalog grew.

Unlike KDP Select, where authors earn per page read, Kindle purchases earn royalties upfront—whether the buyer reads the book or not. I still receive royalties from books I enrolled in KDP Select years ago despite no longer being in the program.

For new authors, you might want to price your first book at 99 cents to encourage initial sales and reviews. It's also a good strategy to enroll your book in KDP Select, especially for fiction, as it helps increase exposure. Remember, reviews are essential for boosting your book's rank, so a lower starting price can help generate those first crucial sales and reviews. You can always raise the price later as the book gains traction.

If you already have a strong social media following, KDP Select may not be as crucial. However, for most new authors, allowing Kindle Unlimited members to borrow your book can help generate feedback and sales. And it's only a 90-day commitment, so you can always reevaluate later.

With fiction, I enroll my books in KDP Select and run free promotions to boost visibility. I'll discuss promotion strategies in another chapter, but offering a free promotion can improve your book's ranking and help build a mailing list.

Many new authors feel uncomfortable pricing their books at a low price point, but the Kindle marketplace is highly competitive. Most successful authors start by offering their books at lower prices to generate reviews and build an audience.

It took years before I could confidently price my Kindle books at $9.99.

Terms & Conditions: The final field you need to review is the Terms & Conditions. Be sure to click the link provided and agree to them before proceeding.

Publish Your Kindle eBook: Once all fields are filled out and you're confident everything is correct, hit the orange **Publish Your Kindle eBook** button. Amazon typically takes up to 72 hours for your book to go live. You can still make changes to most fields after publication. If your book is set for pre-order, the button will read Submit for Pre-order instead.

Paperback & Hardcover Books: Creating a paperback is similar to uploading the Kindle version, with the primary difference being the cover files. Once your Kindle eBook is published, it will appear in your KDP account's **Bookshelf**. Click on the **+ Create paperback** link to get started or select **+ Create hardcover**. I usually create the paperback first since most fields carry over to the hardcover version. If you're uploading only a paperback (like journals or activity books), click **+ Create** from your KDP account homepage under the **Create a new title or series** section.

If you've already uploaded a Kindle version, many fields—like **Language**, **Book Title**, **Series**, and **Keywords**—will pre-fill but can be edited.

Book Title & Subtitle: Unlike Kindle eBooks, you can't change the title or subtitle for paperbacks or hardcovers after publication. Make sure these fields exactly match your book cover to avoid any issues with Amazon.

Categories: As discussed earlier, choosing the right categories is crucial for discoverability. Remember, Kindle and paperback/hardcover categories differ, so you'll need to select different ones for each format. You can pick three categories for each version.

Keywords: The strategy for selecting keywords is the same as for Kindle. Study similar books and choose categories that are popular and relevant to your content.

Low-Content Books: For notebooks, planners, journals, or activity books, check the **Low-content book** option. If not selected, Amazon will return your book to draft status.

Large-Print Books: For books with a font size of 16 points or larger, be sure to select the **Large-print book** option.

After completing this section, click **Save and continue** to move to page two of your paperback details.

Print ISBN: Unlike eBooks, printed books require an ISBN. As discussed earlier, you can purchase your own ISBN on Bowker.com or use a free KDP ISBN provided by Amazon. If you can afford it, I recommend buying your own, but for low-content books, I use the free Amazon option since I don't publish them outside of Amazon.

Remember, if you purchased your own ISBN, the **Publisher** name must exactly match what you used when purchasing the ISBN. If using Amazon's free ISBN, no additional input is required.

Print Options: Unlike eBooks, paperback books offer various options for page interiors. Amazon provides the following **Ink and Paper Types**:

- **Black and white interior with cream paper:** Higher quality, often used for fiction and memoirs.
- **Black-and-white interior with white paper is** Amazon's default, commonly used by most authors, including myself.
- **Standard color interior with white paper:** This option is affordable for books with some color and recommended for those with minimal images.
- **Premium color interior with white paper:** Best for full-color illustrations and graphics, ideal for

children's books.

Trim Size: Unlike Kindle eBooks, paperback books require selecting a **Trim Size**—the exact dimensions of the pages. Once chosen, the trim size is permanent and cannot be changed after publication.

Most fiction and non-fiction self-published paperbacks on Amazon are sized at 6x9 inches. However, Amazon offers other sizes, such as 7x10 inches for journals and 8.5x11 inches for notebooks. Children's books are often sized at 8.25x8.25 inches. More on selecting trim sizes will be covered in the print-on-demand chapter later in this book.

Bleed Settings: According to Amazon, setting your interior to "bleed" allows content to be printed to the edge of the page, which is mainly used for images and illustrations. Most books use "no bleed" unless you have a specific reason to apply it. Changing the bleed settings doesn't affect manufacturing costs.

For books I have created in Word or Kindle Create, I select **No Bleed**. For print-on-demand products like planners and journals (PDF files), I choose **Bleed (PDF only)**.

PRO TIP: Bleed is a publishing-specific term, but in layman's terms, it's the white space margins of a book. If you are reading the paperback version of this book, for example, you will notice the works do not go to the edge of the paper. However, if you look at a children's book, you'll notice the illustrations cover the entire page, leaving no white space between the image and edge of the page.

Paperback cover finish: According to Amazon, paperback covers are printed on 80# (220 GSM) white paper stock with either a glossy or matte finish. A **glossy** finish is shiny, making black covers darker and the artwork more vibrant. It's common for textbooks, children's books, and non-fiction. A **matte** finish has a minimal sheen with a polished look, typical for novels and other fiction.

For my fiction and non-fiction books, I usually opt for a **Glossy** cover with the default settings. For my no-and-low content books, I often choose a **Matte** cover with various sizes and **Bleed** settings.

Manuscript: This is where you'll upload your paperback book file. Amazon supports the following formats for paperback uploads:

- **PDF**
- **DOC**
- **DOCX**
- **HTML**
- **RTF**

I typically use the file created with **Kindle Create** for both my eBook and paperback interiors. However, for print-on-demand products, I upload **PDF** files that I create using specialized software. I'll cover this in more detail in the last chapter of the book.

You can also upload a **.DOCX** file directly from Word to Amazon. Still, I prefer using **Kindle Create** for my formatting.

Book Cover: In this section, you can either use Amazon's Cover Creator or upload your own print-ready PDF file. We'll dive deeper into cover design in the next chapter, but remember, your paperback cover is different from your Kindle version—it includes a spine and back cover, whereas Kindle eBooks only require a front cover.

AI-Generated Content: Just like with your Kindle eBook listing, you'll need to disclose any **AI-generated content** here.

Book Preview: After uploading your manuscript and cover, click **Launch Previewer**. Amazon can take some time to process your files, so I save your progress and returning to check after a few minutes. You won't be able to proceed to the next page until you've previewed and approved your book's complete file.

Once you've reviewed the assembled cover and interior, Amazon will show you the **Your Printing Cost** in the **Summary** section, automatically deducted from your book's sale price.

Finally, click **Save and continue** to proceed to the last page.

Territories: The first section of your paperback is on the third and final page of uploading it. As with your Kindle version, I always choose **all territories (worldwide rights)** for the widest possible distribution.

Primary Marketplace: This field will default to the country you're uploading from, such as **Amazon.com** for U.S. publishers.

Pricing, Royalty, and Distribution: Unlike eBooks, paperback royalties are set at 60%, with printing costs deducted from the purchase price. For example, a journal priced at $11.95 might have a printing cost of $2.34, leaving you with $4.83 per sale after Amazon takes their 40% cut.

The **printing cost** varies based on the book's trim size and page count, so longer and larger books will cost more to print.

You can also select **Expanded Distribution**, which will place your book in additional marketplaces. However, paperback books don't reach as many platforms as eBooks.

Terms & Conditions: Before publishing, you'll need to agree to Amazon's **KDP Terms and Conditions** to confirm compliance with their guidelines.

Request a Book Proof: You can order a proof copy of your book at a discounted rate before publishing. However, proofs will have a large **watermark across** the cover, making them unsuitable for resale.

PRO TIP: After publishing, you can buy **author copies** at a discounted rate. However, these don't count toward sales rankings. I prefer to purchase regular copies from Amazon's site. This way, I not only earn royalties from my purchase, but my book also gets a **sales rank**. A sales rank shows how well your book is performing in its categories. If you see a book without a rank, it means no one has ever purchased it—so boosting your rank with a sale is worth the few extra pennies!

Publish Your Paperback Book: Once you've set your paperback's price and reviewed your details, click **Publish Your Paperback Book** at the bottom of the page. Double-check your title and subtitle, as these cannot be changed after publication.

Unlike Kindle eBooks, which are typically approved within a day, paperback books can take several days, sometimes up to a week, to be approved. This extra time allows Amazon to thoroughly check your paperback for potential printing issues, ensuring the book will print correctly when ordered.

Hardcover: If you decide to upload a hardcover version of your book, simply click on the Create hardcover option in your book's section in your KDP account. The process for uploading a hardcover book is the same as a paperback book. However, you will need to use a different ISNB number.

And that's it! You, my friend, are now a published author!

CHAPTER THIRTEEN: CREATING BEST-SELLING BOOK COVERS

You've likely heard the saying, "You can't judge a book by its cover," but when it comes to selling books on Amazon, that's not necessarily true. Customers often decide whether to click on your book based solely on its cover. A well-designed cover is just as important, if not more so, than the content of the book itself. Since the cover is the first thing potential readers will see while browsing, it's crucial to make sure yours is captivating and professional.

Before I teach you how to design your book covers, let's go over some publishing terminology that may be new to you but that, as an indie author, you will need to learn:

Trim size is the final dimensions of your printed book after it's been trimmed, meaning after the pages are cut. For example, 6" x 9" is the standard trim size for most Amazon KDP fiction and nonfiction books.

Bleed: This means your design extends beyond the trim size to the edge of the paper, ensuring no white edges appear when the book is trimmed. It's essential for full-page images, such as in children's books or photography books. It's also common when creating no-content notebooks, as the lines go to the edge of the page.

No Bleed: Choose this if your design doesn't extend to the edge of the page. Most nonfiction and fiction books have no bleed on their pages because the text stays within the margins.

Pixels vs. Inches: Pixels are used in digital design to measure image size, while inches measure physical dimensions. For example, a Kindle cover might be 2560 x 1600 pixels for high resolution, while a paperback cover is measured in inches based on your trim size.

Now, let's tackle actually creating your book covers. There are three main ways to create covers for Kindle and paperback/hardcover books:

1. Design your own covers using graphic design software.
2. Use Amazon's Cover Creator tool.
3. Hire a designer to create your covers.

Each option has pros and cons, and I have used all three during my self-publishing journey. Before exploring these options, it's important to know the cover requirements for Kindle eBooks on Amazon.

Design your own covers using graphic design software: For Kindle covers, Amazon requires the cover image to have a height/width ratio of 1.6:1, which means for every 1,000 pixels in width, the height should be 1,600 pixels. The recommended cover dimensions are 2560 x 1600 pixels to ensure high quality on HD devices, with a minimum size of 1000 x 625 pixels and a maximum of 10,000 x 10,000 pixels. The file size should be no larger than 50MB.

In other words, Kindle and most eBook covers should measure 2560 x 1600 pixels.

Paperback book covers are different from Kindle eBook covers because the file must include the back cover, spine, and front cover as a single image. The dimensions depend on your book's page count and trim size. We'll discuss creating paperback/hardcover book covers in a moment, but let's first stick with creating Kindle covers.

To design a book cover, you need a graphic design program that allows you to lay out your book's size and add graphics and text. Here are several popular options:

- **Adobe Photoshop**: Plans start at $20.99 per month for individuals.
- **Canva Pro**: $119.99 per year or $12.99 per month.
- **VistaCreate**: Free plan available; Pro plans start at $10 per month.
- **Easil**: Starts at $7.50 per month.
- **Design Wizard**: Starts at $9.99 per month.
- **Keynote**: Available for free in the Apple Store.
- **PowerPoint**: Available with Microsoft 365, starting at $6.99 per month.
- **Snappa**: Starts at $10 per month.
- **Stencil**: Starts at $9 per month.
- **Visme**: Plans start at $15 per month.

When it comes to creating book covers, **Adobe Photoshop** and **Canva Pro** are two of the most popular tools:

Adobe Photoshop is highly versatile, offering advanced tools for custom design, layering, and typography. It's ideal for authors who want complete control over their design, including the ability to manipulate images, create custom textures, and add intricate design elements. However, it has a steeper learning curve, making it best suited for users with design experience or those willing to invest time in learning the software.

Canva Pro, on the other hand, is a more user-friendly option that allows for easy drag-and-drop design. It comes with a vast library of templates, fonts, and graphic elements, which simplifies the process of creating professional-looking covers. There are even book cover templates that you can add text to, change the colors and fonts, and even add elements.

Canva is great for authors without extensive design skills who want to create eye-catching covers. You can enter your book's dimensions and use stock images or illustrations or upload your own. Canva Pro also provides millions of stock images and icons for commercial use with a paid subscription, allowing users to experiment with different styles easily.

If you're planning to design your book cover, you'll need design elements like fonts, colors, and images. These can be sourced from various platforms if you aren't able to create them yourself:

- **Canva Pro**: Pro members can use Canva's graphics for print-on-demand products, including book covers.
- **Creative Fabrica**: Offers fonts, graphics, and POD templates. Be sure to check for print-on-demand licenses, especially for paperback covers.
- **Pixabay**: Provides royalty-free vectors and images. Always double-check for commercial use eligibility.
- **Shutterstock**: An expensive but leading source for professional images, with subscriptions starting at $29 per month.

PRO TIP: Before you purchase any design program, try its free version to get a feel for the platform. Also ensure that any images you use come with a **print-on-design license** that covers paperback books. When an image is printed onto a physical product, such as a tee shirt or book cover, and then sold, it is called **print on demand.** Creative Fabrica and Shutterstock are two that have different licenses on their images, so be sure the ones you buy can be used for print-on-demand.

Here's how to **create a Kindle eBook cover using Canva's free version:**

1. **Sign Up/Log In to Canva.com**

2. **Create Custom Dimensions**: On the homepage, click **Create a design** and select **Custom Size**. Enter 1600 x 2560 px for the Kindle cover size.

3. **Choose a Template**: Canva offers free book cover templates, or you can start with a blank canvas. Search for "book covers" to see the available options and add one to your page.

4. **Play Around**: Customize the template by changing the fonts, font sizes, and colors. Add or delete any images. Try uploading some photos of your own to add in and edit to get comfortable with the platform.

5. **Save/Download**: Once satisfied with the design, click **Share** and choose **Download**. Save your cover as a **JPG file**, which is the preferred format for Kindle covers.

Remember, the free version of Canva provides limited access to templates and design elements. To use more advanced features and to use their elements for paperback/hardcover books (print-on-demand), you'll need to upgrade to Canva Pro.

Creating a paperback cover is more complex than a Kindle cover because you need to account for the front cover, back cover, and spine. The size of your paperback cover depends on the book's page count and trim size.

To simplify this process, **use Amazon's free cover calculator at kdp.amazon.com/cover-calculator**. After entering your book details, Amazon will give you the exact dimensions for your cover. You can also download a template to overlay in Canva, ensuring everything fits within the printing margins. Save the template and upload it to Canva to place over your design.

When uploading your paperback/hardcover book cover to Amazon, you have two options:

Use Cover Creator: Upload your own cover image or use KDP's stock images.

OR

Upload a print-ready PDF: You can save your Canva file as a PDF. However, I recommend uploading the JPG version because it tends to work better in Amazon's system. Using Cover Creator allows you to easily add your author bio, headshot, and book description, ensuring everything is positioned correctly.

When using *Cover Creator*, choose a layout that keeps your cover image on the front with a solid color on the back and spine. Amazon offers several layout options, but this setup ensures your design looks like your original Canva creation.

Here's how to **create a paperback/hardcover book cover using Canva Pro:**

1. **Open Canva Pro**: Select **Create a New Design** and set the custom dimensions based on the size provided by Amazon's cover calculator.

2. **Insert Kindle Cover**: Upload your Kindle cover file and position it on the front cover section.

3. **Set Background**: Choose a solid color background for the spine and back cover.

4. **Template Overlay:** Use the template you downloaded from Amazon, placing it over your design to ensure the graphics and text are within the print area.

5. **Save the File**: Once finished, save it as a JPG file.

6. **Upload to Amazon**: Select **Cover Creator** in the KDP listing and upload your Canva-created image file.

7. **Add Text**: In Cover Creator, add your spine and back cover text. You can also add your author photo or delete the photo placeholder.

8. **Review and Finalize**: Double-check the layout, preview the cover, and ensure all elements—front, spine, and back—are properly aligned.

Using Amazon's Cover Creator Tool: Amazon's Cover *Creator* is a good alternative if graphic design software feels overwhelming. I usually use it for simple books like my yearly reselling planner and accounting ledgers, which don't need to grab attention like fiction or nonfiction books.

To get started, upload your manuscript to KDP, then click on **Cover Creator**. This ensures Amazon sizes the cover correctly based on your book's trim size and page count. You can then browse Amazon's image gallery for options, including solid colors and marbled effects. You'll also have access to various text layouts, so experiment with different designs to see what works best for your book.

While *Cover Creator* simplifies the process, its limitations make it better suited for straightforward books like textbooks and ledgers than for the eye-catching designs needed for fiction or nonfiction.

Hiring a Designer: If you're new to graphic design or find the process overwhelming, hiring a designer is a great option. Many self-published authors hire professionals to create their covers. A good designer understands your genre and knows how to create covers that attract readers.

Many indie authors hire book cover designers from one of two sites: **Fiverr.com** or **UpWork.com**.

Both platforms allow you to post jobs for freelancers to apply for or contact sellers directly. Freelancers list their gigs, complete with resumes and examples of their work, which you can browse. A simple search for "book cover designer" will bring up hundreds of freelancers. You can narrow your search by experience, location, rating, and other factors.

Here's what I look for when hiring a book cover designer:

- **Positive feedback**: Check reviews from previous customers before hiring.
- **Portfolio of completed covers**: Ensure the designer has experience creating covers for your genre.
- **Fluent English speakers**: Communication is key. Narrow your search to freelancers who speak the same language fluently.
- **Revisions**: Ensure the designer offers at least two revisions, as it's unlikely the first draft will be perfect.

On both platforms, there are beginner, intermediate, and expert designers, and pricing reflects experience. Sometimes, new designers offer lower rates to build their portfolios. I've had excellent results from hiring new designers eager to gain reviews.

Typically, UpWork provides higher-quality products, but it's worth checking out both sites. Don't forget to tip your designer if you're happy with the work—they've likely put in a lot of effort to meet your expectations. And if you love their work, you can hire them again. Building a relationship may also get your pushed to the front of the line or even a discount.

Video Tutorials: If you're a visual learner, there are plenty of video tutorials available on YouTube. A search for "create Kindle book covers" or "design KDP book covers" will yield many helpful resources, with creators walking you through each step using your chosen design program.

CHAPTER FOURTEEN: PRICING YOUR BOOKS

I've touched on book pricing several times already, but in this chapter, I'll dive deeper into the topic. Pricing your books isn't just about determining your profit—it's also about attracting customers to actually buy them. While many writers are driven by a love of the craft, making a living from writing is even better!

Books priced too low can come across as low-quality. Amazon is filled with 99-cent books, and in some genres, this is the norm. However, in other genres, such a low price may make potential buyers suspicious of the book's quality. On the flip side, books priced too high may deter buyers, although higher pricing can sometimes suggest better quality.

Finding the sweet spot for your book's price requires balancing its value with the need to appeal to the largest possible customer base.

I'll divide my pricing advice into three categories:
- Fiction (Kindle and paperback/hardcover)
- Nonfiction (Kindle and paperback/hardcover)
- Low-Content (paperback/hardcover)

Pricing Fiction Books: Writing fiction is a labor of love. Authors pour their hearts and souls into their characters, crafting intricate worlds and stories. When writers finish a novel, they're often left physically and emotionally spent, but with the hope that readers will find their book and fall in love with it. The dream for many fiction writers is to land a movie or television deal as their book gains traction.

With hundreds of millions of fiction readers worldwide, you might assume that such a lovingly crafted product demands a high price. Right?

Well, when it comes to fiction, prices can be surprisingly low, whether the books are traditionally published or self-published on Amazon. A $19.99 hardcover from a bestselling author often drops to $9.99, then $6.99 in paperback, and the eBook may end up selling for only a dollar or two. Even if a book is adapted for film or TV, its price typically shrinks when rereleased in mass-market paperback.

Traditional publishing houses can afford to lower prices because they print books in large volumes, reducing per-copy costs and passing those savings on to customers.

For self-published authors, however, it's different. You won't be able to price your first fiction book at $20—or even $10—if you want to build an audience. Your early works likely won't make much money at first, and that's a reality many new authors face.

Pricing Fiction Kindle Books: For self-published fiction on Amazon, consider enrolling your first book in Kindle Select, allowing Kindle Unlimited subscribers to read it for free. You'll earn a small portion of the Kindle Unlimited membership fees, but don't expect much. Currently, you make just one cent for every **two** pages read.

Of course, your book will also be available for outright purchase, allowing you to earn 70% royalties. If you price your book at $2.99, you'll make around $2 per sale. However, when starting, it's tough to make many sales. You'll likely rely more on Kindle Unlimited readers borrowing your book to build an audience, improve rankings, and hopefully generate good reviews.

Money? With any luck, that will come later as you build momentum.

So why are fiction eBooks priced so low? And how does anyone make money writing fiction?

Fiction is the most popular book genre, with hundreds of sub-genres (or "tropes") continually fed by self-published authors. Avid fiction readers, especially those with Kindle Unlimited memberships, devour books rapidly—some even reading a book a day!

Self-published books are typically shorter than traditionally published ones and are released much faster. For instance, a traditionally published romance novel may average around 80,000 words, with historical fiction or fantasy series surpassing 100,000 words. These longer books can take even dedicated readers several days to finish.

In contrast, self-published fiction books can be as short as 30,000 words and still qualify as full-length novels. Amazon also offers short story categories where books are around 10,000 words. This means readers can consume multiple self-published books in the time it takes to finish just one traditionally published novel.

Self-published fiction also caters to niche audiences. For example, while Nicholas Sparks writes sweeping, gut-wrenching romance novels, Kindle Unlimited readers often seek particular, niche romance tropes.

To demonstrate how this works, I looked up "Alpha Male" under Romance on October 1, 2024. The top book, *The Unplanned Wedding* by L. Steele, was priced at $5.99 for the Kindle version but was also enrolled in Kindle Select, meaning Kindle Unlimited members could read it for free. The author earned 70% royalties for each sale, or around $4.19 per book sold.

However, most earnings came from Kindle Unlimited readers, which resulted in about $1.78 per book read—if the reader completed the entire book. Remember, authors are only paid for the pages readers actually turn in Kindle Unlimited.

You might think L. Steele isn't making much money with such low prices, but according to Publisher Rocket, *The Unplanned Wedding* brings in around $380,000 per month in sales! With 91 books published on Amazon, Steele easily makes over $1 million in royalties every year on Amazon alone.

Steele's success comes from mastering her market. She writes in-demand alpha male romance and earns 70% on each Kindle sale, with Kindle Unlimited providing additional income. While the KU payout may seem small, the volume of readers quickly adds up to significant earnings.

Could she earn this much writing nonfiction? No. Could she have built this income selling books priced at $10 or more? Probably not. And would she make as much working with a traditional publisher? No, because indie authors dominate niche genres like alpha male romances.

Indie authors like Steele thrive by writing to market and pricing smartly. By avoiding the extremes—pricing too low, which could signal poor quality, or too high, which could discourage purchases—they find the balance that works for both readers and profits.

Fiction writing is all about volume. The reader base is huge, and there's a constant demand for fresh content. Indie authors can write shorter books and price them lower, compensating for the smaller profit margin by selling more copies and benefiting from page reads.

You've probably noticed that most Kindle eBooks are priced at $2.99 or higher. Amazon offers two royalty structures for Kindle eBooks:

35% royalties for books priced between 99 cents and $2.98, or $10 and up.

OR

70% royalties for books priced between $2.99 and $9.99.

Why the two-tier system? It's about profit margins and perception. Amazon keeps 30% of the profits for books priced between $2.99 and $9.99, but for books priced below $2.99 or above $10, they take a larger cut—65%. This incentivizes authors to price their books within the $2.99–$9.99 range, benefiting both authors and Amazon.

I should note here that Amazon charges authors a 15-cent per megabyte fee on Kindle files. So, the larger your book file, the more Amazon will deduct from your royalties.

For books enrolled in Kindle Select, Amazon pools the money from Kindle Unlimited subscriptions and, after taking its own cut, distributes the remaining profits to authors whose books were read that month.

However, the main reason Amazon encourages pricing between $2.99 and $9.99 is customer preference. Readers enjoy affordable books—low enough to feel like a bargain but not so cheap that it suggests poor quality. Traditionally published paperbacks or hardcovers at Barnes & Noble cost much more than bestsellers on Kindle, which are often priced under $5.

When customers find quality books at these prices, they continue to buy, making Amazon the go-to for affordable eBooks. As a result, both Amazon and authors profit from the volume of sales. Kindle Unlimited subscribers also benefit from this model, with access to thousands of books for a small monthly fee. That's why Amazon dominates the eBook market.

So, how should you price your fiction Kindle eBooks? I recommend starting at $2.99 for your first book and enrolling your first book in Kindle Select, even if only for the 90-day trial. As a new author, you need to attract readers. A great cover and compelling description are key to getting readers to click on your book and download it.

Study your competition within your genre. You may notice some categories where books are priced at 99 cents, with most profits coming from Kindle Unlimited rather than direct sales. In other cases, authors with a strong following may charge more and opt out of Kindle Select.

Once you've built up a readership, you can re-evaluate your pricing and decide whether to continue with Kindle Select. However, be aware that it can take years to grow the kind of following that allows you to charge higher prices and skip Kindle Select altogether.

Pricing and royalties work differently for fiction paperback books. First, Amazon charges a printing fee for every book sold, in addition to taking a 40% cut of the profits. Your 60% royalty is calculated after the printing fee, which is why you need to price paperback books higher than Kindle eBooks.

Most indie authors on Amazon make the bulk of their income from Kindle eBooks. However, some readers prefer to buy paperbacks from authors they love. However, it usually takes time to build a fan base that is willing to pay more for a paperback.

Pricing Paperback Fiction Books: When setting a price for fiction paperbacks, it's essential to research what other authors in your genre are charging. For instance, an author may sell their Kindle eBook for $2.99 and their paperback for $7.99. As authors grow more established, they often increase the prices of both formats, but when you're just starting out, keeping your prices affordable is key.

Pricing Nonfiction Kindle eBooks: Nonfiction is my primary writing category, and while nonfiction books don't usually sell as much as fiction, they tend to command higher prices. Nonfiction covers a wide range of topics, from cookbooks with full-color images to textbooks filled with data, and successful nonfiction authors often make more from paperback sales.

Even though my main revenue comes from paperbacks, I still sell Kindle versions of my books. Since my nonfiction titles are niche-specific, with limited competition and a strong sales history, I can price my Kindle eBooks at $9.99. This allows me to earn the 70% royalty, making around $7 per sale. Pricing higher than $9.99 would drop my royalty rate to 30%.

For nonfiction, researching competitor prices is crucial. If other authors in your category are selling Kindle books for 99 cents, it will be difficult for a new author to charge more.

Personally, only about 10% of my nonfiction book sales come from Kindle eBooks, with the rest coming from paperbacks.

Pricing for Nonfiction Paperback/Hardcover Books: In 2020, I began publishing new versions of my best-selling books each year, including the one you're currently reading, which is the fourth annual release of this title. I also started publishing my books in paperback, with some even in hardcover.

As I've mentioned before, offering my books in paperback significantly increased my publishing income. Business books, in particular, perform better in paperback than on Kindle. However, to justify a paperback version, your book needs to be longer than the typical Kindle eBook.

Unlike Kindle eBooks, there is a printing fee for paperback and hardcover books, which Amazon deducts from your royalties. After the printing fee is taken out, you earn 60% of the remaining sales price. I price most of my nonfiction paperbacks between $14.99 and $18.99 to ensure I earn a similar amount as I do from Kindle sales. Since printing costs depend on the book's page count, longer books cost more to print, which may require you to increase your price to maintain your profit margin.

Hardcover books cost even more to print, so I price them higher than paperbacks. However, there is a market for hardcover books, and you may miss out on potential sales if you don't offer that format.

That said, I've spent years building my brand. When I first started self-publishing, I couldn't have priced my books as I do now. I had to prove to readers that my books were high-quality resources for topics like selling on eBay, starting a YouTube channel, and making money through Amazon KDP.

Just as with fiction, it's essential to research what other authors in your genre charge for their nonfiction books. A saturated market often leads to lower prices due to increased competition.

Spend time researching the bestseller lists in your category. You'll find a mix of traditionally published and self-published titles. For example, if you're writing a cookbook, you'll see prices ranging from 99 cents on Kindle to over $30 for hardcover editions. Independent authors usually price their books lower, and their covers may not feature a celebrity chef.

It's also helpful to browse the Top 100 Free lists in each category. These are books that are part of Kindle Select and temporarily offered for free, available to all Amazon customers. I like to review the top-ranked free books, check the authors' pages, and analyze their revenue using Publisher Rocket. I also compare their pricing and how their books stack up to mine—are they longer, do they have more reviews, and what's their overall sales performance?

That said, I don't always follow the competition's pricing model. My top three best-selling books are consistently ranked in the top 50 in the Auctions & Small Business category. While there are cheaper books in that category that often rank higher, I choose to price my books higher because I believe they offer more value. Additionally, even if some Kindle versions are priced lower, my paperbacks sell far better. Not all of my competitors offer paperback versions, so when readers find my Kindle book, they often end up purchasing the paperback instead.

Pricing Low-Content Books: No-content and low-content books include journals, planners, notebooks, and activity books. While I'll discuss these in the final chapter, let's touch on their pricing here.

These books can only be published in paperback and hardcover formats, as Kindle isn't an option due to the minimal or no content on the interior pages, which are meant to be written in. Blank or lined notebooks, sketchbooks, and journals are classified as having no content because they contain no text inside. Guided journals and activity books fall under low content because they feature some writing and/or images inside.

PRO-TIP: Most no-and-low content books are published in paperback. However, offering hardcover versions can set you apart from the competition and appeal to customers who prefer that format.

Pricing Notebooks: Notebooks are plentiful on Amazon, much like they are in stores, and tend to be priced on the lower side, even from big brands like Mead and Five Star. One major downside for self-publishing notebooks on Amazon is the lack of a spiral-bound option, which many buyers prefer. Since this feature isn't available, focus on creating eye-catching covers to attract buyers.

Paperback notebooks on Amazon are usually priced between $4.99 and $6.99, depending on size and page count, which directly impacts printing costs. Your royalties on paperback books are 60%, compared to 70% for Kindle books. Successful notebook sellers typically upload thousands of designs and operate as a volume business. Most of my notebooks are 7x10 inches (composition notebook size) or 8.5x11 inches (full-size), with around 120 pages. Because my notebooks are larger than many others on Amazon, I generally price them at $5.99.

Pricing Journals: Self-published journals on Amazon range from blank to guided. Blank journals, typically 6x9 inches with around 100 pages, are priced on the lower end at $4.99 to $5.99, yielding publishers less than a dollar per sale. Just like notebooks, the money comes from volume, as publishers need to offer tens of thousands of designs.

Guided journals, on the other hand, are of higher quality and include text prompts for users to fill out. For example, my line of ancestry-guided journals contains questions about a person's life. Because these journals require more effort to create, they can be priced higher.

Guided journals in 6x9-inch sizes can cost from $6.99 to $9.99, while larger ones tend to cost more. My 8.5x11-inch ancestry-guided journals sell for $11.95 in paperback, and the hardcover versions are priced at $19.95. Due to higher printing costs for hardcover, $19.99 allows me to earn the same profit as the paperback versions.

Planners: Planners are a big seller on Amazon, especially during the fourth quarter (October through December), when people buy them for personal use and as gifts. You can create a variety of planners—daily, weekly, monthly, yearly, or undated—in different sizes. The most popular size is 6x9 inches, but planners can go as large as 8.5x11 inches.

Just like with other paperback books, printing costs are deducted from the sale price. The larger and thicker the planner, the more it costs to print, meaning you'll need to price it higher to make a decent profit.

Pricing Activity Books: Activity books, like puzzle books and coloring books, are a hot trend among self-publishers on Amazon. While they're highly sought after, they also require more time and skill to create. The competition is fierce since both self-publishers and traditional publishers offer these types of books.

Given the high competition, pricing too high can deter potential buyers. I've priced my adult coloring books at $7.99, earning around $2 per sale after printing and Amazon's cut. Like notebooks and journals, creators of activity books usually publish hundreds, if not thousands, of titles to increase their profits.

PRO TIP: In 2024, Amazon slightly increased printing costs and allowed authors to bulk edit their prices to account for the increase. While Amazon has generally maintained stable pricing, you may find yourself adjusting your prices regularly as you learn what customers are willing to pay and monitor your competition. Like other parts of your book's listing, you can update your book's price at any time, even after it's been published.

CHAPTER FIFTEEN: HOW TO MARKET YOUR BOOKS FOR FREE

You've done it! Your book is researched, written, edited, and uploaded, complete with an eye-catching cover and an enticing blurb. Now that it's for sale on Amazon, you can sit back and watch the money roll in, right?

Wrong!

Publishing your book is only the beginning. Now, the real work begins: getting people to buy it!

As a self-published author, you're responsible for writing, editing, uploading, and promoting your book. Without an agent or publishing house backing you, it's up to *you* to spread the word. Indie authors are not just writers and editors but also their own marketing teams. I spend just as much time promoting my books as I do writing them.

There are many self-published authors, me included, making a full-time living through Amazon KDP. However, most indie writers never sell a single book. Why? They don't market their work.

So, how do you promote your book to generate sales—especially on a small budget?

Start by harnessing the power of social media. Platforms like Facebook, Threads, Instagram, Twitter, Pinterest, YouTube, and TikTok are all excellent (and free!) ways to drive traffic to your Amazon listing.

Besides being free, these platforms are easy to use. You're probably familiar with some of them already, so learning to leverage them for book marketing is straightforward. You don't even have to use every platform—certain genres perform better on specific sites. For example, fiction authors often thrive on Facebook and TikTok. My initial sales came from my YouTube followers, and I now use Facebook to reach more readers. Some authors stick to one or two platforms, while others use them all. The choice is yours but start with one and expand as you get more comfortable.

Facebook: Almost all indie authors begin by promoting their books on Facebook. Part of marketing yourself as an author involves "branding," and a Facebook presence is the easiest way to achieve this. Creating a Facebook business page specifically for your author brand helps you connect with readers in ways that other platforms can't match.

A Facebook business page is different from your personal one. However, you must first have a personal account to create a business page. The main difference is that people "friend" you on a personal page, but they "like" and "follow" a business page. Your personal page has a limit on the number of friends you can have, but a business page has no such limits on likes and followers.

It might take some time to build up likes and followers on your business page but setting up a separate page from your personal one is essential. Many authors who rely on personal pages eventually hit the friend limit and then have to switch to a business page. Building a following from scratch can be difficult, so it's better to start with a business page.

Not only does this help with branding, but it keeps your personal life separate from your author persona. This can be especially important if you write in genres like romance and don't want your friends or family to know about your pen names.

To set up a Facebook business page for your publishing business, visit facebook.com/pages/creation.

You can also create a separate page for each of your pen names. Facebook makes it easy to toggle back and forth between your personal account and business page. Just go to your profile picture in the top right-hand corner of Facebook to switch between pages.

I use Facebook pages in various ways to promote my books. My main Facebook page, @anneckhart, promotes all my activities, including my non-fiction books, YouTube videos, and even my no-and-low content books. Although these books are published under a different pen name, my large following allows me to promote them without causing confusion.

On the other hand, I handle my fiction Facebook page differently. There is no cross-promotion between my main page and my fiction page, and most followers of @anneckhart don't know I have fiction books under another pen name—and I prefer it that way.

On my fiction page, I share new book releases and promotions and ask engaging questions to connect with my readers. These could be book-related topics or fun, lighthearted questions to encourage interaction, such as asking about their favorite stories, foods, or hobbies. Engagement is more critical with fiction readers, who enjoy discussing characters and plots, while non-fiction readers tend to be more transactional, simply purchasing the book to gain the information they need.

Encouraging any type of interaction—whether it's a like, comment, or share—is vital for keeping your page active. This also helps gain new followers, especially since Facebook has made it more difficult for business posts to be seen without paying for visibility. This is why it's essential to engage your audience with more than just promotional posts. Even small additions like emojis can catch someone's attention and prompt them to engage with your post or click on your book link.

One of the best ways to foster engagement is to post content that isn't purely sales-driven. A good rule of thumb is to post one business-related post followed by three general posts. While it's tempting to share only book links, mixing in other content shows your audience that you want to connect with them, not just sell to them.

One easy way to create engagement outside of posting links to your books is by sharing funny memes or photos. Keep this content clean unless you write spicy fiction, as you'll want to appeal to a broad audience. These types of posts always generate a lot of interaction. I post a variety of memes, not just book-related ones. To find book-themed memes, simply do a Google search, and you'll discover countless funny graphics that are quick and easy to share.

Your posts don't always have to relate to your books. Building a personal relationship with your readers is key, and one way to do that is by sharing different aspects of your life. For instance, my Facebook followers love it when I share pictures of my dogs, home projects, or vacation snapshots.

However, if you're using a pen name and want to keep your real identity private, be careful about what you post. It's common for authors to use their own headshot as their profile picture, but this could lead to revealing your real name. I avoided this by using a graphic of my pen name as my author photo, which worked well.

Another benefit of getting people to "like" or comment on your posts is that their engagement could show up on their friends' feeds. This could encourage others to check out your page and "like" it, too. You've probably seen this happen on your own Facebook feed—where it shows that a friend liked a post or page, and the convenient "like" button is right there for you to click as well.

As your audience grows, you may notice that some readers will want to "friend" you on your personal Facebook page. Even if you're not promoting it, people will often still find it, especially if your author's business page is the same name as your personal page.

Unless it's a reader you've gotten to know well offline, I highly recommend *not adding* readers as friends on Facebook. It's important to maintain privacy and create a boundary between your personal and professional life. While many of my friends and family "like" my Facebook business pages, not all of them do. Additionally, none of them know my fictional pen names, as I've kept those a secret.

I've also set up my personal Facebook page with the highest security settings for added protection, and I've turned off the private messaging feature on my business pages to prevent people from sending direct messages. At one point, I was flooded with lengthy messages from people seeking advice on writing books or just wanting to chat. While most messages were harmless, responding took up a lot of time and energy. However, some authors do allow direct messaging, so it's a personal choice.

PRO TIP: I like to schedule Facebook posts one to two weeks in advance. Every day, I promote one book by sharing a direct Amazon link, which automatically includes the book cover in the post. I add a "sales pitch" and relevant hashtags, scheduling the post to go live in the evenings. This helps keep my books in front of followers without the hassle of posting daily.

Facebook Groups: Another valuable tool for fiction writers is Facebook Groups. Many authors create private groups tied to their business pages, and this is particularly popular in the fiction community. Having a group dedicated to your fiction pen name allows you to build a closer connection with your readers. Fans love feeling like they are part of a community, and creating a private group is a great way to achieve this.

You can link a Facebook group to your corresponding business page and invite followers to join. In the group, you can engage directly with your readers by answering questions, hosting giveaways, and sharing exclusive updates about upcoming books.

To promote your group, include a link in the back of your books, on your Facebook page, and across your social media platforms. Facebook groups are ideal for fostering reader engagement, especially with fiction.

Note: Many indie authors also use Facebook Ads to promote their books. Later in this book, I'll dedicate an entire chapter to Facebook advertising.

Threads: Launched by Meta (Facebook's parent company) as a rival to Twitter, Threads is a text-based social media platform integrated with Instagram. For authors, Threads can be an effective tool to promote books and engage with readers alongside their Facebook business pages.

Because Threads emphasizes real-time conversations and quick updates, authors can use it to share insights into their writing process, announce book releases, post quick snippets or teasers from their books, and interact directly with followers. Since Threads is linked to Facebook and Instagram, it's easy to transition followers from one platform to another.

You can also use hashtags on Threads, just like you would on Instagram and Twitter. Hashtags help categorize your content and make it more discoverable by users who search for or follow specific topics. For authors, using relevant hashtags on Threads can help reach a wider audience interested in books, writing, and genres. Examples of effective hashtags for book promotion might include #BookRelease, #FictionWriter, #AmWriting, or #BookRecommendations.

Take time to search Threads for authors and author groups, as well as fans of the genre you write in. Finding hashtags that relate to your niche will help you broaden your reach, too.

Instagram: Owned by Facebook, Instagram is another easy, free, and fun way to interact with readers and gain followers for your publishing business. Instagram allows you to share photos and short videos and "like" or comment on others' content. Since Facebook owns Instagram, you can link your accounts, allowing you to share posts on both platforms simultaneously.

If you have multiple pen names, Instagram makes it easy to manage separate accounts, preventing overlap in your content. For example, you wouldn't want to mix promoting clean romances with horror novels.

Instagram only allows one clickable link in your profile. If you have only one pen name, linking directly to your Amazon Author Page is fine. However, if you have multiple businesses like mine, you'll want to use a link tree service such as **linker.ee** to create a landing page with all your relevant links accessible via one link.

Instagram is a great way to connect with readers on a more personal level. Share vacation photos, snapshots of your pets, or funny memes to engage with your audience. Avoid controversial topics like politics or religion unless your books focus on those subjects. The goal is to build a personal connection with your audience while subtly promoting your books.

Hashtags are crucial for discovery on Instagram. As with Facebook, Threads, and Twitter, Instagram users find content through hashtags. Popular ones for authors include #writersofinstagram and #authorsofinstagram. These hashtags can help potential readers discover your work and even connect you with fellow authors.

Twitter (now "X" but still commonly called Twitter): Twitter is another free and simple way to connect with readers and drive traffic to your books. Amazon even makes it easy to "tweet" your book by clicking the Twitter icon on your book's page.

Twitter allows 280 characters per post, enough space for text, a link, and hashtags. Hashtags are keywords preceded by a pound (#) sign. For example, when promoting my book *101 Items to Sell On eBay*, I use hashtags like #ebay, #thrifting, #reselling, and #homebasedbusiness to attract relevant audiences.

Readers and savvy Twitter users search hashtags, so using them can significantly boost visibility and sales. I've seen a notable increase in book sales since using targeted hashtags. You can also use hashtags like #author and #writer to connect with other authors and the broader writing community.

Pinterest: Pinterest is like a virtual bulletin board where users can post, and share "pins" related to their interests. While it's often associated with crafts, recipes, and design, Pinterest is a powerful tool for self-published authors to promote their books. There is an active reading community on Pinterest. As an author, you can utilize the platform to help you reach them. Authors can create pins featuring their book covers, quotes, or excerpts, directing users to their Amazon Author Page to purchase their books.

By using relevant keywords and hashtags pin descriptions, authors can better target potential readers. Additionally, creating themed boards related to their books' genres or topics helps attract readers interested in specific themes, such as romance, self-help, or writing tips. Pinterest's search functionality works similarly to Google, meaning your pins can be found long after you post them, giving your books continued visibility over time. You can create engagement by consistently pinning content and repining content from fellow authors.

YouTube: One of the best ways I have promoted my books is through my YouTube channel. Over the years, I have shared everything from business tutorials to personal content. My subscribers were the first people to buy my first book, helping me become a full-time author. And they are still among the first readers of my new releases.

There is an active self-publishing community on YouTube, from authors and readers to those teaching how to make no-and-low content books. As with most social media platforms, it's best to lurk a bit before starting to engage directly so you can get a feel for the community. Some authors love to collaborate with others who do not.

You don't even have to create your own videos to be an active member of the YouTube community. You can get a free YouTube channel page by signing up for a Google account. You can dress that page up and add your links. Then, when you comment on others' videos, they'll be able to click on your profile picture and check out your links. You can also post static content, such as book releases, on your account's community tab.

TikTok: The newest social media platform, TikTok, is all about short videos. Though it started with young people creating dances to popular songs, it has now attracted all ages and demographics, including authors and readers. Popular hashtags like #authortok and #booktok are widely used in the publishing community.

If you're a fiction writer, a popular video format is to read a short summary of your book from a character's perspective, especially one ending with a question. For instance: "My husband left me for another woman, but now he wants me back. What should I do?" Of course, readers must read the book to find out!

Like Instagram, TikTok allows only one link in your profile. The link becomes clickable only if you switch to a TikTok business account. This switch is free, and if you decide to return to a personal account, it's easy to switch back.

If you're only promoting your Amazon Author Page, that link should be in your bio. But if you have more pages or businesses, use a link service like linktr.ee to consolidate them.

As a beginner on TikTok, aim to post three times a day. One post can focus on your books, and the other two can be lighthearted or funny. Consider posting book-related content in the evening when TikTok traffic is higher. As with any social media, balance selling posts with general content to grow your followers without making them feel like you're constantly selling.

Take it one step at a time: I realize that I just gave you a lot of information and that you may feel overwhelmed. After all, you probably just want to write a book and get it published. But to make money in self-publishing, you must also market and promote your work. Utilizing social media is key to selling self-published books, so plan to carve out time each day to build your following.

Here is a step-by-step list to follow that will help keep you on track:

1. Look into purchasing a URL for your pen name from a site such as GoDaddy. For example, I own the URL AnnEckhart.com. There is a slight cost to this, but you want to make sure you have your name or pen name locked in so no one else can use that web address.

2. Sign up for a Linktr.ee account to organize all of your links so that you can provide one main link for readers.

3. Create a Facebook page for your pen name, even if it is your legal name.

4. Create a Facebook reader group. Add a link to the group on your Facebook page and in the *About the Author* section of your books so readers can find it.

5. Create a Threads account for your author name.

6. Create an Instagram account for your author name.

7. Create a Twitter account for your author name.

8. Consider creating a TikTok account and a YouTube account for your author name. You don't have to utilize either, at least not immediately, but lock in the names as soon as possible. Even if you don't create your own content, set up the pages so that when you comment on others' videos, they can check out your profile and click through to your links.

9. Make sure all of the links in your Linktr.ee are up to date and organized by importance, with your *Amazon Author* page at the top.

10. Commit to a posting schedule that works for you!

CHAPTER SIXTEEN: GETTING BOOK REVIEWS

Reviews help sell books—well, *good* reviews help sell books. Bad reviews can kill a book's momentum instantly. Unfortunately, getting readers to leave reviews on Amazon is tricky. Most readers don't bother, and some leave negative reviews just because they can. Waiting for your first review is nerve-wracking, and a bad review can feel devastating.

So, how can you encourage good reviews? The first step is to ask! Many authors include a note at the end of their books: "If you enjoyed this book, please consider leaving an honest review on Amazon." You can also request reviews on social media from readers who enjoyed your book.

Still struggling to get reviews? Here are more ideas to try:

Free Book Promotions: If you've enrolled in KDP Select, you can offer your Kindle eBooks for free for up to five days during each 90-day enrollment period. However, free book promotions have both pros and cons.

The pros are clear: giving your book away helps build recognition and boosts your book's ranking on Amazon's free best-sellers list. It's also a chance to collect reviews, which are essential for future sales.

But there's a downside: people who download free books are often more likely to leave negative reviews. I've had two instances where I offered a book for free and received immediate one-star reviews. While every book eventually gets bad reviews, it's rough when the first review is a negative one.

It's demoralizing—trust me, I've been there. Seeing a bad review can feel devastating, especially when it's the only one up for a while. It's even worse when it affects the book's launch, as reviews help drive sales. However, over time, more reviews usually roll in, burying the negative ones, which eventually boosts the book's standing.

BETA Readers: Want to ensure your book launches with positive reviews? BETA readers are critical! BETA readers get an advanced copy of your book to proofread and, in return, agree to leave a review on launch day.

How do you find BETA readers? Remember those Facebook groups I mentioned earlier? That's where I find mine. I simply post in my group, offering a free digital copy in exchange for feedback and a review.

To manage BETA readers efficiently, I use **BookFunnel.com**, which starts at just $20 a year. It distributes your book and sends reminders about their reviews to readers.

If you don't yet have a Facebook group or don't have very many members, here are some other ways you can find BETA readers:

Goodreads: Goodreads groups often have dedicated sections for finding and exchanging BETA reading services. Look for the category you write in to find readers who would be interested in reading your work.

Reddit: Reddit is an online message board with thousands of topics. Look for reader groups and then search for subreddits like r/BetaReaders and r/DestructiveReaders to find potential

BETA readers.

BookSprout: This platform is explicitly designed to connect authors with readers who are willing to provide early reviews. Note that this is a paid service with different tiers, but they do have a free version you can use that you only pay for when you start getting reviews.

Instagram: Not only are there active author and reader communities on Instagram, but you can also search relevant hashtags like #betareaderswanted to reach readers who would love to be BETA readers.

Mailing List: In the fiction world, a mailing list is the ultimate tool. Building an email database of fans who will buy every book you publish is what separates successful authors from those who struggle to sell even one copy. A mailing list provides readers for your private Facebook group and BETA readers who will happily review your books.

But how do you build a mailing list before publishing a book?

First, you need a mailing list provider. There are numerous websites you can use to build your mailing list, such as AuthorEmail.com, ConstantContact.com, ConvertKit.com, MailerLite.com, and MailChimp.com. I use MailChimp.

Prices and features vary among these websites, but all allow you to collect email addresses and send out mass email campaigns. You need a reader magnet to entice people to sign up.

A reader magnet is a freebie offered in exchange for a subscriber's email address. For authors, this is often a short story, the first chapter of a book, or even an entire novel. Non-fiction authors might offer a how-to guide or tutorial. Whatever you choose, the reader must subscribe to your email list to get it.

BookFunnel is an excellent platform for distributing reader magnets. You can upload your reader magnet to BookFunnel and share the link on social media. Once people click the link, they sign up for your email list to access the freebie.

BookFunnel not only sends the magnet but also collects email addresses, which you can integrate into your mailing list. You can even set up an automated "welcome" message that invites new subscribers to join your Facebook group.

Work with Influencers: Influencers on social media, particularly on Instagram and TikTok, can help promote your books. On Instagram, search hashtags like #readersofinstagram or #bookgram, and on TikTok, look under #booktok to find influencers passionate about fiction. Find content creators who enjoy your genre (e.g., #smalltownromance) and look for those who accept books in exchange for reviews. Reach out to ask if they'd like a free copy of your book to share with their followers. While unpaid influencers aren't obligated to post, smaller creators often appreciate free products to grow their audience.

Friends & Family: While it may seem logical to ask friends and family to leave positive reviews for your books, you need to be cautious. Amazon strictly forbids paid reviews and can flag reviews from accounts linked to yours. For example, suppose you've sent someone a gift through Amazon, and they leave a review without purchasing your book. In that case, Amazon may assume it's a paid review. This could lead to Amazon removing reviews or, worse, banning your account. It's safer to avoid reviews from those close to you.

How Amazon Views Reviews: While you shouldn't pay for reviews or have friends and family leave them, BETA readers are a safe option. Amazon detects paid reviews when accounts post mass reviews or use review services that leave suspicious patterns. Similarly, friends and family reviews can be flagged if their accounts are linked to yours (e.g., through shared addresses or gifts). BETA readers, however, have no such connection to your account, so their reviews are safe. Just avoid sending them gifts through Amazon to prevent any association.

Do's & Don'ts: Here are good rules to follow when it comes to getting Amazon reviews for your books:

DO....

Engage with Readers: Reply to readers who leave positive reviews on social media, showing appreciation and encouraging them to leave more reviews for future books. Giving their posts a "thumbs up" or "love" heart and replying with a simple "thank you" goes a long way towards building a loyal audience.

Use Call-to-Actions (CTA): At the end of your eBook, ask readers directly for an honest review, making it easy with a link to your **Amazon Author Page.** You can also put this ask at the end of paperback and hardcover books to remind people to go to the *Orders* section of their Amazon account to leave a review for your book.

Leverage Book Bloggers: In addition to finding readers through social media, bloggers review indie books, especially if they fit their niche. Reach out to them with a personalized message offering to send them a free book in exchange for a write-up. Note that those with a large following may charge for this service; make sure you aren't asking the blogger for reviews but for them to share your book with their audience, who will then hopefully leave you reviews.

DON'T....

Offer Incentives: Never offer a gift, discount, or financial compensation in exchange for a review. This violates Amazon's guidelines. Providing BETA readers with a free book copy in exchange for their honest review is okay; sending them gifts to ensure they leave you a positive review is now.

Flood Review Requests: Don't over-ask your audience for reviews. It can come across as pushy and turn readers off. And it can put you in a position where your audience will only review the books you give to them for free rather than purchasing them.

And in the long run, you want to sell books, not give them away.

Completely Ignore Negative Feedback: If you get a bad review, don't respond negatively. Instead, focus on constructive criticism to improve your future work. Eventually, any negative reviews will get drowned out by positive ones!

CHAPTER SEVENTEEN: FACEBOOK ADS FOR AUTHORS

Using free social media platforms to promote your books is a great way to start marketing. However, the most successful indie authors often use paid advertising, especially on Facebook.

In addition to creating a Facebook page for your pen name and a group for your readers, Facebook offers advertising options that can be highly effective for selling books. In fact, Facebook ads are second only to Amazon Ads in popularity among authors. (We'll cover Amazon Ads in the next chapter.)

Once you have a business page and start posting, Facebook will offer the option to boost your posts. Boosting a post essentially means paying to have Facebook show it to more people. Facebook offers two main ways to advertise:

- **Boosting Posts:** Pay to show a status update or link to a broader audience.
- **Facebook Ads:** Create an ad specifically to promote your book to a targeted audience.

Boosting a post and running a Facebook ad are similar in promotion; the difference is how the post is created. Boosting turns an existing post into an ad, while Facebook Ads are designed specifically for advertising.

To boost a post, simply click the blue **Boost Post** link under an active post. To create an ad from scratch, navigate to the **Meta Business Suite** from your page profile, then click **Ads**. Alternatively, from your page, click **Ad Center** on the left-hand side, then the blue **Advertise** button.

Under **Choose ad type**, you'll see three options:

- **Get started with Automated Ads**
- **Create new ad**
- **Boost a post**

Get started with Automated Ads: This option lets Facebook create an ad for you by determining your audience based on answers you provide about your product. They'll test up to six different versions of your ad to find the best one, making it a great starting point for beginners.

The system will ask you, "What are some topics your audience might like?" Be sure to include "reading" and "books," along with your book's genre and well-known authors in your genre. This helps Facebook target readers already interested in similar books. Note that only authors with followers of 100,000 will show up as an option, meaning most indie authors will not be on Facebook's list. Choose authors who write in a genre similar to yours, even if they aren't exactly the same.

After you complete all the steps, Facebook will preview your ad. Set a **Daily Budget**(start with at least $5 per day) and **Duration** (run it for about seven days). Add a payment method, then click the blue **Publish** button.

Create new ad: This option skips the steps in Get Started with Automated Ads and takes you directly to a single page where you can make all selections manually.

Under **Goal**, choose **Get more website visitors** to drive sales by directing people to your Amazon Author Page.

Next, design your **Ad Creative**. Under **Select Media**, upload up to five images, typically your book cover. Some authors create custom images using Canva or hire designers on Fiverr or UpWork.

Choose **Shop Now** as your **Button Label** for selling books. For the **website URL**, provide a link to either the specific book or your Amazon Author Page.

Under **Additional Contact Method**, select **None** unless you want to offer WhatsApp or phone contact.

If you've uploaded multiple images, you can use the **Advantage + Creative** option. This feature allows Facebook to deliver different ad variations based on user data to maximize ad performance, which is especially helpful for beginners.

PRO TIP: Find other indie authors in your genre on Facebook to see how they structure their ads. Do they simply use their book cover or create more detailed graphics? Do they use photos or videos? While you don't want to copy someone else's ad, you can get a sense of what designs resonate with readers and create similar ones.

Special Ad Category: This is primarily for businesses hiring employees, so you can leave this off.

The **Audience** field is critical when creating your Facebook ad. If you choose to run an Automated Ad, Facebook will select this data for you using the **Advantage Audience** option. However, you can fine-tune the audience by editing details like Gender, Age, and Location. For example, if you write a later-in-life romance, you may not want to target 18-year-old men. If most of your readers are in one country, you can narrow the audience by location.

You can also deselect **Advantage Audience** and choose from the following:

- **People you choose through targeting**
- **People who like your Page**
- **People who like your Page and people similar to them**
- **Create new**

People you choose through targeting: Click the pencil icon next to **Audience Details** to adjust the Gender, Age, Locations, and Detailed Targeting. Customer location data can be found under the **Reports** tab in your Amazon KDP dashboard.

Detailed Targeting is where you can narrow down your audience further. One effective strategy for beginners is targeting well-known authors in your genre. Note that these authors need at least 100,000 followers to appear in Facebook's targeting system. Most indie authors won't have that, so aim for traditionally published authors. For instance, if you write horror novels, you might target Stephen King fans; if you write steamy romance, Nora Roberts might be a good choice.

People who like your Page: This option is generally not recommended unless you have a large following, as it limits the potential audience.

People who like your Page and people similar to them: This is a solid option if you want to grow your audience by targeting people connected to your current followers.

PRO TIP: Facebook recently introduced the **@followers** feature. When you post something on your page, type **@followers** in the comment section. This will tag your followers, helping to ensure your post is seen. Use this sparingly, though, to avoid overwhelming your audience.

Next, you'll set your **Duration** and **Daily Budget**. Many authors suggest running ads continuously with the highest budget you can afford, but starting small (like $5/day) is a good strategy for beginners to test the ad's effectiveness.

How to Know if an Ad is Working: Facebook will charge you for clicks, but neither Facebook nor Amazon will tell you if those clicks result in book sales. The best way to gauge success is by tracking your book's rank on Amazon. If your ad is driving clicks and your book's rank rises, the ad is likely contributing to sales. You can test this by turning off the ad and seeing if your rank drops.

If your ad is getting clicks but your book's rank isn't moving, it's time to tweak your audience or try a new ad entirely.

Finally, remember you can pause or delete an ad at any time. However, running an ad for at least a month will give you more data to work with. Finding your audience takes time, and most authors constantly test and refine their ads. Stick to a budget, and don't be discouraged if it takes a while to find what works.

Meta is continually making changes and improvements to their advertising platform. I encourage you to play around with all of their features to see what types of ads it can create, even if you don't end up using them. As you become more comfortable running ads, consider these advanced techniques:

A/B Testing: Always test different versions of your ads to see what resonates with your audience. Change one element at a time (like an image, text, or headline) to measure its impact.

Retargeting: Use Facebook's retargeting feature to show ads to people who've already visited your website or engaged with previous ads.

Use Facebook Pixel: If you have a website, install Facebook Pixel to track conversions and optimize your ads based on accurate data.

Track Key Metrics: Monitor click-through rate (CTR), cost-per-click (CPC), and conversion rate to evaluate performance and adjust your strategy.

Budget: When it comes to budgeting for Facebook ads, I recommend starting with at least $5 per day. As a new author, I know it can feel nerve-wracking to spend money but running an ad for at least a week is essential to gather enough data to see how Facebook places it and how many clicks it gets. While you don't have to run ads, they really can work for authors and become a wise investment in your business. Think of it as paying to reach readers who wouldn't otherwise find your books organically. By sticking with it and testing small budgets, you'll get a better sense of what works and where to invest more down the road.

If you're hesitant about the cost, remember that a small daily spend over time can add up to significant exposure without breaking the bank. By carefully monitoring your ad's performance and tweaking it as needed, you can maximize the value of your investment. Think of it as a way to get your book in front of readers who are actively searching for books like yours.

In business, you sometimes need to spend money to make money, and Facebook ads can be worth the price if you see your sales increase!

CHAPTER EIGHTEEN: AMAZON ADS FOR AUTHORS

Some books sell well organically on Amazon. Whether it's because the topic is in a relatively niche genre with little competition, like the nonfiction business guides I write, or because readers have latched onto a specific trope, there are self-published authors who do very little, if any, paid marketing for their books.

But for the rest of us, the book market is crowded—both with big-name publishing houses and tens of thousands of self-published authors. Getting your book noticed by Amazon customers can feel nearly impossible.

Thankfully, Amazon offers one tool to help you get your books in front of potential buyers: **Amazon Advertising**, usually referred to as **Amazon Ads.**

With Amazon Ads, you can promote your books directly on Amazon's website, where customers are already searching for their next read. Now, I know it might feel frustrating to pay for visibility on the platform where your book is already published but remember—you're competing with millions of other books. Unless you have a best-seller right out of the gate, you'll likely need Amazon Ads to generate Kindle Unlimited borrows and paperback sales, especially if you write fiction or are uploading low-content books like planners, journals, notebooks, and activity books—categories where competition is particularly fierce.

Amazon controls 80% of eBook sales and 65% of print book sales. Plus, 83% of e-reader users own an Amazon Kindle. There are over 12 million Kindle books available on Amazon, with new ones being uploaded daily. Even if you have the best title, cover, description, and keywords, it will still be nearly impossible for your book to be discovered in search without doing some form of marketing. While social media and Facebook ads are great tools, Amazon Ads remain the most effective way to boost visibility.

How effective are Amazon Ads for selling books? According to Amazon's data:

- **76%** of global book buyers surveyed who researched a book on Amazon recall seeing an ad for the book on the site.
- **62%** of surveyed buyers who discover a title or author on Amazon go on to purchase that book or other works by the same author, either on Amazon or elsewhere.
- **55%** of surveyed buyers say Amazon provides the information that makes them feel confident in their purchase, helping maintain Amazon's position as the number one bookseller.
- The average Amazon advertising conversion rate for book ads is about **9.96%**. Compare that to the rate for general merchandise, which is only 1.33%. This means that Amazon Ads for books are highly effective at converting clicks into sales.

Amazon offers two key methods for advertising books:

Sponsored Products: These are cost-per-click (CPC) ads that promote individual product listings. Sponsored Product Ads appear prominently on Amazon, including on the first page of shopping results and individual product pages. You set a budget for how much you're willing to spend per click, and you only pay when a customer clicks on your ad. A daily budget helps control costs, making this option flexible and budget-friendly for new authors.

Sponsored Brands: These ads also use a CPC model but focus on promoting multiple products along with your brand logo and a headline. They are ideal for promoting a series or multiple books by the same author. They appear in shopping results and help drive the discovery of your brand as a whole. Just like with Sponsored Product Ads, you only pay when a customer clicks on the ad, and you control both the click price and daily budget.

To start with Amazon Advertising, you first need to create an account at advertising.amazon.com. The process is free and straightforward. Since you'll be paying for ads, you'll need to provide a payment method, such as a debit or credit card, or you can opt to have funds withdrawn directly from a bank account.

Once your account is active, setting up your first ad is easy. The default page you'll see in the Amazon Ad dashboard is the **Sponsored Ads Campaign Manager**. This is where you will manage all your ad campaigns. I suggest bookmarking this page for quick access, as you'll be checking it frequently to monitor your campaigns.

Sponsored Products are the ad option most widely used by new authors, so we will begin with this section. In the *Sponsored Products* box, click on the blue **Continue** option. The **New campaign** window will open for you to make your selections.

The first field you will see is **Ad Format**. Here, you can select from one of two options:

- **Custom text ad:** Add custom text to your ad. Your ad will appear in a box on Amazon's site with whatever text you add. You can only advertise one book per Custom text ad.

- **Standard ad:** Create an ad with no box or custom text. Your book will appear on Amazon's site with "SPONSORED" in small text. You can add multiple books to a Standard ad.

Custom text ads are a more advanced option. You really need to know your audience to create an effective ad with text. If you're just starting out, I recommend using the Standard ad option. In fact, I only run Standard ads as they are faster to create and often get just as good, if not better, results than a custom advertisement.

For this example, let's focus on creating a **Standard ad.**

The next field is titled **Products**, which refers to the books you choose to add to your ad. For example, if you have a series of crime novels, you could add all of the books in that series into one campaign. I use this tactic to run a single ad for multiple books in the same genre. For instance, I have one ad that includes all of my eBay books and another with all of my Etsy books, and I also create ad groups for my guided journals.

However, you don't have to use this technique. You can create an ad using just one title, especially if it's the first book in a series. If you are promoting your first and only book, you'll obviously have just one book to add. You can also run separate ads for the Kindle and paperback versions of your book. Still, I almost always include all formats (including hardcover, if available) in a single ad. Amazon will decide which version to show customers.

You can check the data after the ad has been running for a while to see which version is getting the most exposure. If, for example, Amazon is primarily promoting the Kindle version, you might decide to create a second ad focused solely on the paperback version.

PRO TIP: If you have an extensive library of books, you can use the **Search** bar to quickly find specific titles instead of scrolling through all your listings. However, make sure you match the capitalization of the book title exactly. For example, if I want to find one of my Etsy books, I need to type "Etsy," not "ETSY," into the search bar, as the capitalization must match. Also, the list will include any books you've unpublished. I have published over 731 titles over the years, but less than 400 are currently available for sale.

The next section of the page is **Targeting**, where you can choose between **Automatic Targeting** or **Manual Targeting**. If you're new to self-publishing, you might want to start with Automatic Targeting. With this option, Amazon selects keywords and products similar to the one in your ad to help your book get matched with other relevant books on the platform. For instance, if you're advertising a romance novel, Amazon will try to match your book with other romance titles.

As you become more comfortable with ads, you'll likely want to switch to **Manual Targeting**, where you can handpick the keywords and products you want your ad to appear next to. This gives you more control over where and how your book shows up in search results.

PRO TIP: Amazon constantly updates its ad platform, so what works today might not work tomorrow. For example, I successfully used Automatic Targeting for nearly two years. However, after Amazon adjusted its algorithm, I had to switch to manual targeting with keywords. It's always a good idea to test out both options to see what works best for your books and to be prepared to adapt as Amazon's system evolves.

Because there are different options within **Manual Targeting**, we will use that for this example.

When you choose **Manual Targeting**, a new field appears offering two choices:

- **Keyword Targeting:** Select keywords that you think customers would type into Amazon's search bar to find your book.

- **Product Targeting:** Select specific products or categories alongside which to target your ad.

Most new authors begin with **Keyword Targeting** because it allows you to choose particular keywords or short phrases that shoppers often use when searching on Amazon. You can create a keyword list, use Amazon's suggested keywords, or do a mix of both. Some authors even use keyword-generating software like **KDP Rocket**, which you can purchase at publisherrocket.com.

For example, let's say I'm setting up a **Keyword Targeting** ad for one of my eBay books. As soon as I choose the book I want to promote, Amazon generates a list of suggested keywords related to it. For my eBay books, this list usually includes terms like "eBay," "eBay business," "home-based business," "how to sell on eBay," "selling on eBay," "eBay what to sell," and dozens of other related phrases.

PRO TIP: Amazon recently updated the data available to authors when selecting keywords. They are currently Beta testing **Keyword Groups**, which leverage Amazon's data to automatically provide keywords related to similar books in your category. Additionally, next to some suggested keywords, you'll notice codes like **IS** and **IR**:

- **Impression Share (IS):** This represents the percentage of impressions you're receiving for a specific keyword relative to all the impressions that the keyword generates across the platform.
- **Impression Rank (IR):** This shows your IS's share of impressions for the same keyword compared to other advertisers.

This new impression data helps you select keywords that are more likely to appear on the first page of a buyer's search results. I focus on choosing keywords with **IS** and **IR** data, which helps narrow down the most effective options for my ads.

You'll notice that many keywords consist of two or three words together because this mirrors what Amazon customers typically type into the search bar. For instance, someone looking for a book about selling on eBay isn't typing out, "I am looking for a book about how to sell things on eBay." Instead, they're using shorter phrases like "eBay book" or "eBay guide" or even just typing "eBay."

As customers begin typing into Amazon's search bar, Amazon will start auto-filling suggestions for them. When I type "eBay" into the search bar, several options like "eBay gift card," "ebay.com," and "eBay tape" appear.

Now, you might be thinking that "eBay tape" isn't an ideal keyword for an ad about my eBay book. However, the fact that Amazon is suggesting "eBay tape" means people are actively searching for it. And if they're purchasing eBay tape, they might also be interested in learning more about selling on eBay, making "eBay tape" a potentially useful keyword to include in my ad.

Let's return to the **Keyword Targeting** section. Amazon provides you with Suggested keywords, but you also have the option to add your own by selecting **Enter list**. Suppose you already have a keyword list saved. In that case, you can upload it using the **Upload a file** option (compatible with CSV, TSV, or XLSX formats). Since uploading files is a more advanced technique, we'll stick with using the **Suggested** and **Enter list** options for now.

Before you start selecting keywords, you need to determine your bidding price. Next to **Bid**, you'll see a bar labeled **Suggested bid**. Clicking on this brings up a drop-down menu with the following choices:

- **Suggested bid**: This uses past bidding data to predict the bids that are most likely to win.
- **Custom bid**: This allows you to customize bids for each keyword.

- **Default bid**: This applies the same bid value to multiple keywords.

Suppose Amazon has a Prime Day or other significant sales event coming up. In that case, you may see a temporary option related to those events, as bids tend to be higher during these periods.

When I first started running Amazon Ads, the biggest mistake I made was using the **Suggested bids**. Remember, Amazon wants your money, so their **Suggested bids** are much higher than necessary for effective ads. Using these bids can quickly eat up your advertising budget, as it did mine. **Do not use them!**

Instead, I recommend selecting **Custom bid**, which allows you to set the same rate for each keyword. I also suggest starting your ads with a **low bid**.

You'll notice that the **Suggested bids** provided by Amazon are pretty high—often in the 50-cent to $1 range, and some are even several dollars. Instead, enter a **low Custom bid** of under 30 cents to start, especially for fiction or nonfiction books, and even lower for low- and no-content books. For example, I might start a nonfiction book ad at 25 cents per click, but for a journal ad, I would only bid around 15 cents.

PRO TIP: To be competitive against other advertisers, consider using an odd-numbered bid. Most advertisers choose even numbers, like 20 cents. So, bidding 21 cents could give you a slight advantage as you compete for ad placements.

Once you've set your bid rate, it's time to select your keywords. Amazon divides keywords into three types:

- **Broad**: This method matches your keywords to search terms that are not only exact but also related, including synonyms, misspellings, and variations. For example, entering "eBay" as a broad match could show your ad next to books from searches like "eay" (misspelled), "reselling," or "auctions."

- **Phrase**: Matches search terms that include your keyword in any order. For instance, "eBay" as a phrase match could place your ad next to searches like "selling on eBay" or "eBay sales."
- **Exact**: Matches only the exact search term. For example, suppose you use "eBay" as an exact match. In that case, your ad will only be shown to users who specifically search for "eBay" without any other variations.

When you're starting out, it's perfectly fine to select all three options. In fact, Amazon defaults to having all three pre-selected. As you get more experience with Amazon Ads, you'll likely identify which of these types works best for your campaigns. Some advertisers prefer using just one type, while others mix and match. You can also allow Amazon to show all three options initially and manually refine your selections later.

Amazon will present you with a long list of keywords. While you can click **Add all** to select them all, I recommend taking the time to review each one. Often, irrelevant keywords will be included. For example, while setting up an ad for an eBay book, Amazon's system pulled the word "bay" from "eBay" and added keywords related to a San Francisco Bay Area spice company. Clearly, those keywords weren't going to help me sell eBay books, so it was essential to select the relevant ones manually.

When you set up your first ad, carefully look at Amazon's suggested keywords and manually add each, choosing between **Broad**, **Phrase**, and **Exact** matches. Not all keywords will have a suggested bid amount, but that's okay if you still want to use them with your **Custom bid**. Sometimes, Amazon's reporting system lags, and the suggested bids don't show. If you feel a keyword is a good fit for your book, go ahead and include it.

Once you've added keywords, they'll appear in the right-hand column of the ad setup page. You can still review and delete any keywords you don't want before publishing your ad. Even after your ad is live, you can make specific keywords inactive by pausing them. You can also add new keywords at any time.

Above the **Keyword targeting** section, next to **Suggested**, is the **Enter list** option. This is where you can manually enter keywords by typing them in or pasting them from a file. Tools like KDP Rocket can provide targeted keywords based on your book's genre.

Publisher Rocket: Publisher Rocket, sometimes also referred to as KDP Rocket, is a subscription-based Amazon KDP research tool used by most self-published authors, including myself. It allows you to research keywords and categories, see what other authors are earning on their books, and generate keyword lists for your Amazon Ads. One helpful feature is the ability to export keyword lists into an Excel spreadsheet, which you can then copy and paste directly into your Amazon ad keyword field. To learn more about Publisher Rocket, visit publisherrocket.com.

I typically use a combination of Amazon's suggested keywords, keywords from Publisher Rocket, and those I've come up with on my own. When starting an ad campaign, it's a good idea to include as many keywords as possible—literally 200 or more. This will help you see where Amazon is placing your ad. As your ad runs, you can narrow down the keyword list and focus on those that are driving the most traffic.

PRO TIP: While Amazon doesn't allow you to use competitor author names or book titles in your book's metadata or description, you *can* use them in your Amazon Ads. For example, if your book is similar to *Harry Potter*, you can include *Harry Potter*-related keywords in your ad. You may even want to create a dedicated ad using keywords explicitly related to popular books in your genre.

Why not put every single competitor author and book into one single ad? The answer lies in **Impressions**. Amazon can only place your ad in so many spots. These placements are called

Impressions. You don't pay for Impressions; you only pay when someone clicks on your ad (Clicks). However, if Amazon focuses on just a few of your keywords, it means the other keywords you've selected are not being utilized, which essentially wastes your ad potential.

You can run as many ads as your budget allows, so creating multiple ads with different targets makes sense. This strategy also helps you identify which keywords resonate with customers and which targets aren't delivering results, allowing you to adjust your ads more effectively.

Product Targeting: If you choose Product Targeting instead of Keyword Targeting, the dashboard will change to offer two different options:

- **Categories:** Under Suggested, Amazon will show you the categories where your book is already listed. You can also search for additional categories under Search.
- **Individual Products**: Amazon suggests books that are likely similar to yours. You can also manually search for specific products or enter ISBNs under **Enter list**. You can even generate ISBN lists using Publisher Rocket.

Between the two, I recommend starting with Categories. As you progress in your author journey and gather data on which books are performing well in your category, you can start targeting specific books individually.

When you click on Categories, Amazon will show you the three categories you selected when setting up your book listing. However, you can use the Search feature to add more categories. Just like when you initially selected your book's categories, it's a good idea to look at where similar books are listed. If you didn't get to include all the categories you wanted in your book's listing, now is your chance to target them through ads. Publisher Rocket can also help you research categories for better ad targeting.

Regardless of whether you choose a keyword or category ad, the next section of the listing field is **Negative Targeting**. If you are running a keyword ad, this section will be labeled **Negative Keyword Targeting**. If you're running a category or product ad, it will be titled **Negative Product Targeting**.

This section is optional but can be pretty helpful in refining your ad targeting. It helps weed out potential search terms or categories that Amazon might use to target your ad, even if those terms have nothing to do with your book. To make the most of Negative Targeting, however, you'll need to have some data on your book's sales and ad performance.

For example, if you've written a clean Christian romance, you don't want your book shown to people searching for horror novels or erotica. Sometimes, your book's title or cover might make it appear in unexpected genres. If a customer clicks on your ad for the wrong reasons, you'll still be charged for that click, even though they won't buy your book. Adding Negative Keywords helps prevent Amazon from wasting impressions and clicks on customers who are searching for something completely different.

You can also add negative keywords or products to an ad after it's already running. Suppose you notice that your ad is getting clicks from a particular keyword that isn't resulting in sales. In that case, you can go back and add that keyword to your Negative Keyword list to optimize your ad's performance.

The next section of the page is **Campaign**, where you will select your Campaign bidding strategy. Amazon gives you three options:

- **Dynamic bids, down only**: Amazon will lower your bids in real-time when your ad is less likely to convert into a sale.
- **Dynamic bids, up and down**: Amazon will raise your bids (by up to 100%) in real-time when your ad is more

likely to convert to a sale and lower them when it's less likely.

- **Fixed bids**: Amazon will stick to your exact bid without adjusting based on the likelihood of a sale.

Most self-published authors choose Dynamic bids – down only because it's the best way to control costs. Amazon loves spending ad money, so restricting them to only lower your bid when necessary ensures you won't go over budget.

Next, you'll find an option to Adjust bids by placement. This allows you to increase your bid (by up to 900%) to get your ad to appear at the top of search results or on product pages. This is a more advanced feature, and I've found that it can be costly without delivering better results than a regular bidding strategy. So, for now, we'll leave this section as-is.

The last section is **Settings**. Here, you'll enter your **Campaign name**. It's easiest to start by naming your campaign after your book. As you get more experienced, you may end up running multiple campaigns for the same book, so you'll want to create distinct names later on. The system won't let you use the same name twice. I usually name mine based on the type of targeting I'm using, like "Beginner eBay: Keywords."

Next, you will choose **Portfolio**, which is simply the "folder" where you want your ad to be filed. You can create Portfolios from the main screen of your account. Until you've done that, the system will default to No Portfolio. After the ad goes live, you can create a portfolio and select the ad you want to place in it. I have a portfolio called Active Campaigns for all ads currently running. Amazon doesn't allow you to delete old campaigns, even when they're inactive. So, I file all my inactive campaigns under a portfolio titled Inactive Campaigns.

Next, you'll choose the **Start and End dates** for your ad. Unless you're running an ad for a specific promotion, you'll likely leave the default date, which is the day you create the ad. I only set an End date for limited-time offers or books focused on specific holidays. Otherwise, I leave it as *No end date*.

The **Country** section will automatically select your advertising country. If you set up your account in the U.S., the United States will already be selected for you. You can also create separate accounts to advertise in other countries like Canada and Mexico.

Now, you need to set your **Daily budget.** I recommend starting with at least $5. If your ad proves successful, you can always increase your ad spending.

PRO TIP: Spending money on ads can be scary, especially when you're paying per click. Starting at $5 a day is a good entry point, but as you start earning from your books, consider increasing your budget. I sometimes run 20+ ads at a time with daily budgets totaling $100 or more. Does all that money get spent? No, because I'm cautious about setting strict parameters and controlled bid amounts. However, setting a higher budget gives Amazon the flexibility to show your book more often. The more impressions your book gets, the better the chance a customer may click on it and eventually buy.

After filling in all the fields, you can click on **Save as draft** or **Launch campaign**. Once launched, your campaign will be listed as Active under the Portfolios section of your advertising console. It might take a few minutes for an ad to launch officially, but once it's live, you can always edit, pause, or stop it.

Sponsored Brands: Sponsored Brands is a more complex ad option that Amazon offers to help an author build their brand. These are sizable ads displayed in prime spots on Amazon, like at the top or alongside shopping results, and link directly to a landing page of your choice. Amazon offers the following options for Sponsored Brands:

Product collection: This format lets you promote multiple books from a custom landing page. You'll get to feature your brand logo, a custom headline, and three or more of your books.

When shoppers click on a book image, they'll go to that book's product detail page. If they click on your logo or headline, it takes them to your **Amazon Author Store** or a custom landing page where you've grouped your books.

Video: Video ads can be a great way to grab attention by featuring a single book in a video format. These ads link directly to the book's product detail page and appear in shopping results on both desktop and mobile. Video is particularly useful for low content books to show how the book will look in someone's hands as they flip through the pages and write or color inside.

Both ad types are cost-per-click (CPC), so you only pay when someone clicks on your ad. Plus, you control the budget by setting how much you want to spend per day and how much you want to bid per click.

Amazon will review your ad to ensure it follows their guidelines. Once it's approved, you'll get an email, and your ad will go live. If changes are needed, they'll notify you before it's launched.

In late 2024, Amazon completely overhauled Sponsored Brands, including now requiring authors to provide their custom ad images. Before, Amazon simply used the book cover.

Editing an ad is easy: Just like you can edit your book files and covers after publishing, you can also adjust your ads at any time. Simply click on the ad, and you'll be taken to a page where you can view specific data, such as *Total targets,* which refers to the keywords, categories, or products you've selected to target.

For example, let's say your ad has low impressions and targets only the Historical Romance category. Imagine you're running an ad for a book about YouTube that only targets the Social Media category. By clicking on *Total targets*, Amazon will display all your targets and their respective bid amounts—let's say your current bid is 21 cents.

If the impressions are low, it likely means your bid is too low, and other advertisers are outbidding you, so Amazon is showing their ads instead of yours. To improve your bid competitiveness, you could raise it to, say, 31 or 41 cents. After adjusting the bid, let the ad run for a couple more weeks to gather more data.

If your ad starts getting more impressions but still isn't generating clicks, you might consider dropping that category. Similarly, if your ad gets clicks but no sales, it could indicate that your targets—keywords or categories—aren't the best fit. It could also point to issues with your book listing, such as the cover not matching the genre, a description that isn't compelling enough, or insufficient reviews. Worse, several bad reviews could be deterring buyers. In that case, it's worth revisiting the strategies discussed earlier in this book to refine your listing and improve your reviews.

Monitoring your ads: So how do you check an ad's performance beyond simply looking at how much money it's spending? Go directly to the ad within your campaign dashboard and click on it to bring up all the detailed statistics.

I like to keep all my active campaigns in a folder I've cleverly titled Active Campaigns. Some advertisers prefer to organize their ads differently, for example, by maintaining ads for different fiction series in separate portfolios. You can experiment to find the organizational method that works best for you.

If you haven't yet set up portfolios, you can start by clicking on **Portfolios**, which will show you all your current ads. From here, you can click Create portfolio and begin organizing your campaigns.

Amazon offers the following **column settings**, which you can customize according to your preferences:

- **Active**: Indicates whether an ad is enabled and running or disabled. This is a default column that cannot be removed.

- **Campaigns**: This column displays the name of the ad campaign. It is another standard column that cannot be removed.
- **Status**: Shows if the ad is in review, pending, or currently delivering. This column is also fixed.
- **Type**: Specifies whether the ad is a *Sponsored Product* or *Sponsored Brand* and whether it uses *Automatic* or *Manual Targeting*.
- **Start Date**: The date the ad began delivering.
- **End Date**: The date the ad is scheduled to stop running.
- **Budget**: The daily budget allocated for the ad.
- **Impressions**: The number of times Amazon has displayed the ad on its website.
- **Clicks**: How many times someone clicked on the ad.
- **CTR** (*Click-Through-Rate*): The ratio of clicks to impressions, calculated as clicks divided by impressions. This helps you gauge how often customers click on your ad when it's shown.
- **Spend**: The total amount spent on the ad campaign.
- **CPC** (*Cost-Per-Click*): The average amount you've paid for each click on the ad.
- **Orders**: The number of orders placed by customers after clicking on your ad.
- **Sales**: The total dollar value of the products sold to shoppers within the ad campaign's time frame. Note that this is the total sales amount, not your earned royalties.
- **ACOS** (*Advertising Cost of Sales*): The percentage of sales you made from advertising, calculated as ad spend divided by total sales from the ad.
- **KENP read**: The estimated number of pages read by Kindle Unlimited subscribers attributed to your ad. Your book must be enrolled in KDP Select to earn

money from KENP reads.

- **Estimated KENP**: The estimated royalties earned from Kindle Unlimited pages read. Current payouts are approximately one cent for every two pages read.

I know there is a lot of data here, but the good news is that you do not necessarily have to pay attention to most of it. In fact, if you do not find specific data fields helpful, you can adjust the settings only to show the columns you are interested in.

I have my grid settings set to show me the following data:

Type: This indicates whether the ad is a Sponsored Product or a Sponsored brand and whether it's using Automatic or Manual Targeting. Sponsored Products typically promote individual items, whereas Sponsored Brands highlight multiple products or brands.

End Date: This column shows when the ad is scheduled to end. Unless you are running a limited-time promotion or seasonal ad, it's best not to enter an ending date so you can gather as much data as possible.

CTR (Click-Through Rate): This data point calculates how often shoppers who see your ad click on it. It's an essential metric for measuring how compelling your ad is. A higher CTR suggests that your ad copy, book cover, or keywords are catching customers' attention.

Spend: This is the total amount you've spent on the ad campaign to date. It helps you track how much you're investing in the ad's performance over time.

CPC (Cost-Per-Click): This shows how much, on average, you're paying for each click on your ad. Lower CPC rates mean you're spending less for each potential reader to view your product page.

Orders: This column tracks the number of individual orders placed after a customer clicks on your ad. It's important to measure the effectiveness of your ad in converting clicks into sales.

Sales: This column shows the total value of sales generated from your ad. However, note that it's the gross sales value, not your royalties.

ACOS (Advertising Cost of Sales): This metric is a ratio of your ad spend to your sales revenue. For example, if you spend $10 on ads and make $100 in sales, your ACOS is 10%. It helps you gauge your ad's profitability, with lower ACOS values indicating higher profit margins.

KENP read: This column shows the estimated number of **Kindle Edition Normalized Pages (KENP)** read by Kindle Unlimited subscribers attributed to your ad.

Estimated KENP: This column provides an estimate of your royalties earned from Kindle Unlimited pages read, which is calculated as approximately one cent for every two pages read.

Once you have located your list of ads, you can analyze them either all together or individually by clicking on each one. Amazon provides an abundance of information about your ads, which can sometimes be overwhelming. When reviewing all the ads in one portfolio, you can select five statistics to display at the top of the page. Based on my experience, the most valuable statistics for my fiction books are:

- **Spend**: How much have I spent on all ads within a given period?
- **Sales**: The total revenue generated from ad-related book sales. Keep in mind that this reflects gross sales, not your royalties.
- **Orders**: The number of books purchased directly through your ads.
- **Estimated KENP royalties** are the estimated earnings from Kindle Unlimited page reads resulting from someone downloading your book through an ad.

- **KENP read**: The total number of Kindle pages read that can be attributed to someone downloading your book from an ad.

However, for my nonfiction and no-and-low content books, which are not enrolled in Kindle Select, the Kindle Unlimited data (KENP) isn't applicable. For these types of books, I prefer monitoring the following five statistics:

- **Spend:** So I can monitor how much money I'm spending.
- **Sales:** The amount of money the books have made from the ad. Note that this is the gross sales number, not the royalties you will earn.
- **Orders:** The number of orders that resulted from your ad.
- **Clicks**: The number of times someone has clicked on one of my ads.
- **CTR (Click-Through Rate)**: The percentage of impressions that resulted in clicks, calculated by dividing clicks by impressions.

Several options are available to customize the data shown at the top of the page. However, you'll gain the most insight and can edit individual ads within the grid where your campaigns are listed. If you've organized your ads into a portfolio, clicking on it will narrow down your view, making it easier to manage your campaigns.

You can also customize the graph and filter results by date range, with options such as:

- Today
- Yesterday
- Last seven days
- This week
- Last week

- Last 30 days
- This month (this is my default setting)
- Last month
- Year to date
- Lifetime

I regularly check my daily stats and month-to-date numbers to get a clearer picture of how my ads are performing. These date ranges are flexible, so try experimenting with them to find which ones provide you with the most helpful information.

What I'm always watching is my total ad spend versus sales. The goal is to ensure that I'm making more than I'm spending. For example, if you earn $3 for every book sold and manage to sell ten books from one ad, you'll need to pay $30 to break even. If you're earning $30 but spending $40, you're losing money. On the other hand, if you spend only $10 but earn $30 or $40 in return, your ad is doing well, and you might consider increasing the budget to scale up those profits.

To explain things further, let me give you two examples of how I monitor my ads:

Let's say I have an ad for a fiction book set to target specific keywords. I set my cost-per-click at 21 cents, and the ad is getting a lot of clicks. However, I'm not seeing any sales from those clicks. Each click costs me 21 cents, but I have no book sales or KENP page reads to show for it. Since this is a fiction book, I'd be concerned and would consider turning off the ad if, after two weeks, there are still little to no sales.

However, if the same ad was for one of my nonfiction books, I might leave it running. This is because even though that particular book isn't selling, I might see a spike in sales for one of my other books. For example, if I run an ad for 101 ITEMS TO SELL ON EBAY that isn't generating sales, but I notice an increase in sales for my BEGINNER'S GUIDE TO SELLING ON EBAY, I might guess that the ad is helping boost sales for my other books. I could test this theory by pausing the advertisement for a while to see if my sales for the other book drop.

Unfortunately, Amazon doesn't tell you if someone clicked on an ad for one of your books but ended up buying a different one. Regardless, a sale is a sale! The only way I can guess if a specific ad is leading to other sales is to turn the ad off temporarily and watch for changes in sales.

As more people self-publish, the cost-per-click rates have continued to increase, with the average CPC now around $0.50 to $1. This means that your bidding strategies need to be more calculated. Low bids may not get you many impressions, but starting at 30 cents per click is still a safe way to test campaigns, especially for fiction or niche nonfiction.

Now, let's say the ad is working well, and people are buying the book I'm advertising. I can tell this because I'm earning more in royalties than the ad is costing me. Suppose the ad is doing really well, and my $5 daily budget is being fully used. In that case, I might decide to increase the budget, hoping that the additional spending will lead to more sales.

Now, let's look at a different ad type, one where I'm targeting categories. Suppose I set up an ad for my BEGINNER'S GUIDE TO YOUTUBE book, targeting the Social Media book category. If the impressions are very low, Amazon will not be showing the ad to customers. This could be because Amazon doesn't think my ad is relevant to the category or because my bid is too low. It's usually the latter, so this is when I would go into the ad and increase my bid to be more competitive.

Upping your budget: Once a book has started selling and has gathered some reviews, I often increase my advertising by running multiple ads with different targets. For example, with 101 ITEMS TO SELL ON EBAY, I might run one ad targeting the Antiques and Collectibles category, another focusing on

E-commerce, and a third aimed at Home-Based Business categories.

Just like with Keywords, you can choose a Custom bid or cost-per-click for Product targeting. Again, I recommend starting with a low bid and then monitoring the ad to see how it performs. You can always adjust your bids later. This approach is known as the "low and slow" method for running KDP ads.

One advantage of targeted ads over keyword ads is that the cost-per-click is usually lower. I've had difficulty keeping keyword bids below 50 cents for my nonfiction books. Still, I've been able to run successful category-targeted ads with bids as low as 20 cents.

Running ads for low-content books can be trickier since these books are usually priced lower and don't sell as frequently as fiction or nonfiction books. If you're advertising a notebook priced at $5.99, you probably won't want to spend more than 10 cents per click. Unfortunately, it's tough to find keyword bids that low on Amazon. That's why I rarely run ads for no-content books like notebooks and blank journals. Instead, I focus on my higher-priced, low-content guided journals and adult coloring books, where I can afford slightly higher bids, though still lower than for my nonfiction titles.

Regardless of your bidding strategy, give the ad time to perform before making any changes. It's tempting to stop an ad after a day or two, especially if you're spending money without seeing immediate results, but patience is vital.

So why wait? While Amazon will start displaying your ad within a few hours of activation, their reporting tends to lag. Most authors agree that you should let an ad run for at least two weeks before tweaking it, as it can take that long for Amazon to provide enough data. Some even suggest waiting six weeks to get a complete sense of the ad's performance.

Impressions are important: If an ad is not getting many

Impressions overall, you might want to consider increasing the bids for each keyword or target. But what if some keywords or targets are getting Impressions while others aren't? You have two choices: either disable the underperforming keywords/targets altogether or disable them and create new ads using just those keywords/targets to test them further.

Remember, Amazon wants to make money from ads but also from book sales. It's in their best interest for your ads to be successful. If you have an ad where specific keywords are generating Impressions and sales, that's great! In that case, you'll want to focus on those winning keywords by disabling the ones that aren't working.

However, that doesn't mean the underperforming keywords/targets are useless. They might just be overshadowed by the more successful ones in that particular ad. It can be worth taking those underperformers and creating a separate ad to focus on them. You can easily do this by turning off the weak keywords/targets and copying them into a new ad.

This strategy has worked for me on several occasions. In fact, I've seen cases where the keywords Amazon wasn't using much in the first ad performed better in a new, separate ad. As I mentioned earlier, it's common to start ads with hundreds of keywords. Still, as you refine your strategy, you'll want to trim that down to a more manageable number—ideally, less than fifteen. Turning off underperforming keywords and creating new ads is all part of the process you'll go through when running Amazon Ads.

ACOS: Another essential piece of data that Amazon provides advertisers with is **ACOS** or **Advertising Cost of Sales**. This metric is displayed both on the main campaign page and within each ad.

When reviewing the ACOS on the main campaign page, you're looking at the combined data for all your keywords and targets.

Ideally, you want ads with the lowest ACOS percentage, as that shows you're getting the best return on your investment. A general rule is that anything over 50% indicates you're losing money on that ad.

However, sometimes ads with a higher ACOS are worth keeping on. They may be driving traffic to your other books. For instance, I often run ads for one of my books about selling on eBay, but if the ACOS is higher than 50% for that ad, I look at my overall sales. If I see an increase across all my eBay books, it suggests that people may have found my other titles because of that ad. In such cases, even if I'm losing a little money on that specific ad, I'll keep it running because it helps increase my overall income.

Amazon also provides ACOS data for each keyword or target within an ad. I often find some keywords have an extremely low ACOS, meaning they're performing well. On the flip side, other keywords or targets may show an ACOS of over 50%, meaning they aren't working as effectively. When that happens, I usually turn off those keywords/targets and focus on the ones that show lower ACOS percentages.

Search Terms: Another valuable piece of data Amazon provides within individual ads is **Search Terms**. When you click on a specific ad, you'll find **Search Terms** listed in a column on the left-hand side of the page. Clicking on **Search Terms** will show you the exact terms customers typed into Amazon's search bar, which led them to see your ad and click on it.

For example, one of my eBay book ads might reveal that a customer searched for "thrift store reselling." Since I had "thrift" as a keyword, Amazon displayed my ad. If I notice that this search term led to a sale, I might consider adding it as a permanent keyword in the ad or even creating a new ad with that exact term. To add it to the existing ad, I simply check the box next to the search term, which brings up the **Add as keyword** icon. Clicking this will immediately add the search term to the ad's list of targets.

On the flip side, if I see that specific search terms are generating clicks but not sales (thus wasting my ad spend), I can click on those terms and add them to the **Negative keywords** list. This will help ensure that Amazon stops using those search terms in future ad displays, saving you money and helping your ad perform better.

Bottom Line: Amazon Ads are one of the trickiest parts of self-publishing. These ads can certainly work but perfecting them takes time and experimentation. Start with a $5 ad and be prepared to lose a little money as you figure out which methods work best for your books.

A common piece of advice, especially for new authors on Amazon KDP, is to go "low and slow" with Amazon Ads. This means setting your bids low and letting them run for a more extended period to gather data. The idea is to test what works without burning through your budget too quickly.

However, as you gain more experience with ads, you might try the opposite approach—setting your bids higher to get quicker data. While this will cost more upfront, it allows you to see faster which keywords and targets are most effective.

Every author has lost money on advertising; it's part of the business. However, with the tips and tricks in this chapter, I hope you can avoid some of the costly mistakes I made when I first started with Amazon Advertising. Start small with one ad to test the waters, and over time, you'll learn what works best for your specific books.

CHAPTER NINETEEN: USING A+ CONTENT TO SELL MORE BOOKS

If you've ever browsed Amazon and clicked on a product listing, you may have noticed some listings with large, visually rich sections in the middle of the page—essentially advertisements for the product. This is called **A+ Content**, and it's a feature you can add to your book product pages.

When looking at a fiction or non-fiction book listing on Amazon from a desktop (not a mobile device), you'll typically see a "Look Inside" feature above the book cover. This feature allows shoppers to preview the first few pages, helping them understand what the book is about and decide whether to purchase it. Think of it like browsing in a bookstore—you wouldn't just grab a book off the shelf and head to checkout. You'd likely flip through the pages and read the back cover before making a decision. The "Look Inside" feature serves the same purpose for online shoppers.

However, the "Look Inside" feature is often missing from books with no and low content, such as notebooks, journals, planners, and activity books. A few years ago, Amazon removed this feature from these books, although some titles published before the change may still have it. If you're publishing these types of books now, keep in mind that customers won't be able to preview the interior pages, which can severely limit your ability to make sales.

That's where A+ Content comes in. While some fiction and non-fiction authors use A+ Content to really "sell" their book by providing additional graphics, quotes, and recommendations, the best use of A+ Content is for no-and-low content books. It allows publishers to show customers photos of the inside pages, which is crucial for these types of books.

Amazon provides templates to create A+ Content, but it's up to the authors to produce the images. To see how A+ Content might work best for your books, start by checking out some listings in your category. However, not all book listings have A+ Content, so you might need to search around a bit to find good examples.

You can create one A+ Content project and apply it to multiple ASIN listings. For example, I have a line of genealogy-guided journals under my Jean Lee pen name. While there are different options for various family members (mom, dad, grandma, grandpa, etc.), the interior pages maintain a consistent look. I created one A+ Content project where I show examples of the pages, but I applied that same project to all 16 journals.

A book must be published before you can add A+ Content to it. To access the A+ Content dashboard, log into your Amazon KDP account and click on the **Marketing** tab at the top of the page. A+ Content is located in the middle of the page.

The steps to create A+ Content are as follows:

1. Under the **Marketing** tab in your Amazon KDP dashboard, scroll down to the A+ Content section.
2. Choose your **Marketplace** (Amazon.com for the American site).
3. Click on **Manage A+ Content** (you may have to log in a

second time for security purposes).

4. Click on the **Start Creating A+ Content** button.
5. Enter a **Content name** (this can be anything, but the field must be filled out).
6. Click on **Add Module**.
7. A pop-up window will appear with several different A+ modules from which to choose. You can add multiple modules within the same listing, but you'll need to work on them one at a time.
8. Clicking on each module will open a new window with the image specifications.
9. In this new window, you will also have the option to click **Add Module** again.
10. Continue adding modules until all your images are uploaded.
11. Use the up and down arrows to rearrange your modules.
12. Click on **Next: Apply ASINs**.
13. Go to your book listings on Amazon to find their ASINs (the ASIN is located where your book's rank is listed).
14. Copy and paste the ASINs for the books you want the A+ Content applied to.
15. Click on **Review & Submit**.
16. Click on **Submit for Approval**.

It can take Amazon up to seven days to approve A+ Content, but mine usually gets approved within 24 hours.

So, how do you actually create images for A+ content?

Just like Canva is excellent for designing book covers, I use it to create my A+ content as well. I make modules that incorporate both the book covers and images of the interior pages, especially for low-content books. Since I design all of my low-content book interiors, it's easy for me to add those images to the A+ modules.

When formatting images for A+ Content, here are the guidelines you need to follow (reworded from Amazon's requirements):

- **Image and text formatting:** You must use **jpg or png** file formats, and the images must be in **RGB color mode** (not CYMK). Each file must be **under 2 MB** in size, and the resolution should be at least **72 dpi**. **Animated images** (like GIFs) aren't allowed.
- Avoid using blurry, low-quality, **or watermarked** images or images with small text that would be hard to read on mobile devices.
- Your **image alt-text** needs to accurately describe the image, especially to help users with screen readers. If the description doesn't match or is vague, your content could be rejected.
- Make sure your images and text for A+ Content are **unique**. Don't reuse images that already appear in the product image gallery. A+ Content should show something **distinct** about your product.
- **Logos and icons:** Use only one **brand logo** and include icons that help the reader navigate through the text. As a self-published author, any logos you use should be ones you made or hired someone else to create.
- When it comes to text, **spell out numbers under 10**, use **consistent punctuation** (including serial/Oxford commas), and **capitalize each major word in a header**. Avoid mistakes like grammatical errors, overuse of bold/italic formatting, all-caps, or redundant information, as these could result in your content being rejected.
- Lastly, make sure the content is written in the language you've specified. **HTML tags** or text in another language are not allowed.

Amazon also has a list of things you **cannot** include in your A + Content, and it's important to follow these guidelines closely. Here's what you need to avoid:

- **Pricing or promotional details:** Don't include pricing, discounts, or promotional information in your A + Content. You should also avoid phrases like "affordable," "bonus," and "free" and direct calls to action like "buy now," "add to cart," or "get yours today."

- **Customer reviews:** You can't include customer reviews in your A+ Content. However, if you want to add editorial reviews, you can do so through Amazon Author Central by setting up an Author Page.

- **Time-sensitive language:** Avoid terms like "new," "latest," "on sale now," or any mention of holidays. This even includes references to Kindle Unlimited.

- **Publication quotes:** You can use a maximum of four quotes or endorsements, but they need to come from well-known publications or public figures. Be sure to include the author's name and, if it's from a publication, the title of the publication.

- **Guarantee information:** Any mention of off-Amazon return or refund policies is strictly not allowed in A+ Content.

- **KDP Terms and Content Guidelines:** You must follow Amazon's KDP Terms and Conditions and Content Guidelines at all times.

- **Shipping details and personal info:** Don't include mentions like "free shipping" or any personal info like phone numbers, email addresses, or physical addresses.

- **Quotes or attributions:** You can't use quotes from individuals or customers. However, you can use up to four quotes from recognized publications or public figures as long as you credit them properly.

- **Competitor references:** Don't reference or compare your book to competitors, whether by name or by

- **Comparison charts:** A comparison chart can only compare books in your KDP account.
- **Trademark and copyright symbols:** These are allowed only if they are part of your packaging or logo. You can't just add them wherever you want in the text.
- **Web links or redirects:** No links or mentions of external sites are allowed in A+ Content.
- **Prohibited content:** Amazon will not accept any content they deem offensive, which includes things like hate speech, content promoting child exploitation, pornography, or anything that glorifies rape, terrorism, or other inappropriate material.
- **Off-Amazon customer service:** You can't include phrases like "contact us if you have problems" or provide any phone numbers or email addresses for customer service outside of Amazon.
- **Amazon logos and references:** Don't try to mimic Amazon's logos or headings. However, you can reference Amazon-supported programs or branded products when relevant.

For low- and no-content books such as journals, planners, notebooks, and activity books, my favorite A+ Content module is the **Comparison Chart**. You may have seen this feature while shopping for products on Amazon—it's a section that shows several products side by side with a chart comparing them, such as dimensions or other details. The best part of this module is that you can click directly on the books to view them. Since Amazon no longer allows low-content books to be listed as a series, the Comparison Chart lets you showcase similar books with direct links.

For example, I have a series of school year-guided journals where kids can record memories for each year of school. While

Amazon won't let me group these into a series, I use the A + Content Comparison Chart to show the other available titles so customers can easily navigate between them. I also included another module with examples of the interior pages since these journals don't have the Look Inside feature. Without A + Content, customers wouldn't know what the inside of the journals looks like or what other grades are available.

UPDATE: In late 2024, Amazon updated the Comparison Chart guidelines, allowing only one chart per listing. I used to include two charts in some listings, as each chart only shows six books. For my school journals, for example, I used two charts to display all 12 titles. Now, I can only show six, so I list the high school journals on high school pages and use different modules for junior high and elementary school journals.

My advice for A+ Content is to focus on what your potential customers actually need. If you write fiction or non-fiction, customers can use the Look Inside feature to preview your book. They don't necessarily need additional images of text pages. However, they may want to know more about you as an author, so A+ Content could be used to share your author brand or promote your other books.

Check out other books in your category. Are bestsellers using A + Content? If so, it's probably a good idea to include it in your books as well. However, if they aren't, you can choose to skip A + Content for now and maybe come back to it later when you're more comfortable with the process.

For no- and low-content books that don't have the Look Inside feature, it's in your best interest to provide page examples. If you're selling coloring books, for instance, showing a few sample pages can help customers see what they're getting. The same goes for guided journals, planners, and other activity books. Since you create these types of books yourself, you can easily use a program like Canva to design sample pages for your modules.

While I hate to add another task to your plate, if you're producing low-content books without the Look Inside option, you'll need A+ Content to help drive sales. The good news is that you don't need to create a ton of modules—just a few page examples can make a huge difference. And if your books have a consistent look, you can reuse the same modules across multiple listings.

Finally, Amazon has a comprehensive A+ Content section within the KDP dashboard. Under the A+ Content section in the Marketing tab, you'll find tutorials and examples that can help you create modules to boost your sales!

CHAPTER TWENTY: PUBLISHING ON PLATFORMS OTHER THAN AMAZON

Suppose you've decided to opt into Amazon's KDP Select program for Kindle Unlimited subscribers. In that case, your eBooks must remain exclusive to Amazon. This means you cannot sell your eBooks on any other websites—not even your own. However, if you're not in Kindle Select, you have the freedom to sell your eBooks on any platform, including your own website. Additionally, Kindle Select's exclusivity doesn't apply to paperback or hardcover books, so you're free to sell those on other platforms as well as on Amazon.

Selling books on sites other than Amazon is often referred to as "going wide." While Amazon is the largest bookseller in the U.S., there are different platforms where indie authors can self-publish and where customers regularly buy books.

In previous editions of this book, I've discussed several options for self-publishing outside of Amazon. However, this year, I'm excited to highlight one site that has become both easy and free to use for publishing eBooks and paperbacks: **Draft2Digital**.

For years, Draft2Digital was the go-to platform for self-publishing eBooks outside of Amazon. Since merging with Smashwords, they now offer a full range of publishing services, including fiction, non-fiction paperbacks, and even low-content books.

Before this merger, many self-published authors turned to **IngramSpark** to publish their paperback books. While IngramSpark remains a viable option with a dedicated user base, in my opinion, Draft2Digital has emerged as the best choice for new indie authors looking to publish paperbacks. IngramSpark has always been more complex to navigate, and it requires payment to publish a book. Furthermore, IngramSpark isn't a traditional publishing platform; instead, it's a printing company. You don't earn royalties from IngramSpark—you earn commission payouts based on the number of book orders Ingram fulfills from bookstores and libraries.

Draft2Digital distributes eBooks to the following websites:

- Amazon (if you aren't already published there; if you are, just deselect Amazon so a second listing of your book won't appear)
- Apple Books
- Barnes & Noble
- Kobo
- Smashwords Store
- Tolino
- OverDrive
- cloudLibrary
- Everand
- Baker & Taylor
- Hoopla
- Vivlio

- BorrowBox
- Odilo
- Palace Marketplace
- Gardners

You might be surprised to see Amazon on that list! Some authors choose to sell their books on Amazon through Draft2Digital because the royalty payout can be higher. For example, a book priced at $4.99 directly on Amazon will earn you 70% royalties. However, if you sell the same book through Draft2Digital, you could earn 85% royalties.

Paperback books are also distributed through all the sales channels listed above, including independent bookstores and libraries.

If your eBook is already published on Amazon, Draft2Digital will automatically detect it and prevent the listing from being duplicated. Additionally, if your book is enrolled in KDP Select, Draft2Digital will catch that as well and won't publish your book to avoid violating Amazon's exclusivity terms.

Do you have to publish your book to all the websites Draft2Digital distributes to? No, you can select the sites where you want your eBook to appear. However, there's really no reason not to pick them all, as it increases your book's visibility.

Publishing your eBooks on Draft2Digital is incredibly easy—actually, it's even easier than Amazon's process. To start, you'll need to create an account at Draft2Digital.com. Like Amazon, you'll be required to enter your financial information so you can get paid. Draft2Digital doesn't withhold taxes from your earnings, but it will report your earnings to the IRS. This means you'll also need to complete a tax interview, where you'll provide your Social Security number.

There is no up-front cost to publish your eBooks on

Draft2Digital. Authors generally earn around 60% in royalties for eBooks. For print books, indie authors make about 45% of the list price minus the base printing cost. Each platform Draft2Digital distributes to has its own fee structure, so your royalties will vary depending on where your book is sold. And while Draft2Digital's royalty payouts are lower than Amazon's, the platform's ease of use and the ability to publish for free makes it a strong choice for many authors.

One of Draft2Digital's best features is how easy it is to upload your manuscript. Draft2Digital currently accepts Word Doc and Docx files, ODT, Rich Text documents, and pre-formatted ePub files. If you've already formatted a Word document for Amazon, you can upload that file directly to Draft2Digital. Just make sure to upload the Word file, not the Kindle Create version.

Draft2Digital will convert your document into an eBook file, allowing you to double-check the formatting and make changes before your book goes live. You can play around with fonts, type styles, line spacing, and extra features within the program. And if you get stuck, their customer service is excellent and responsive.

For eBook covers, Draft2Digital accepts files in .jpeg format, ideally measuring 1600x2400 pixels. However, they state, "All we really need is a tall rectangle." For paperback books, the cover files need to be either in PDF or PNG format. If you've created your covers on Canva, you should be able to upload those duplicate files to Draft2Digital. Once uploaded, the platform will guide you through adding text for the spine and back cover.

Just like Amazon, Draft2Digital offers free ISBNs for the books you publish there. However, it's always better to purchase your ISBNs outright from a site like Bowker.com. Different ISBNs on the same book can cause them to show up as separate versions on Amazon.

You may wonder if Draft2Digital is so easy to use that

you should skip Amazon altogether and publish only there. However, there are two big reasons why Amazon should still be your first choice. First, Amazon is the largest platform for book shoppers by far. Second, you have more control over your author brand on Amazon, with features like an author page, the ability to run ads and detailed sales data.

Draft2Digital pays out royalties once a month and offers four payment options: check, PayPal, direct deposit, or Payoneer. They also provide tax forms at the end of the year to help you accurately report your royalties.

Keep in mind that each of Draft2Digital's store partners has its own policy for royalty releases. Like Amazon, Draft2Digital generally pays you 60 days after the end of the sales month. For instance, royalties earned in January will be paid out at the end of March. You'll receive individual sales reports from each partner site as well as a combined monthly total from all platforms.

Other Self-Publishing Platforms: While Amazon and Draft2Digital are the only platforms I currently use to upload new books, there are other options you might want to explore.

IngramSpark: While Amazon dominates the eBook market, IngramSpark (often referred to simply as Ingram) is the largest distributor of self-published paperback and hardcover books outside of Amazon. They distribute to over 40,000 retailers and libraries worldwide. However, unlike Amazon or Draft2Digital, publishing with IngramSpark comes at a cost, and the platform is known for having a more challenging interface, making the process of uploading files difficult. For these reasons, many indie authors, including myself, now prefer Draft2Digital, which also supports paperback books, including low-content ones. Note that IngramSpark does not allow print-on-demand (POD) books like journals, planners, or notebooks—only fiction and non-fiction titles.

The most significant difference with IngramSpark is that you have to pay to distribute your book through their platform. It costs $49 to publish each physical book. Since IngramSpark only prints copies when a retailer or library orders them, there's no guarantee you'll make back that initial investment.

This upfront cost often deters authors from using IngramSpark for physical books. And with Draft2Digital's increasing support for paperbacks (and expected lower costs), it may be worth considering waiting or using Draft2Digital instead.

Another hurdle with IngramSpark is that most bookstores won't purchase books that cannot be returned. Many self-published authors can't afford to offer returns because enabling that option means covering the cost of not just printing but also shipping to and from bookstores.

Why not enable returns? It boils down to the cost. If bookstores order your books in bulk but don't sell them, they can return the unsold stock. But as the author, you bear the total cost of those returns—both the printing and the shipping fees. You're responsible for reimbursing the store for what they paid and covering the shipping costs both ways. You can choose to have the unsold books shipped back to you, but you never know what condition they'll be in.

For this reason, most self-published authors do *not* enable returns on IngramSpark, which makes it challenging to get their books into bookstores. Even top-selling self-published authors struggle to get bookstores to carry their books if they can't guarantee returns.

Lulu: Before Draft2Digital began supporting low-content books, many self-publishers turned to Lulu.com. Lulu allows you to publish your books for print-on-demand (POD) sales on their website and order your own printed copies to sell yourself. Lulu has been especially popular for no-and-low content books, which IngramSpark doesn't print, and it offers some options that Amazon doesn't provide.

On Lulu, you can create a variety of products, including:

- Print Books
- Photo Books
- Notebooks
- Calendars
- Comic Books
- Magazines
- Cookbooks
- Yearbooks
- eBooks

You can publish both paperback and hardcover books, and Lulu boasts over 3,000 possible formatting, color, and size combinations. One big draw for Lulu is the ability to create spiral-bound books, which are popular for notebooks and planners. You can sell directly on Lulu's website, and you can also order bulk cases of your books to sell on your own.

I recommend Lulu for authors who are already full-time in the no-and-low content book market. Suppose you've successfully built a brand of notebooks, journals, planners, or activity books on Amazon. In that case, it might be worth expanding to Lulu for additional sales on their platform.

However, like IngramSpark, uploading your books to Lulu involves fees. Although you can sell your books on the Lulu.com bookstore, the customer base is smaller compared to Amazon or Draft2Digital.

Lulu offers many customization options, particularly for no-and-low content books. However, because of the costs and smaller customer reach, it may not be the best option for most authors. If you've built a larger brand or want to print products to sell yourself, Lulu is a strong choice for printing large quantities at a reasonable price.

Blurb: Blurb is a self-publishing platform that emphasizes visual and design-heavy books, such as photography books, cookbooks, planners, journals, and even magazines and notebooks. Blurb also offers spiral-bound books, which is a great option for those who create planners and notebooks. You can sell your books directly on Blurb's website, and the platform also offers distribution through Amazon, Ingram, and other retailers.

BookBaby is another self-publishing platform that offers a wide range of services to indie authors. BookBaby provides everything from book design, formatting, editing, and distribution to both eBooks and print books. However, these services come at a high cost. Unlike platforms like Amazon or Draft2Digital, where you can publish for free and only pay a portion of your royalties, BookBaby has significant upfront fees for services.

Selling Directly To Customers: Some successful indie authors decide to sell their books directly to readers via their own websites. Platforms like GoDaddy, Shopify, and Wix offer user-friendly tools to create e-commerce websites where you can sell both digital versions of your books and paperback copies. However, selling paperback books directly means you'll need to either link your store to a POD (Print On Demand) site like Lulu.com or order copies in bulk and handle the shipping yourself.

Setting up a direct-selling website is a lot of work. Not only do you need to build and maintain the website, but you also have to create and manage the digital files for your eBooks, as well as establish a system for delivering these files to your customers. For paperback sales, you'll be responsible for order fulfillment, which includes packing and shipping books yourself or coordinating with a POD service.

Another important consideration is handling taxes. Unlike Amazon, which collects and remits sales tax for authors, if you sell directly, you will be responsible for collecting and remitting sales tax in the states where it is required. Since almost every state in the U.S. requires sales tax collection on orders placed by residents, the bookkeeping involved is a significant undertaking and may deter many authors from direct selling.

That said, it is possible to sell directly to customers. However, it's something to consider only after you've built a successful publishing business on Amazon and have established a large reader base. Direct selling is best suited for authors who have the infrastructure and customer following to support this additional layer of business complexity.

CHAPTER TWENTY-ONE: MAKING MONEY WITH NO-AND-LOW CONTENT BOOKS

Now that we've covered the basics of self-publishing fiction and nonfiction books—both as eBooks and paperbacks—it's time to shift our focus to another lucrative category: print-on-demand (POD) journals, planners, notebooks, and activity books, also known as no-content and low-content books.

While we've touched on no-and-low-content books throughout this guide, this chapter is fully dedicated to explaining how to research, design, upload, and promote these types of books to make money on Amazon.

As you may recall from earlier, when you upload a new book in your KDP dashboard, the default option is to create a Kindle eBook, followed by the paperback and hardcover options. Most authors follow this route—publishing the Kindle version first, then adding the paperback and hardcover editions to the same listing.

But here's something you might not know you don't have to publish a Kindle version at all! In fact, many books on Amazon are available only in paperback because they contain little to no text. These are your no-and-low-content books, which Amazon prints on demand—meaning they're only produced when a customer orders them. That's why they're called POD (Print-On-Demand) books. Believe it or not, there are people who make a full-time living just by selling these types of books!

Although all paperback books on Amazon are technically POD, the term is more often used to describe books like journals, planners, and activity books with little or no interior text.

So, to keep things simple, we'll refer to these as POD books from here on out.

The market for POD (Print-On-Demand) books has exploded in recent years, especially on platforms like Amazon and Etsy. Unlike traditional fiction or nonfiction books, these types of products don't require extensive writing or months of drafting and editing. Instead, you focus on creating ideas for journals, planners, notebooks, and activity books to sell.

Just like Amazon requires an interior (pages) file and a cover file for regular paperbacks, the same process applies to POD books. In fact, you upload these using the same "Paperback" option in your KDP dashboard as you would for fiction or nonfiction books. The only difference is that there's no Kindle version of these books.

There are four main types of POD books that people typically create and upload on Amazon:

Journals: Journals can range from no-content (blank or lined pages) to low-content (some text included). Guided journals, which contain question prompts for people to answer, fall under the low-content category. Journals come in various sizes, with 6x9 inches being the most popular. Larger options, like 8x10 or 8.5x11, are also common for those who prefer more writing space.

Planners: Planners can be designed for different timeframes—

daily, monthly, yearly, or even perpetual (undated). They may follow a typical calendar year or an academic year (July to June), and some planners cover two years. At a minimum, planners include calendar pages, but you can add other elements like contacts, lists, goals, and more. Sizes vary from pocket-sized planners to larger 8.5x11-inch ones. However, the most popular size is 6x9 inches, especially as gift items around the holidays.

Notebooks: Notebooks are usually no-content, meaning their pages are either blank, lined, or have grids or blocks for writing. Like planners and journals, they come in different sizes. Sketchbooks also fall into this category. Composition notebooks (7x10 inches) are trendy on Amazon, while full-size notebooks are typically 8.5x11 inches. Some people prefer smaller, purse-sized notebooks around 5x7 inches for on-the-go use.

Activity Books: A rapidly growing category in the low-content space is activity books for both children and adults. This includes puzzle books, coloring books, and educational workbooks. Although these require more effort and skill to create compared to planners and notebooks, the audience for these books is much larger. Plus, you can often price activity books higher than simple notebooks.

So, what makes self-published planners, journals, notebooks, and activity books so successful on Amazon? Aren't there already large companies producing these items?

The answer is yes—big brands like Hallmark and Mead create tons of stationery products, and traditional publishing houses release a variety of activity books. You've likely seen word search or crossword puzzle books produced by large publishers near the checkout at grocery stores. However, what these companies lack is variety in niche designs and themes.

You might visit an office supply store and find an entire aisle dedicated to planners. Still, while the colors and sizes vary, they're all pretty standard. Most are plain or come in basic patterns. Even stores like Hobby Lobby and Michaels, which offer a wider range of fun planners and accessories, only release a limited number of styles each year.

That's where self-published authors can truly stand out with POD products. Whether you're creating fiction, nonfiction, or low-content books, the key to success is tapping into underserved niches. Big brands can't always cater to niche markets, so there's room for you to offer more specific, unique designs that fill that gap on Amazon.

Instead of producing generic notebooks with plain designs, you want to create items that cater to particular groups. For instance:

- A notebook for nursing students who also enjoy hiking in their free time
- A planner for someone following a plant-based diet who loves traveling to national parks
- A guided journal for retired military veterans living in Arizona
- A guided journal for a newly single woman who enjoys gardening and birdwatching
- A notebook for high school students where a falcon is the school mascot
- A notebook featuring the names of popular beach towns in California
- A coloring book with illustrations of adorable sloths
- A crossword puzzle book for people who enjoy camping in the Rocky Mountains

Many creators uploading POD products to Amazon are focused on producing *a high volume* of items. We're talking about hundreds, even thousands, of notebooks, often using the same interior pages but switching up the covers. The strategy here is all about quantity rather than quality. With so many different products available, these sellers are able to capture a variety of customer interests, which naturally leads to consistent sales over time.

However, this approach of mass uploads has led to a significant oversaturation of low-content books on Amazon. Much like when Amazon addressed the surge of short eBooks taking advantage of the Kindle Select program, in late 2023, they introduced a new policy limiting the number of books you can upload per day.

Previously, there was no cap, and you could publish as many books as you wanted. Now, Amazon restricts new uploads to just three per day per account. This change was largely in response to the growing use of artificial intelligence (AI) tools like ChatGPT and MidJourney, which some creators were using to quickly generate books, both in text and images. This new limit makes it even more essential to focus on creating high-quality books. Personally, I view this as a positive step because it curbs the flood of low-quality uploads, helping customers discover well-crafted books more easily.

I've always prioritized quality over quantity, and this limit plays to that strength. While some may have relied on mass uploads, I prefer crafting longer nonfiction books and putting more effort into creating well-designed POD products. By focusing on creating books that I personally enjoy, not only do I find more satisfaction in the process, but I also create products that have broader appeal to customers.

Maybe you're into gardening. Think about all the different types of gardens people maintain—from vegetable and flower gardens to hydroponics and indoor herb gardens. What kinds of tools and knowledge do gardeners need? You could create specialized journals for people to track their plant growth, planners for seasonal garden tasks, or notebooks specifically designed for documenting their favorite plant varieties. Creating word searches or crossword puzzle books that include gardening terms could be a unique product idea for that niche.

If you're a music lover, explore the wide range of instruments and musical styles people are passionate about. While guitar and piano might come to mind first, there are also many other instruments like the violin, saxophone, or even the harp. You could create practice planners for different instruments, journals for aspiring songwriters to jot down lyrics, or themed notebooks for orchestra members. Music teachers, students, and enthusiasts alike would appreciate these niche products.

Animals, pets, food, academics, music, movies, TV shows, leisure activities, health, fitness, and travel—these categories already have an established presence on Amazon and are fantastic topics for creating your own POD products. The key is to get creative and brainstorm unique ideas that align with these popular themes.

One of the best ways to gather inspiration and see what's already out there is by browsing Amazon for existing POD products. It's important to differentiate what large stationery companies produce from what independent creators are offering. Here's a simple way to start:

Head to Amazon and type in "planners," "journals," or "notebooks" into the search bar. Let's use "planners" for this example.

When you search "planners," you'll notice a massive number of results, including many from office supply categories. But if you look under the "Department" filter, select "Books," and you'll narrow the results down to book-style planners. Now you're likely to see over 70,000 results—don't panic!

Next, to further refine your search for self-published products, click on "Paperback" under the "Book Format" section. Self-published planners on Amazon KDP aren't spiral bound, so focusing on paperbacks will weed out many of the big-name stationery brands that typically use spiral binding.

From there, you can further refine your search by clicking "English" under the "Book Language" filter and selecting "Last 30 days" under "New Releases" to focus on what has recently been uploaded. While the overall product count may remain high, what you're left with will mostly be self-published books, giving you insight into what's currently trending.

Finally, for some fun research, try searching for niche ideas like "alpaca yoga planner" or "avocado recipe notebook." You'll notice that most results are from self-publishers, which shows the wide variety of unique ideas others are exploring.

But how can you tell if these products are actually selling? One quick trick is to adjust the way search results are displayed. In the upper right-hand corner of the search results, you'll find the "Sort by" option. Select "Avg. Customer Review" from the dropdown menu, and Amazon will sort the listings based on the best-rated items. Typically, the books with the highest number of positive reviews are the ones generating the most sales.

That said, just because a book doesn't have any reviews doesn't mean it isn't selling. Many of my own POD books, some without a single review, sell regularly. As I mentioned earlier, most Amazon customers don't leave reviews, even for products they love. For example, I recently sold 30 copies of a journal I published back in 2020, which still has zero reviews. While reviews can be a helpful indicator, the length of time a product has been available on Amazon will likely affect whether or not it has reviews.

Another good sign of how well a product is selling is to check the categories it's listed under. If you don't see any categories mentioned, the product may not have sold yet. But if there are two or three categories with rankings, it means at least one sale has been made. The lower the number, the better the product will rank on Amazon.

To dig deeper into how POD products are performing, you

might want to invest in software like Publisher Rocket, which I've mentioned before. Publisher Rocket's Competition Analyzer feature helps you see how books are selling by searching for various keywords. This tool can help you identify categories worth targeting. You can check it out at PublisherRocket.com.

For example, a quick search for "2024 Planner" might show results ranging from books making only a few dollars a month to others pulling in thousands. By looking at the high earners, you can find inspiration for your own products, targeting niches that aren't yet fully served.

Just remember—you don't want to replicate someone else's work. Instead, focus on gaps in the market where your unique product can fill a need. For example, while there's already a sea of planners for nurses, teachers, and moms, exploring other professions or hobbies could reveal untapped opportunities.

Publishing humorous or sarcastic versions of traditionally serious planners is a proven strategy for success. Funny, tongue-in-cheek products have a huge following. With Publisher Rocket, I've seen examples like a "Teacher Misery Planner" pulling in close to $30,000 a month. Often, the inside pages of these planners are simple and functional; it's the catchy or witty covers that drive the sales. You can use one basic interior and then focus your creative efforts on designing multiple covers. Humorous covers are especially effective during the fourth quarter when people are on the lookout for unique and amusing gifts.

If you want to succeed in selling POD products, thinking outside the box is essential. It's all about finding those unique, underserved niches. In fact, research is likely to take up more of your time than the actual creation process. I recommend keeping a notebook handy to jot down ideas whenever inspiration strikes—you never know when it will hit!

Tracking down self-published POD books on Amazon can

be a little tricky since they are mixed in with traditional publications. But there are a few clues to help you spot them. First, most self-published POD books are only available in paperback, as Amazon doesn't yet allow most users to produce spiral-bound or hardcover books (though they are beta-testing hardcover options).

Secondly, the covers of self-published POD products tend to be simpler, often relying more on text than intricate graphics. Once you become familiar with the POD world, you'll start recognizing self-published books just from their cover designs.

Lastly, click on the author's name and are directed to their author page. You'll often see multiple similar books that vary only by cover design. This is another strong indicator that the books are self-published. It's also worth noting that many POD publishers use different pen names for different niches. As I've shared before, I use multiple pen names for my various nonfiction, fiction, and POD books. Many publishers create even more pen names, dedicating one to their teacher-themed planners and another to, say, cat-themed notebooks.

Just like you want to create a recognizable brand for your nonfiction and fiction books, the same idea applies to POD products—especially when dealing with niche markets like political or religious items, which might not appeal to everyone. Amazon doesn't restrict how many pen names self-publishers can use, so it's a good opportunity to keep your pen names aligned with the specific genres you're publishing.

For my own work, I use a separate pen name for my POD products, keeping them distinct from my fiction and nonfiction books. While you might think that putting all my books under one name would help sales, I've found that it could actually hurt my business. Customers who buy my eBay guides might not understand why I also sell notebooks with cat-themed covers, leading to confusion.

It's a good idea to start by focusing on one niche and building a brand around it before expanding into other areas. For example, if you're thinking about creating adult coloring books, you could launch a pen name dedicated to that niche, develop an Amazon Author Page, and set up a dedicated Facebook page for it. Then, if you decide to create a series of religious-themed guided journals, you could launch a separate pen name and brand for that, complete with its own social media presence. This way, you keep your products well-organized and cater to the right audience without alienating potential customers.

Creating POD Products: Similar to how you need both interior and cover files when uploading nonfiction and fiction paperbacks to Amazon, the same applies to POD products. Since these are physical books that customers will write in, you'll need to put together the pages. Still, this process differs slightly from creating traditional books in Word. For planners, journals, notebooks, or activity books, you'll need more specialized programs to design your POD products. And, of course, there's a bit of a learning curve to creating these types of interiors.

POD Book Interiors: Creating a POD product means designing the interior pages for your book, which you'll then save as a PDF file. If you're comfortable with programs like Adobe, you might choose to design your interiors from scratch. But suppose you're looking for an easier option. In that case, you can also buy pre-made interiors or subscribe to a service that offers ready-to-use templates.

There are two main ways to get POD book interiors: You can buy individual pages or page sets from designers and assemble the files yourself, or you can subscribe to a service that provides both templates and tools to create and export your interiors as PDF files, ready for uploading to Amazon.

Several websites specialize in selling complete packages for POD products, including templates and the software needed to put the pages together. Two of the most popular sites for creating POD books are BookBolt and Tangent Templates.

BookBolt: This platform is packed with features to help you design and create POD books. It includes research tools, a cover creator, interior design tools, a drag-and-drop editor, over 1,200 fonts, and access to more than one million royalty-free images. It also has a range of puzzle templates you can use. Plans start at $9.99 per month, making it an affordable option for beginners. Plus, BookBolt offers a variety of free interior templates under its "Interior Wizard" section that you can download, even if you're not a subscriber. Some of the free interiors include:

- Birthday reminders
- Blank pages with page numbers
- Blood pressure log pages
- Body measurements tracker
- Career plan
- College-ruled notebook paper
- Comic book pages
- Daily planners
- Diabetes log pages
- Dot graph paper
- Dot line notebook paper
- Dream journal pages
- Finals planning tracker pages
- Fishing logbook pages
- Fitness calendar pages
- Food journal pages
- Graph paper
- Graph, picture, and notebook combination pages

- Gratitude journal pages
- Guest list wedding planner pages
- Guitar tabs pages
- Habit tracker pages
- Handwriting paper
- Hexagon paper
- House sitting pages
- Lined journal
- Mileage log pages
- Monthly planner pages
- Monthly to-do list
- Mood tracker
- Music sheets
- Numbered pages
- Online shopping tracker
- Password tracker pages
- Personal expense tracker pages
- Pet information pages
- And many more

The paid version of **BookBolt** offers even more downloadable options, including a variety of additional pages. There's also an add-on feature for creating activity books, puzzles, and coloring books. This opens up a whole new avenue for producing more complex and engaging POD products.

Beyond the templates, BookBolt allows you to select from several download options, including:

- No Bleed or Bleed
- Various book sizes, from 5x8 to 8.5x11

- Customizable page counts

Once you've selected the options that fit your project, you can download the file directly to your computer. From there, you can upload the file to Amazon, create your cover, and start selling your product.

For example, let's say you want to create a notebook. Using Book Bolt's **Interior Generator**, you would choose the **College-Ruled notebook paper**. You can select **Bleed**, set the size to **8.5x11**, and enter the **page count**—let's say 100 pages. Then, click **Download** and the PDF file for your 100-page notebook will be saved to your computer.

Once your file is ready, log into your Amazon account and click the yellow + **Create** button. On the second page of the listing, under **Manuscript**, click the yellow **Upload paperback manuscript** button, and select the PDF notebook file you just downloaded.

BookBolt also offers an **Interior Generator Pro**, which lets you create book interiors with up to **240 pages**. This tool allows you to combine multiple PDF files into a single book. For example, if you're working on a planner, you might have separate PDFs for calendar pages, contact logs, and to-do lists. With the Interior Generator, you can upload each of these PDFs and arrange the pages in the exact order you want. Once finished, you can download the entire interior as a single file and upload it directly to Amazon.

Another great feature of BookBolt is its **KDP Keyword Finder**, which is available to paid subscribers. This tool helps you find keywords to use in your listings and Amazon Ads, and it also shows you the competition level for each keyword. For example, I typed in "planner" and got 14 related keywords. The keyword "planner" had high competition, but "planner for" had low competition. So, I'd make sure to include the phrase "planner for" in my title, description, and keywords. I might also add phrases like "planner for women, moms, teachers, students" to target specific audiences.

The tool also shows frequently used keywords related to your search. For "planner," I saw the following:

- Planner daily planner
- Planner for
- The happy planner planners
- Budget planner
- Planner monthly planner
- Weekly planner

These frequent keywords provide insight into what customers are actively searching for. For example, "budget planner" appeared on the list, meaning people are regularly searching for budget planners. Now, while budget planners are common, you could carve out a niche with more targeted planners. How about a **budget planner for single moms** or **college students**? Or even a **budget planner for retirees**? By focusing on specific niches, you can help your planner stand out from the competition.

So, is BookBolt worth it? I recommend starting with their free interior pages to get comfortable with the different sizes and layouts available. If you like the platform and plan to create a variety of POD products, then BookBolt could be a worthwhile investment. They also offer video tutorials to help guide beginners through the book creation process.

You can learn more about BookBolt at **bookbolt.io**.

Tangent Templates: Tangent Templates is a user-friendly software suite designed specifically for creating no-and-low content books like planners, journals, and notebooks. For a one-time fee of **$59**, users gain lifetime access to a wide variety of templates that simplify the process of creating professional-looking interiors. This software is handy for indie authors looking to break into the print-on-demand (POD) market with minimal upfront costs.

Tangent Templates provides over **100 templates** with different types of interiors, ready for customization. These include everything from the most basic options, like **blank numbered pages** and **lined paper**, to more specialized templates, such as:

- **Dot grid paper** and **graph paper** for bullet journals
- **Sheet music** and **guitar tabs** for music-related products
- **Recipe pages** for cookbook journals
- **Sermon paper** and **habit trackers** for more niche categories
- **Knitting paper** and **gardening logs** for hobby-related planners

In addition to the wide range of templates, Tangent Templates allows users to export their projects as PDF files, which are perfectly formatted and ready to upload to Amazon KDP or other POD platforms.

For beginners and seasoned POD creators alike, Tangent Templates streamlines the design process, helping users create attractive and functional book interiors without having to start from scratch. If you're planning to create a diverse range of POD products, the templates offered by Tangent can save you time and provide professional results.

Tangent Template's **Dynamic Templates** feature is one of its best tools, especially for creating customized pages. With **Prompts**, you can build guided journals and other content-heavy pages where you'd like to include specific text prompts or questions. The **Planners** section offers flexibility, allowing you to design yearly, monthly, weekly, or daily planners with a wide range of font options and customizable features, making it perfect for creating unique planner products.

You can download pages in various trim sizes, from **5x8** to **8.5x11**, with options for **bleed** or **no bleed** to match your preferred print style. The **Interior Designer** tool gives you the ability to craft entirely custom pages—something I often use for my business planners, where I design several pages myself to create a tailored product.

The **Tangent Builder** tool is another standout feature. It allows you to assemble your books and export them as print-ready PDFs, which makes uploading to Amazon simple and fast.

Tangent Templates also comes with additional helpful features, such as the **KDP Helper**, which assists in figuring out interior and cover dimensions for your books, and the **Listing Helper**, which helps you generate titles and keywords for your listings.

Lastly, the **Category Explorer** is a useful tool for researching book categories. While I personally prefer Publisher Rocket's category search tool, Tangent's built-in explorer is a fine option, especially if you're just starting out and want to avoid investing in multiple programs.

For more information on Tangent Templates, visit templates.tangent.rocks.

BookBolt versus Tangent Templates: When it comes to choosing between **BookBolt** and **Tangent Templates**, I tend to favor Tangent Templates as the more user-friendly option, especially for those who are new to POD publishing. One of the biggest perks of Tangent Templates is its **one-time fee**, which makes it more affordable than BookBolt's monthly subscription. Plus, Tangent Templates comes with an active **Facebook community** and a **YouTube channel** where users can find tutorials, tips, and answers to their questions. This makes the learning curve easier for beginners.

That being said, many POD publishers ultimately decide to use **both programs** since each has its strengths. For example,

BookBolt's **research tools** and free templates are valuable for gaining experience in designing no-and-low content products. Even if you don't use BookBolt's free interiors for your final products, they provide a hands-on learning experience.

As for me, I use both programs, but I find myself using **Tangent Templates** more often. I began learning POD with Tangent, so my preference is somewhat biased. However, BookBolt's **keyword research tools** are handy for tracking competition and optimizing your product listings, which is an advantage that Tangent lacks.

Additional Websites for POD Content: You can also explore **Etsy** and **Creative Fabrica** to purchase pre-designed interiors. Both sites offer ready-to-upload template bundles and individual pages, including journal, notebook, and planner interiors similar to what BookBolt and Tangent provide. These sites are convenient for finding **activity book pages**, like those for adult coloring books, puzzle books, or other more intricate designs. For POD creators looking to expand their product offerings, these websites are treasure troves of creative options. If you subscribe to **Canva Pro**, you can also use their templates and design elements to create books.

Activity Books: Puzzle books, coloring books, and workbooks fall under the Activity Book category. These books are often more complex to produce than notebooks and journals, but the upside is that they have a much larger and more loyal customer base.

Activity books work similarly to fiction in that their audiences are always eager for new material. Just like avid fiction readers eagerly awaiting the next romance or thriller, puzzle enthusiasts and coloring book fans are always on the lookout for fresh content. For example, my father loved crossword puzzle books and could go through one quickly, meaning I was constantly buying him more.

The same applies to **adult coloring books**, which have become a growing trend. I'm a fan of adult coloring books myself and frequently buy new ones, which inspired me to start making my own. Coloring books for both kids and adults have a steady market, making them a fantastic option for print-on-demand (POD) creators.

While you can create these books from scratch, many designers purchase ready-made interiors from **graphic websites** and individual designers. Below are some software **programs and websites** that can help you create custom puzzles or coloring book pages:

- **BookBolt**: As discussed earlier, BookBolt offers more than just planner and notebook interiors. Their Puzzle Creation Software is available through their **Monthly Pro Plan**, priced at **$19.99 per month**.

- **Tangent Templates**: Recently, Tangent released a guide for creating coloring book pages using **MidJourney AI**. If you're interested, you can explore their Facebook page first before purchasing the course.

- **Canva**: If you're subscribed to **Canva Pro**, you can access various puzzle templates and coloring images that you can use in POD books. They have options for both children and adults.

- **Creative Fabrica**: Offering thousands of **puzzle and coloring book pages**, Creative Fabrica operates on a subscription basis, or you can purchase individual files. Just make sure that what you buy includes a **print-on-demand license**, allowing you to use the material for resale.

- **Fiverr**: If you don't want to create interiors yourself, you can hire a designer on Fiverr to do it for you. They'll create both **interiors** and **covers** for your activity books.

- **InstantMazeGenerator.com**: For just **$67**, this site allows you to create **custom maze puzzles** for both kids and adults.

- **UpWork**: Like Fiverr, **UpWork** allows you to hire freelancers to create your puzzle books or other activity book content.
- **WordUnscramble.io**: A free tool that lets you generate **word scramble** and **anagram puzzles** for your activity books.

POD Book Covers: Earlier in this book, we covered how to create covers for paperback books. The process for making covers for POD books like journals, planners, notebooks, and activity books is similar. However, one major difference is in the **sizes of** these products. While most nonfiction and fiction books are typically sized at **6x9 inches**, POD books often come in **larger sizes**, such as **7x10 inches** or **8.5x11 inches**. Though 6x9-inch POD books do exist, creating larger products can help yours stand out in an already crowded marketplace.

In addition to size, the **style of the covers** for POD products tends to be more visually creative compared to nonfiction and fiction books. For example, **vector graphics** (rather than photographs), **bold fonts**, **vibrant colors**, and **patterned backgrounds** are commonly used. This design approach helps planners, journals, and coloring books catch the attention of shoppers as they scroll through Amazon's listings. Considering the platform is flooded with new POD books daily, anything that makes your cover pop is a plus.

Once you start researching your competition, you will likely notice a sea of **6x9-inch POD books** with **plain black covers** and **white text**. These designs are often from publishers who rely on the **quantity over quality** approach. While this method can bring in sales if you have thousands of notebooks listed, Amazon's recent changes limiting uploads to **three books per day** will make it harder for sellers to flood the market with hundreds of simple designs. Because of this, you are focusing on **quality creative covers, which is now** more important than ever for standing out.

My Process: The best way for me to walk you through how to create print-on-demand products is by sharing my step-by-step method. Let's say I want to make a dog-themed pug planner. First, I log into **Tangent Templates** and browse their selection of planner pages to figure out what I want to include. If I want to add extra features, like sections for internet passwords and contacts, Tangent already has templates for those pages, so all I need to do is mix and match.

For this planner, I'd start by choosing the planner page styles I like—Tangent offers several options. In this case, I want to include a yearly calendar grid, a monthly calendar grid, and a weekly calendar grid. I download each of these files to my desktop, a process Tangent walks me through step by step, so it's pretty simple. If I catch an error, I can easily go back and re-download the corrected file.

Next, I use Tangent's **Builder** feature to combine these pages into a complete book. I upload each of the calendar pages I saved, and then I add any extras like password logs or contacts pages from their site. Once I'm happy with how everything looks, I select the size I want my planner to be. I prefer the larger **8.5x11-inch** size because it offers more writing space compared to the smaller 6x9-inch size. Then, I simply download the finished PDF file to my desktop—Tangent provides a handy download button for this.

Tangent also gave me the cover dimensions for the planner, which I downloaded along with the cover template. I open **Canva** and use the measurements provided to create the cover. From there, I can add commercial-use graphics I've purchased from sites like **Creative Fabrica**. I tweak the colors and fonts until the cover looks exactly how I want it to.

Using the cover template from Tangent helps me see exactly where everything will be on the printed book, including the spine. I center everything and adjust the placement of the text, so it's aligned properly on the spine and cover.

When it comes to POD books, text on the back cover isn't as common as it is for fiction and nonfiction. I usually leave the back cover blank for planners, notebooks, and basic journals. Still, I'll add some text for **guided journals** or **activity books**.

Once my cover is ready to go, I save it to my desktop and head over to **KDP** to upload my book. I click on the yellow **+Create** button, just as I do for a regular nonfiction or fiction book. The process is almost identical—you need to enter your title, subtitle, description, and keywords. On the second page of the setup, you upload your interior and cover files, just like with any other book.

Note: For low-and-no-content books, Amazon no longer offers free ISBNs. If you want your book to have an ISBN, you'll need to purchase one from **Bowker**. I usually skip the ISBN for simpler products like notebooks. Still, for higher-end products like **coloring books** or **guided journals**, I buy my own ISBNs so I can maintain ownership. ISBNs can be costly, but you can buy them in bulk, which saves you money in the long run.

Lastly, on the final setup page, I set the book's price. Since the POD market is competitive, it's essential to price these books lower than you would traditionally books. For basic notebooks, I usually start at **$4.99**, while more complex planners or journals might be priced between **$8.99 and $14.99**. It's important to look at the market and see what similar products are selling for. Once my book starts gaining reviews, I might increase the price gradually.

When I start selling, I often set a lower price to attract buyers. For example, I might start a notebook at **$4.99**, but if it starts selling and gets positive reviews, I'll bump it up to **$5.99** or **$6.99**. The same goes for planners—I might launch them at **$6.99**, but after gathering reviews, I might raise the price to

$9.99.

Printing Costs: Just like with fiction and nonfiction paperbacks, Amazon deducts the cost of printing your POD books from the sale price. This naturally affects your profit margins. The exact printing cost depends on the book's trim size and page count. For low-priced books, your royalties might be quite small after the printing costs and Amazon fees are deducted.

Amazon will show you the estimated earnings for each sale during the listing process, which helps you decide how to price your products. It's common to make only a dollar or two in royalties for no-and-low content books, so I usually focus on creating higher-quality journals and planners where I can charge a bit more.

Marketing & Advertising POD Books: The strategies I covered in earlier chapters about promoting your books through social media, Facebook ads, and Amazon Ads apply to your POD books, too. However, one big difference is your cost-per-click bid when running Amazon Ads. Because POD books are generally priced lower than fiction and nonfiction books, you'll need to keep your keyword bids low—typically around 10 cents or even less to start with.

I rarely advertise my basic notebooks or blank journals and tend only to run ads for planners around the holidays. However, I do run low-bid ads for coloring books that have gathered some reviews. For my guided journals, which are priced between $11.95 and $14.95, I can afford to bid a bit higher because the higher royalty payout makes it worthwhile. I've also had success running automated ads on these journals, as their strong sales history helps Amazon know where to place them to generate more sales.

POD as a Business: I view my POD products as a separate business from my fiction and nonfiction books. Even though they're all housed under the same Amazon KDP account and their royalties get lumped together, I use a different pen name for my POD books, and I maintain separate social media channels for them. For me, creating POD books is a more creative outlet than writing, and it's something I can work on when I need a break from my other projects.

Currently, my POD books account for roughly 20–25% of my total monthly royalties. Sales spike dramatically in the fourth quarter as many customers buy planners, journals, notebooks, and activity books as holiday gifts—December is by far my best-selling month. Plus, these products are evergreen, meaning I don't have to constantly update or re-release new versions. Once I upload them, they remain on Amazon indefinitely unless I choose to take them down.

POD is definitely a competitive space on Amazon. Still, with some thoughtful research and creativity, you can generate a steady stream of passive income from no-and-low content books. My only regret is that I didn't start making POD books sooner!

CHAPTER TWENTY-TWO: THE EMERGENCE OF AI

You've probably heard the term **artificial intelligence** (AI), which refers to the creation of machines or software that can perform tasks typically requiring human intelligence. This includes learning from experience, recognizing patterns, solving problems, understanding language, and making decisions.

Essentially, AI is about teaching computers to "think" and make decisions on their own, often by analyzing large amounts of data. While it's still in its early stages, AI is rapidly evolving and influencing many aspects of our daily lives.

AI systems use **algorithms** (step-by-step instructions) along with data to "learn" and improve over time. Several key techniques enable AI to function, including:

- **Machine learning**: Where computers analyze data to improve their performance.
- **Neural networks**: These are where algorithms are modeled after the human brain to recognize patterns.
- **Deep learning**: The most advanced form, using multiple layers of data processing to understand complex inputs.

While AI might seem like a brand-new invention, we've actually been using it for years. Examples include voice assistants like **Siri** and **Alexa** and content recommendations from platforms like **YouTube** based on what you've watched before.

The pros of AI are clear: it helps automate repetitive tasks, solves complex problems faster than humans, and analyzes vast amounts of data that would be impossible for a person to process. However, the cons include:

- The risk of AI taking over human jobs.
- Concerns about security.
- A lack of transparency in understanding exactly how AI systems make decisions.

For authors, AI presents both opportunities and challenges. On one hand, AI tools can drastically cut down on editing time and help streamline the writing process. On the other hand, some may attempt to rely on AI entirely to write books, causing fear about the potential for AI to replace human writers altogether. As a society, people worry that AI could eventually take over all the creative jobs traditionally performed by people.

However, there are two things I always remind myself about AI: First, AI only knows what we, as humans, have taught it. Second, humans are still better at most tasks than AI in many areas.

I remember when personal computers first came onto the market. I was excited about the technology, but others feared that computers would take over everyday life. Yet here we are in 2025, and computers have mainly served to help us, not replace us. We taught computers how to assist us, and the same is true for AI.

I once heard an interview with an AI expert who described AI as a helpful coworker—someone you can bounce ideas off of. This is exactly how I use AI as an author. AI doesn't write my books for me, but it helps me proofread and edit my work more intuitively than tools like Grammarly. While Grammarly is excellent for catching spelling and punctuation errors, AI excels at editing for clarity and flow, making my writing more polished.

Many major platforms are now incorporating AI into their features. For instance, eBay has an AI tool that generates listing descriptions, and even Grammarly has added AI functions. However, from my experience, these AI features aren't quite there yet. On eBay, the AI often produces lengthy descriptions with incorrect information about the item. Grammarly sometimes rewrites sentences in a way that misses the intended meaning altogether. While these tools may improve over time, at the moment, they can be more of a hindrance than a help.

In addition to text-based AI, there are now AI programs that create images. This has allowed me to start writing children's books, something I never thought I could do because I'm not an illustrator and couldn't afford to hire one. Using AI, I've been able to create illustrations for my "Pug Dog Tales" series, which features my pug dogs. However, it's not as simple as clicking a button and getting the perfect image. I have to "train" the AI by providing it with my photos to work from, and then I experiment with different prompts. Often, it takes dozens of attempts to generate a usable image. Even then, I still have to edit the image in Canva to get it ready for the book.

As an author, here are some AI programs that may help you with your writing:

AutoCrit: AutoCrit is an advanced AI tool explicitly designed to help fiction authors refine their manuscripts by providing comprehensive editing and analysis. Unlike general writing software, AutoCrit tailors its feedback to storytelling elements, such as pacing, dialogue, and word choice. It is a go-to tool for novelists and other fiction writers looking to polish their work. It's ideal for authors aiming to take their storytelling to the next level by improving the flow, emotional resonance, and reader engagement of their narratives.

One of AutoCrit's standout features is its ability to analyze a manuscript in comparison to best-selling books in your genre. This allows authors to see how their writing measures up to the genre's conventions, whether they are writing mysteries, romance, or fantasy. For instance, the tool can highlight overused words, adverbs, and filler content while giving genre-specific suggestions to improve your manuscript's pace and readability. By pinpointing areas where the story might drag or feel rushed, AutoCrit provides actionable feedback that helps writers refine their narrative structure and keep readers hooked.

AutoCrit also provides deep insights into dialogue. It helps authors craft realistic, engaging conversations by analyzing sentence length, tone, and patterns specific to your chosen genre. Whether you're writing fast-paced thriller dialogue or a more reflective literary work, AutoCrit ensures your characters' conversations feel natural and enhance the overall narrative.

ChatGPT: ChatGPT is one of the most popular and advanced text-based AI programs available today, developed by OpenAI. It's known for its ability to respond to questions and prompts conversationally, providing detailed and coherent responses. ChatGPT leverages a vast public database of information along with real-time data (for users with internet access) to help users with everything from writing projects and content creation to brainstorming ideas. This tool can handle a wide range of tasks like drafting emails, creating marketing copy, and even composing creative content like short stories or poetry.

For my author business, ChatGPT has been an invaluable resource. I use it to help me write compelling Facebook ads that grab attention and boost engagement. When I'm publishing a new book on Amazon, I turn to ChatGPT to assist in crafting captivating book descriptions that draw readers in. It also helps me organize book outlines, whether I'm working on a fiction novel or a nonfiction guide, by generating ideas, suggesting chapter structures, and even offering advice on pacing.

Beyond writing, ChatGPT is a handy tool for keyword research. It helps me identify relevant keywords that can improve my book's visibility on Amazon, Facebook, or Google. Additionally, when I need to optimize my social media presence, ChatGPT assists in generating trending hashtags, which increases the likelihood of my posts reaching a wider audience.

There's a free version of ChatGPT that anyone can try, but for access to the latest updates and more advanced features, a subscription costs $20 per month. The paid version offers faster responses, more capabilities, and the ability to use more recent data for even better results.

Jasper AI: Jasper AI is a popular tool designed specifically for content creators and marketers. It is a great asset for authors looking to promote their books. While it can assist with various writing tasks, Jasper excels at creating social media content, blog posts, and other marketing materials that authors need to increase their online presence and build a brand.

The interface is user-friendly, with its standout feature being the long-form content assistant, which helps users generate longer pieces like blog posts, articles, or even detailed book chapters. This can be particularly useful if you need help writing a lengthy blog to promote your latest book or to keep your author's website fresh with regular content. Additionally, Jasper offers over 50 templates to make content creation even faster and easier. Whether you're crafting engaging Facebook posts, Instagram captions, or email newsletters, Jasper's templates can guide you to produce high-quality material in minutes.

Another powerful feature Jasper offers is its support for 25 languages, making it an ideal tool for authors with a global audience. Beyond writing assistance, Jasper integrates essential add-ons like a built-in grammar checker, which ensures your posts are polished, and a plagiarism detector, which helps avoid unintentional duplication. Jasper's SEO assistance can also help your content rank better in search engines, boosting visibility for your books on platforms like Google or Amazon.

Pricing for Jasper starts at $39 per month. While it might seem steep, the platform offers a free trial so you can test out its capabilities before committing.

Plottr: Plottr is an intuitive visual planning tool designed specifically for authors who want to outline and organize their books before diving into the writing process. Unlike text-based AI writing assistants, Plottr focuses on helping authors map out their stories, visualize their plotlines, and keep track of characters, scenes, and key events. Whether you're a plotter or a pantser looking for more structure, Plottr offers a way to streamline the outlining process and make your writing more cohesive.

At the heart of Plottr is its **timeline feature**, which allows you to create a visual representation of your plot. You can lay out key scenes, rearrange them with ease, and add subplots, all while seeing how your story flows. This makes it especially useful for authors who write multi-POV novels or complex stories with multiple timelines. You can also customize the timeline with different colors, making it easy to differentiate between characters, story arcs, or settings.

In addition to timeline plotting, Plottr offers a **character and setting bible that** helps you keep track of essential details about your characters and the world they inhabit. This feature is invaluable for authors working on a series, as it allows you to store and organize character backstories, physical descriptions, relationships, and motivations. The setting bible can also help maintain consistency in your world-building, ensuring that essential details about your fictional universe remain intact across multiple books.

Another standout feature is Plottr's **story templates**, which are based on popular plotting structures like the Hero's Journey, the Three-Act Structure, and Save the Cat! These templates guide you through the critical beats of each structure, making it easier to ensure your story hits all the necessary milestones. This is particularly useful for new authors or anyone struggling to structure their story effectively.

Plottr integrates with **Scrivener and Microsoft Word**, allowing you to export your outline and character notes directly into your manuscript. This seamless workflow makes it easy to move from outlining to drafting without losing any of your progress.

Plottr is available for a one-time purchase of $25, or you can opt for their annual plan, which includes all updates and new features. It's a great tool for authors who need a more visual approach to outlining and want to ensure their story structure is solid before they start writing.

ProWritingAid: ProWritingAid is an advanced writing assistant designed to help authors refine their manuscripts by providing detailed feedback on grammar, style, structure, and readability. It combines the functionality of a traditional grammar checker with in-depth writing reports that help authors improve their overall writing technique. Whether you're writing fiction, nonfiction, or even short stories, ProWritingAid offers tools to polish your work and make it publication-ready.

One of ProWritingAid's most notable features is its **20+ detailed writing reports**. These reports analyze different aspects of your writing, such as grammar, overused words, sentence variety, pacing, and even clichés or repeated sentence starters. The software's feedback is incredibly specific, making it a valuable resource for authors who want to fine-tune their manuscripts before sending them off to editors or publishing them.

For fiction authors, ProWritingAid offers features like **dialogue tag suggestions and** analysis of **pacing and emotional tone**. These ensure that your narrative flows smoothly and that the characters' dialogue sounds natural. It also helps with readability, providing guidance on adjusting complex sentence structures or unwieldy paragraphs to enhance the reading experience.

Another major advantage of ProWritingAid is its **integration with popular writing tools like** Scrivener, Google Docs, and Microsoft Word. You can use ProWritingAid within your favorite platform without needing to switch between different applications. This seamless integration makes it easy to edit your manuscript without disrupting your writing workflow.

ProWritingAid also stands out with its **style and structure suggestions**, making it an invaluable tool for both fiction and nonfiction authors. The program doesn't just fix grammatical issues; it offers solutions to enhance your voice, ensuring that your writing remains engaging and clear. Plus, its built-in **plagiarism checker** is an added bonus for authors who want to ensure their content is entirely original.

Pricing starts at $20 per month, or you can purchase a lifetime license, which makes ProWritingAid a flexible and affordable choice for authors at any stage of their writing journey. With its wide range of features, it's ideal for authors who want to go beyond basic grammar checks and truly elevate the quality of their writing.

QuillBot: If you tend to over-explain or get bogged down in wordy sentences, QuillBot may be the perfect AI tool to streamline your writing. QuillBot specializes in paraphrasing, allowing you to copy and paste sections of your work into the program and see how your message can be delivered more concisely. It's beneficial for authors who want to tighten up their writing, making it clearer and more engaging for readers. For example, if you have a passage in your book that feels too wordy, QuillBot can help you trim it down while still maintaining the core message.

QuillBot offers multiple modes for paraphrasing, such as "Fluency" for refining grammar and "Shorten" for reducing word count, making it incredibly versatile depending on your specific writing needs. It's also an excellent tool for rewriting book descriptions, ad copy, or even social media posts in more concise ways.

QuillBot is more than just a paraphrasing tool, though. It also comes with a **plagiarism checker**, which can be particularly helpful when you're quoting research or other sources in your nonfiction writing. You can also use its **article summarizer** to quickly condense long articles into key points—perfect for authors who do a lot of research and need quick, digestible overviews of complex material.

QuillBot's **citation generator** is another fantastic feature for authors, especially those writing academic papers, nonfiction books, or any work that requires detailed referencing. The citation generator supports different formats, like APA, MLA, and Chicago, making it easy to add properly formatted citations to your text.

You can also write directly within QuillBot, and as you type, it will intuitively offer suggestions to improve clarity and style, much like Grammarly. However, QuillBot tends to focus more on rephrasing and reducing redundancy, making it an excellent tool for tightening up your manuscripts.

QuillBot offers a free version with limited features, but paid plans starting at $6.25 per month allow users to access more advanced functions, making it an affordable option for authors looking to enhance their writing efficiency.

Smodin: Smodin is a versatile, user-friendly AI platform that offers a variety of tools for writers, including the ability to generate copy in over 100 languages. For authors, this platform can be a valuable resource not only for creating multilingual content but also for improving your writing process. Whether you're looking to brainstorm new ideas, research facts, or receive feedback on your current work, Smodin has the tools to assist you.

One of Smodin's standout features is its **research capabilities**. If you're writing nonfiction or a fact-heavy book, you can use the platform to gather accurate information quickly. Smodin's fact-checking function can help you validate the data in your manuscript, ensuring your work is both reliable and well-researched—particularly useful for authors writing historical fiction, research-based nonfiction, or academic essays.

Another key feature is Smodin's ability to **give feedback on sentence structure and grammar**, which can help you improve clarity and flow in your work. Whether you're crafting dialogue in a novel or writing a formal essay, Smodin helps polish your writing so it's more readable and professional. This makes it a strong option for authors who want more stylistic feedback beyond basic grammar and spelling checks.

Smodin is also specially designed for those writing **essays and articles**, which means it's ideal for nonfiction authors, bloggers, or anyone working in a more academic or journalistic format. Its algorithms analyze your writing and suggest improvements, particularly with **proper sentence structure** and flow, ensuring that your content is not only factually sound but also well-articulated.

For authors who write in multiple languages or target a global audience, Smodin's ability to generate copy in over 100 languages is particularly beneficial. This feature helps with translating and adapting your book for international markets, ensuring your content is linguistically and culturally accurate for different audiences.

Smodin also aids in **idea generation**, which is perfect for when you're feeling stuck or need inspiration for new chapters, plot points, or content for a new book. It's a flexible tool that caters to various writing needs, from brainstorming ideas to fine-tuning the final draft.

Smodin offers a free version with limited options, allowing users to explore its features before committing to a paid plan. Subscription plans start at $12 per month, making it affordable for authors looking to boost their productivity and refine their writing.

Sudowrite: Sudowrite is an AI-powered writing assistant developed specifically for fiction authors. It's designed to help writers overcome creative blocks, brainstorm new ideas, and improve their storytelling. Sudowrite goes beyond typical grammar and spell-checking tools by offering creative prompts, scene suggestions, and feedback on your manuscript's structure and tone. It acts like a writing partner that can collaborate with you at any stage of the writing process.

One of the standout features of Sudowrite is its "Twist" function, which provides unique plot twists and ideas that can help move your story forward. This feature is particularly helpful when you're stuck on how to progress in your story or need inspiration to add excitement to your plot. Another useful tool is its "Describe" function, which enhances your descriptive writing. If you're struggling to capture a particular scene, you can input a rough draft or a brief outline, and Sudowrite will generate more vivid and creative ways to bring the scene to life.

Sudowrite also helps with character development. Its "Expand" feature can assist you in fleshing out character arcs, building more depth into your characters, and even suggesting dialogue. Additionally, Sudowrite's "Rewrite" function provides various alternative ways to phrase sentences or paragraphs, helping you refine your prose while maintaining your voice as a writer.

What makes Sudowrite unique is its focus on the creative aspects of writing fiction rather than just technical editing. It supports writers who are looking to enrich their stories, create engaging characters, and keep the narrative momentum flowing. Whether you're a seasoned writer or just starting, Sudowrite helps you brainstorm and refine ideas quickly.

Sudowrite offers different pricing tiers, starting at $10 per month.

Writesonic: Writesonic is a comprehensive AI platform that can perform many of the same functions as other text-based programs, but it truly excels in its ability to generate high-quality marketing content, making it an ideal choice for authors who need help with promoting their work. Whether you're running ads on social media, building email campaigns, or developing content for your author's website, Writesonic provides a variety of tools to make the process easier.

One of the standout features for authors is Writesonic's **copywriting abilities**. It is designed to create engaging marketing content such as Facebook ads, Instagram captions, email subject lines, and blog posts—all critical for promoting your books and building your online presence. Writesonic's templates can help you craft persuasive and well-structured marketing copy that can drive engagement and book sales.

What sets Writesonic apart is its focus on **business and marketing**, providing features tailored explicitly for advertising and brand-building. For authors who might feel overwhelmed by the need to market themselves, Writesonic can help simplify the process by generating content that is optimized for different platforms. Whether you're creating a **social media post** to announce a new release or a **landing page** for your book series, Writesonic can craft professional copy that resonates with your audience.

In addition to generating marketing content, Writesonic also offers tools for creating **blog posts, product descriptions, and even website copy**, which can be particularly useful if you're developing a website to promote your author brand. If you're not familiar with writing sales-focused content, Writesonic's templates guide you through the process, helping you create professional marketing materials without needing to hire a copywriter.

Similar to other AI platforms, Writesonic offers a free version with limited features, allowing you to test out its capabilities before committing to a subscription. Paid plans start at $12 per month and provide access to more advanced features like **SEO optimization** and longer-form content generation—important tools for building a strong author platform.

For authors needing graphics and illustrations, particularly those working on children's books or creating visually-driven stories, there are several AI programs designed to generate high-quality images:

DALL-E: DALL-E, integrated with ChatGPT for paid users, allows authors to generate images from detailed text prompts. It's ideal for those needing quick illustrations for children's books or visual elements for book covers. DALL-E excels at creating unique and imaginative visuals, offering authors the flexibility to create entirely custom graphics without needing to rely on stock images. This makes it particularly useful for developing illustrations that fit the specific tone, setting, and characters of your story.

To use DALL-E, you simply describe the image you want, and the AI generates several versions for you to choose from. Whether you need whimsical animals, fantastical landscapes, or even more abstract visuals, DALL-E is capable of producing diverse results that can be fine-tuned based on your prompts. Paid plans for ChatGPT+ include DALL-E access, making it a cost-effective option for those already using the platform for writing assistance.

MidJourney: MidJourney is a powerful AI image-generation tool that's particularly popular among authors and artists for its ability to create stunning, artistic visuals. What makes MidJourney unique is its ability to produce illustrations that look hand-painted or stylized. This is especially useful for creating images with a storybook quality—ideal for authors of children's books, fantasy, or graphic novels.

To use **MidJourney**, users must interact with the AI through the **Discord** platform, which acts as the interface for generating images. The process begins by "feeding" the AI with **detailed text prompts** describing the type of image you want it to create. These prompts are crucial because the AI relies entirely on them to understand your creative vision. The more specific and imaginative your prompt, the more likely you are to get an output that aligns with your needs. For example, instead of just typing "dragon," a more detailed prompt like "a majestic, emerald dragon soaring over a snowy mountain under a twilight sky" will yield much more tailored results.

MidJourney offers flexibility for users to experiment with different art styles, color schemes, and themes. By including additional keywords such as "watercolor," "oil painting," or "fantasy art," you can guide the AI to produce artwork in your preferred style. It often takes a few iterations of prompt refinement to get the exact look you're going for. Still, this trial-and-error process is part of the creative fun.

You can also influence the image by adding **aspect ratio commands** (for wider or taller images), **specific lighting** (like "soft lighting" or "dramatic lighting"), and even **atmosphere** (like "foggy" or "rainy"). For children's books, this level of customization can help you achieve the whimsical, colorful feel you want for your illustrations.

After generating an image, MidJourney gives you the option to **upscale** it for better resolution or to **re-roll** if you want a different variation. You can also create multiple versions of the same image for comparison and further adjustments. MidJourney's flexibility allows for endless creativity, making it an invaluable tool for authors who need unique visuals without the expense of hiring an illustrator.

For more info, you can visit the MidJourney Discord community or their official website to explore tutorials and examples from other users, which can help you get a sense of how to craft effective prompts. You can generate a limited number of images for free. Still, if you need more, there are different subscription levels available.

Artbreeder: Artbreeder specializes in **generative art**, blending and evolving existing images to create new ones. It is great for generating **character portraits**, **landscapes**, and **abstract designs**, making it popular with fantasy, sci-fi, and children's book authors.

The key to using Artbreeder is its **collaborative approach**. You start by selecting a base image and then tweak various parameters to "breed" a new image based on your preferences. You can control attributes like facial features, colors, artistic style, and more. Artbreeder lets you combine different images, leading to creative and personalized results that align with your vision.

To use Artbreeder, you need to upload an existing image or start with one from their massive community-driven gallery. So, if you are writing a children's book about your granddaughter, you could upload a photo of her. You then "evolve" the image by adjusting sliders for different traits, such as "age," "gender," "art style," and even elements like "lighting" or "color balance." The AI will modify the image according to these settings, allowing you to preview and continuously refine the art. This makes it incredibly intuitive for those who don't have design expertise but still want high-quality illustrations.

Canva Pro with AI Integration: Canva Pro is an incredibly versatile design tool that authors can use for both **book covers** and **illustrations**. Known for its **drag-and-drop interface**, Canva is perfect for beginners who want professional-quality designs without needing advanced technical skills. For authors, Canva can be used to create **custom book covers**, **interior illustrations**, **social media graphics**, and even **marketing materials** like book launch posters or promotional ads.

Canva offers a wide variety of **templates** specifically for book covers, whether you're creating a simple notebook cover or an eye-catching design for your novel. With the Pro version, you also get access to a massive library of **premium stock photos, illustrations, and fonts** that can help elevate your design. One of the most useful features of Canva Pro for authors is the ability to **resize your designs** with just one click—so if you're making a book cover and need it for both Kindle and print versions, Canva makes it simple.

Customizing illustrations: While Canva is often associated with graphic design, it's also great for creating illustrations. You can use pre-made elements or start from scratch using vector shapes, textures, and graphics. Many children's book authors, for example, find Canva helpful for creating colorful, attractive illustrations for younger readers. The Pro version includes **access to premium design elements** like characters, animals, and landscapes, which can be a big asset when designing visual-heavy books.

AI features: Canva Pro includes some AI-powered features, such as a **background remover**. This tool can quickly and cleanly remove backgrounds from images, helping you integrate different elements smoothly into your designs. This is particularly useful for layering multiple design elements when creating complex covers or promotional material. Canva also has **Magic Resize**, which lets you automatically adjust designs to different formats, such as social media posts, flyers, and banners.

Team collaboration: Canva Pro offers **collaboration tools**, so if you're working with a designer, illustrator, or even an editor, you can share designs and get real-time feedback. This is a huge time-saver for authors collaborating on illustrations or marketing material. You can share design links, allow others to edit, and keep everything organized in one place.

Pricing: Canva offers a **free version**, but the **Pro plan** comes with a host of premium features that authors will find incredibly useful. At **$12.99 per month** (or **$119.99 per year**), Canva Pro gives you unlimited access to **premium images, fonts, templates**, and other design tools. This can be invaluable for authors who need to consistently create professional-grade visuals for multiple book releases or promotional campaigns.

How To Choose An AI Program: Do you need AI in your author business? Not necessarily. But as with any new technology affecting your industry, it's best to familiarize yourself with the options at least. AI is rapidly evolving; sites like MidJourney update frequently as new features become available.

My advice is to start with the most popular, which is ChatGPT. You can create a free account and play around with the features. Talk to ChatGPT like it is a real person when you ask it questions. AI isn't like an internet search engine; it is much more engaging and intuitive. If you are looking for book illustrations, MidJourney is the most popular graphics AI program, and you can test that out for free, too.

Here are some additional **do's and don'ts** for authors using AI, particularly when creating content for platforms like Amazon:

Do's

1. **Use AI to Brainstorm**: AI is great for generating ideas and titles or brainstorming character names. Use it as a **creative partner** to jumpstart your imagination, not to replace your creative process.

2. **Proofread & Edit**: Always proofread and edit what AI generates. **Fine-tuning and rewriting in your voice**

will ensure the content feels authentic to your readers.

3. **Run a Plagiarism Check**: Before publishing, use plagiarism checkers (like Grammarly or QuillBot) to ensure no part of your content unintentionally borrows from copyrighted material. AI can sometimes reproduce phrases that exist elsewhere, so double-checking is critical.

4. **Modify AI-Generated Graphics**: If you're using an AI tool for illustrations or covers, **tweak or combine elements** to make them your own. You can combine AI-generated images with your own elements using programs like Canva, giving them an original touch.

5. **Use AI to Enhance Efficiency**: Let AI help with repetitive tasks, such as generating social media posts, outlining chapters, or proofreading. It can **improve productivity** without overshadowing your personal style.

Don'ts

1. **Don't Rely on AI to Write Entire Books**: AI can be helpful in assisting with portions of your book but relying on it to write entire chapters or books can result in a **loss of originality**. Readers come to books for human connection and emotion, which AI can't replicate.

2. **Avoid Blindly Copying AI Output**: AI's text can be generic or repetitive. **Never copy and paste directly** from AI into your work without reviewing, editing, and personalizing the content.

3. **Don't Forget Copyright & Trademark Laws**: When generating text or images, **ensure you're not using copyrighted material**. AI can inadvertently pull from existing works, which can lead to legal issues,

especially if it's song lyrics, poems, or brand names.

4. **Avoid Over-Saturation**: Don't use AI to generate dozens of low-quality, identical POD products in the hopes of making quick sales. **Amazon has strict guidelines** against this, and they are increasingly cracking down on accounts that flood the marketplace with mass-produced, low-quality AI content.

5. **Don't Use Trademarked Characters or Logos**: When creating images, avoid using prompts with terms related to **Disney, Marvel, Harry Potter**, or other trademarked characters. AI can generate art that violates copyright laws, and selling these products can result in your account being suspended.

By following these tips, you can use AI as a **helpful tool without** compromising your integrity as an author or running into trouble on platforms like Amazon.

CONCLUSION

Publishing a book has long been a dream for many, and thanks to self-publishing, that dream is more achievable than ever. No longer do you have to rely on traditional publishing houses to get your book into the hands of readers. Self-publishing through platforms like Amazon KDP allows you the freedom to write on your terms, control your creative process, and keep a larger share of the profits.

However, successfully making money through self-publishing is more than just writing a great book. It requires mastering the entire process, from formatting your files and designing a professional-looking cover to navigating promotions and advertising. Self-publishing can be time-consuming and demanding, but with persistence, consistency, and the strategies outlined in this book, you can turn your passion into a source of income.

Whether you're writing fiction or nonfiction or creating print-on-demand (POD) books like journals, planners, or coloring books, there's an active community of self-publishers out there to learn from. Social media groups, YouTube channels, and other platforms are filled with people sharing their experiences and making money. It's important to tap into these resources and stay updated on the ever-evolving world of self-publishing so your books continue to thrive in a competitive market.

In the self-publishing world, the phrase *write, publish, repeat* is the mantra for making money. The more books you have available, the more opportunities you'll create for making sales. With each book you publish, you'll improve your skills in writing, cover design, marketing, and the entire publishing process. My journey began in 2013, and the way I approach publishing has evolved dramatically since then. By sharing my experiences and the lessons I've learned, I hope this book has made your self-publishing journey smoother and more efficient.

So now it's time to take action! Start writing, start publishing, and start making money by self-publishing your books on Amazon KDP!

ABOUT THE AUTHOR

Ann Eckhart is a writer, entrepreneur, and online content creator based in Iowa. She has authored numerous books available about how to make money online from home.

For all of her titles, visit her website at AnnEckhart.com.

You can also follow her on Facebook at @anneckhart.

COPYRIGHT 2024
ANN ECKHART

No part of this book may be reprinted or reproduced without the express written permission from the author.

Cover Design by Ann Eckhart

Made in the USA
Las Vegas, NV
22 February 2025

18533682R00157